S0-BOG-750

Museums and the Law

85-0-1313

AASLH Management Series
Volume 1

This book marks the beginning of a series of handbooks on the varied aspects of management encountered by administrators in museums and historical agencies. The next volume in the series will focus on public relations.

Museums
and the Law

Marilyn Phelan

The American Association for State and Local History
Nashville, Tennessee

AMERICAN CRAFT COUNCIL
LIBRARY

KF4305
.P5
1982

Library of Congress Cataloguing-in-Publication Data

Phelan, Marilyn E.
  Museums and the law.

  Bibliography: p.
  Includes index.
  1. Museums—Law and legislation—United States.
I. Title.
KF4305.P5   344.73′093   81–22912
ISBN 0-910050-60-0   347.30493   AACR2

Copyright © 1982 by the American Association for State and Local History. All rights reserved. Printed in the United States of America. Except for brief quotations used in critical articles or reviews, no part of this publication may be reproduced or transmitted in any form by any means, electronic or mechanical, including photocopying, recording, or any information storage/retrieval system, without written permission of the copyright owner. For information, write to the American Association for State and Local History, 708 Berry Road, Nashville, Tennessee 37204.

Publication of this book was made possible in part by funds from the sale of the Bicentennial State Histories, which were supported by the National Endowment for the Humanities.

Designed by Gary Gore

To
Harold and my children,
Pat, Scott, and Kim

Contents

Preface

Museum directors or curators generally are selected on the basis of their reputations in the sciences, humanities, or arts. Such people often are ill prepared to handle the complicated legal problems that have plagued museums in recent years. Museum directors must make numerous decisions that can result in lawsuits. They must file a variety of reports and must monitor activities in such a manner that the tax-exempt status of their museum organizations will not be endangered or lost. When they seek legal counsel, museum directors may find that a lawyer is not familiar with those laws peculiar to the museum profession. Because the museum director may find it difficult to communicate with counsel, solutions to such problems may not be readily available. This book was written to present the law relating to museum organizations in a simple and concise form and, thus, to provide museum personnel with a guide in solving minor legal problems and a management tool to help prevent future legal complications. The book is not intended as a substitute for good legal advice.

It is not possible to predict the specific issues that may confront each museum; consequently, I have dealt most heavily with those issues that I perceive to be most common to all museums. The book is intended to be a reference source on the general law relating to museums; it is not written to solve all legal problems of every museum. That would be an impossible task. For example, each state has laws peculiar to that state—regulations that may change the applicability of the general law as presented in the text. In addition, the way the general law applies to an individual transaction depends on the individual facts in question. Hence, the book cannot serve as a substitute for legal counsel on individual transactions.

Sample contracts and other legal aids are provided in the appendixes. These can be very useful documents to the museum director; however, they must always be used with caution, as specific clauses may not apply in certain situations and, in some instances, will not cover a transaction at all. State law should be consulted to determine the applicability of the forms in that state and to determine whether certain clauses should be added or deleted. Still, I hope that these sample documents will help solve recurring problems.

The discussion of tax problems in chapter 2 is long and covers complicated tax areas; consequently, it is not easy reading. The reader may feel the material is too weighted in the tax area; however, it is not possible to cover the complexities of tax law for exempt organizations, such as museums, more concisely without eliminating some important area. Though a tax-exempt museum would normally pay no income tax, the very fact that it is exempt from income tax liability causes substantial controls on its operation by the federal government, to assure that its exempt status is not being abused. Given that type of supervision, reporting requirements can be quite extensive. Though chapter 2 may not be light reading, it should prove extremely helpful, not only in meeting requirements to assure the preservation of exempt status, but to provide guidance for both the donor and the institution in handling gifts to the museum. Placing this chapter at the end of the text was considered, as a museum director would normally consult these materials only in the event of particular tax problems; however, the information more appropriately follows that of chapter 1, on the organizational structure of museums. Further, in actual practice, tax laws may be considerably more important to the museum director than are other legal issues. Reading the first two chapters together will provide a basic understanding of the legal principles that apply to different types of museums. A comprehensive study of these opening chapters will provide a substantial working knowledge of the legal ramifications with which museum directors must deal.

The remaining chapters in the book provide concise, "hornbook" coverage of laws that have particular relevance to museums. Chapter 3 summarizes the law of torts, contracts, and copyrights and explains how such laws apply to museums. Chapter 5 discusses the law applicable to museum acquisitions—purchases, gifts, and loans—and summarizes statutes and regulations on historical preservation and systematic collections. A working knowledge of these laws is almost a necessity for all museum personnel.

Museum directors should also be familiar with laws regarding employee relations, as summarized in chapter 6.

Further, all museum employees should be concerned with conflict-of-interest problems, discussed in chapter 7.

With the sample documents provided to illustrate practical applications of some of the legal principles discussed, the book should prepare museum directors with a working knowledge of all important areas of law with which they may be confronted. For personnel of small museums lacking regular legal counsel, the book should provide information on possible areas of concern and guidelines for solving recurring problems. For readers who are not familiar with legal terminology, a glossary of legal terms is provided in the appendix.

I thank Dr. J. Knox Jones, Jr., Vice-President for Research and Graduate Studies and Graduate Dean at Texas Tech University, for his suggestions and over-all help in preparing this text. Dr. Jones conceived the idea of a program in museum science at Texas Tech University and wanted a course in museum law to be part of the curriculum—hence the evolution of this book. I also wish to thank JoAnn Chilton and Judy Snellings for their help in preparing the manuscript.

1

Organizational Structure of Museums

Museums are of two categories—public and private. Private museums normally have nonprofit status and are organized as tax-exempt organizations providing charitable deductions for donors. A public museum may be created by a state, a city, or a county. It may be part of a university and hence subject to statutes pertaining to educational institutions. Knowledge of the legal structure of a museum becomes relevant for several reasons. Legal constraints concerning funding, policies, and programs of public institutions vary from state to state and per type of institution. In addition, liability under various statutes is not the same for different organizations. For example, officials of state institutions are subject to Fourteenth Amendment constraints, whereas officials of private institutions generally are not. Public institutions are subject to governmental control; private institutions may be subject to governmental regulation, but they are controlled by their members. The differing rules and regulations applicable to the varying types of museums are discussed throughout this book.

A private museum will normally have one of three forms—trust, association, or corporation. A public museum may be either a charitable trust or a corporation, or it may simply be an unincorporated agency of a political subdivision or of the state.

Trusts

In a trust arrangement, an equitable obligation is imposed upon a person called a trustee, who is bound to deal with trust property for the benefit of the beneficiaries. The legal and equitable estates are separated; the legal estate is vested in the trustee and the equitable title in the beneficiaries (certain designated individuals) of the trust. It is essential for the existence of any trust that there be trust subject matter and that there be a separation of the legal estate from the beneficial enjoyment. There are few restrictions on the kind or nature of trust property—it may be real or personal property. The rights and powers of the trustee depend on the nature of the trust, the terms of the trust instrument, and the purpose for which the trust was created. The authority of the trustee in the management of the trust is governed by state statute, the instrument creating the trust, and the common law rules governing trusts and trustees. A person acting as a trustee does not become a separate entity, as does a corporation, but continues to be the same natural person that he is in his individual capacity.

A trustee is deemed to possess the powers conferred on him by the terms of the trust or those that are necessary to effect the purposes of the trust. Acts within the scope of his authority bind the trust property and the beneficiaries. Those acts outside his power are void. By accepting the trust, a trustee becomes bound to administer the property in accordance with provisions of the trust instrument and the intent of the grantor. He can be relieved from all or part of his duties only by consent of all the beneficiaries or by placing administration of the trust in the hands of a court.

Powers of a trustee are either mandatory or discretionary. A power is mandatory when it authorizes and commands the trustee to perform some positive act, while a power is discretionary when the trustee may either exercise it or refrain from exercising it or when the time, manner, or extent of its exercise is left to his discretion. The measure of discretion possessed by a trustee must be determined by the trust instrument as construed in accordance with established principles of law. It is the trustee's paramount duty to preserve and protect the trust estate in compliance with the terms of the trust. He is the representative of the beneficiaries and as such owes the beneficiaries those duties which the law imposes upon a fiduciary.[1] (See chapter 7 for a discussion of the duties of a trustee.)

A museum may be established in the form of a charitable trust. In such an organization, the beneficiaries of the trust would be the general public. The so-called cy pres doctrine (discussed in chapter 5) requires that administration of such a trust be carried out with as close an approximation to the scheme of the donor as is reasonably practicable.

Such charitable trusts are normally represented by the attorney general of the state. (See appendix A for a sample charitable trust indenture.)

A museum may have some other legal structure but may be funded by a trust which is separate and apart from the museum. The trust in this case would be passive in that it would exist only to administer the trust fund; the trustees would not govern museum operations.

Associations

An association is an unincorporated organization acting without a charter but upon the methods and forms used by incorporated bodies.[2] The laws pertaining to such an organization are uncertain. Establishing an association is relatively simple; however, the operation of such an organization can become difficult and troublesome. A constitution and/ or bylaws ordinarily determine an association's powers, but if the association has neither, it may adopt any reasonable means to accomplish the objective for which it was formed. An unincorporated association may not, without statutory authorization, receive or hold property, though a grant to an association will not fail for want of a grantee—in such a case, title vests in its members. Title to the property of an association may also be vested in trustees to hold for its benefit. Those persons comprising an association would undoubtedly be individually liable for their actions, and for the action of other members, in the operation of the association. For these reasons, it is recommended that a museum not be organized as an unincorporated association.

Corporations

It is preferable that a museum be incorporated. A corporation is a separate, legal entity created by and under the laws of a particular state. Property acquired by a corporation becomes property of the corporation in the same sense that personal property is owned by a natural person. Contracts entered into for the corporation by its authorized officers or agents are contracts of the corporation as a distinct legal entity. Such contracts neither confer rights nor impose liabilities or restrictions on corporate members or shareholders individually. A corporation is vested with the capacity of continuous succession, irrespective of changes in its membership, and of acting as a unit in matters relating to the common purpose of the corporation.[3]

As a consequence of the concept that a corporation is a distinct legal entity, the shareholders or members are generally not liable for torts of the corporation. Further, actions in relation to corporate property and rights must ordinarily be brought by the corporation in its corporate name; the shareholders or members may not maintain such actions, either to recover possession of corporate property or to recover damages. Shareholders may, however, require that corporate officers operate the corporation for the purposes for which it was formed and may sue to enforce proper behavior on the part of corporate officials.

State statutes prescribe the manner and purposes for which a corporation may be formed. A corporation has been defined as an artificial being, invisible, intangible, and existing only in contemplation of law.[4] Being a mere creature of law, then, a corporation possesses only those properties which its charter of creation confers upon it, either expressly or as incident to its very existence.[5] To create a corporation, persons called incorporators file articles of incorporation with the state setting forth the purpose or purposes for which the corporation is being formed. Because the right to act as a corporation is a special privilege conferred by the state, the commencement of corporate existence depends upon a grant from the state, usually in the form of a charter, issued upon acceptance by the state of the articles of incorporation.

A corporation is managed by a board of directors; members of the board are elected by the shareholders. Shareholders do not have management and control of the affairs of a corporation; they are deemed to have consented to control by a board of directors. The directors have authority to transact all the ordinary business of the corporation within the scope of corporate charter powers. The board appoints officers— normally a president, vice president, secretary, and treasurer—to conduct the daily activities of the corporation. Corporate bylaws establish the rights and duties of the members regarding internal management of the corporation.

Corporations may be classified as public, quasi-public, and private. A public corporation is created by the government to act as an agency of the state or of the federal government. Private corporations are created by agreement of the members, either for purely private purposes or for purposes partly private and partly public. The most important distinction between public and private corporations is with respect to governmental control. Public corporations, being instrumentalities of the state, are subject to governmental control. On the other hand, the charter of a private corporation is a contract between the state and the corporation, and because of a provision of the United States Constitution prohibiting state laws from impairing the obligations of contracts, a private corporation cannot be subject to state control.

Corporations are divided into stock corporations and nonstock, or membership, corporations. A stock corporation issues capital stock, divided into shares, to its members. The corporation is authorized to distribute dividends from surplus profits to its shareholders. Membership corporations have no stock; membership is represented in some other form.

If a museum is incorporated, the corporation itself, then, is liable for its actions and not the individuals involved. Further, once incorporated, a museum organization would have power to purchase, hold, lease, improve, and sell property, to make contracts, to incur liabilities, and to sue and be sued. Bylaws of the corporation would determine the administration and regulations of its affairs. An incorporated museum would be managed by a board of directors; restrictions and liabilities would be imposed upon the board of directors by state corporate statutes and by the common law relating to corporations. (See chapter 7 for a discussion of the duties of corporate directors and of museum trustees.)

A museum organization should be incorporated as a nonprofit corporation. Most states have statutes specifically providing for nonprofit corporations. As a general rule (state statutes will vary), to organize, incorporators file articles of incorporation with the secretary of the state pursuant to the state's nonprofit corporate statute. (See appendix A for sample articles of incorporation.) The purpose for which the museum corporation is organized must be fully stated in the articles of incorporation. If articles filed with the secretary of state conform to law, the secretary of the state will issue a certificate of incorporation. Upon receipt of this certificate (or charter), the corporate existence begins. The incorporators and initially named board of directors should have an organizational meeting to elect officers of the corporation and adopt bylaws.

Unless they are exempt, corporations must pay state franchise taxes. A nonprofit corporation should apply for exempt status, generally by submitting to the state comptroller the same information furnished the Internal Revenue Service in its request for exemption from federal income taxation (explained in chapter 2). Normally, nonprofit corporations are not precluded from carrying on business for profit that is incidental to their primary purpose. To acquire tax-exempt status.

however, a nonprofit corporation must not plan to distribute its assets to its members on dissolution. A nonprofit corporation may issue membership cards, certificates, or other instruments denoting membership in the organization, voting rights, or ownership rights.

Public Museums

State statutes normally provide for establishment of public, governmental museums. In addition, some public educational universities are authorized to establish museums. Museums so created are subject to statutory law regarding both establishment and operation. Often such museums are separately incorporated. If citizens of a political subdivision wish to establish a public museum, state statutes must be consulted and followed. Management and supervision of public museums will vary in the several states. It is beyond the scope of this text to examine the statutes of all the states; however, I will briefly summarize a few selected statutes to provide examples.

In Texas, a city or county, either independently or in cooperation, may acquire lands and buildings for historical museums.[6] These local governments may enter into joint agreements to provide for museum services.[7] Condemnation proceedings may be used for such acquisitions if it is necessary to prevent destruction or deterioration of a historical site, building, or structure. The commissioners' court of any county may appoint a county historical commission to operate any museum owned or leased by the county. Cities with a population of 5,000 or more may issue negotiable revenue bonds to fund the establishment and maintenance of such museums and may levy an occupancy tax on hotel rooms to provide revenue for the payment of the bonds.[8] A city with a population in excess of 40,000 may create a park board of trustees to acquire or improve lands or buildings to be used for historical museums. Such a board would have power to employ a manager and to issue revenue bonds payable from its facility revenues.[9]

In California, the legislative body may establish a public museum of natural and historical objects in a city where there is none.[10] Upon receiving a petition signed by one-third of the city electors, the legislative body is required to establish a museum in the city.[11] The mayor appoints a board of five museum trustees to manage the museum, and title to property of the museum vests in the city.[12] The board of supervisors of a county may also construct a historical museum.[13]

Operation of a public museum in the state of New York is somewhat unusual. By majority vote, any county, city, or town in the state of New York may establish a museum and appropriate money raised by taxes to maintain and equip the museum.[14] Within one month of taking office, however, the trustees of the museum must apply to the regents within the state board of education for a charter. Such a museum is supervised by the state board of education, and the regents fix the standards for its services.[15] Tax monies can be used to operate a museum owned by a corporation, but the corporation must have been incorporated with the consent of the regents and must be registered by the regents.

2

Museums and the Internal Revenue Service

General Tax Status

A museum should qualify for exemption from federal income taxation. No organization other than an agency of the state or a political subdivision of the state, is automatically exempt from taxation, however.[1] To acquire exempt status, each organization must apply to a district director of the Internal Revenue Service (IRS). Furthermore, subject to a few exceptions, exempt organizations must file annual information returns, generally on Form 990, specifying receipts and expenditures and indicating their current financial status. An organization which has unrelated business income above $1,000 must file Form 990-T and must pay tax on that income. Further, if an organization is a private foundation, it must file Form 990-PF and pay an excise tax of 2 percent on its net investment income as well as submit detailed information concerning its activities for the year.

The Internal Revenue Code grants exempt status to some twenty-five types of nonprofit organizations. These include: federal instrumentalities; charitable organizations; civic and social welfare organizations; labor, agricultural, and horticultural organizations; business leagues, chambers of commerce, and real estate boards; social clubs; credit unions; war veterans' organizations; and farmers' cooperative associations. Exempt organizations are referred to by their Internal Revenue Code classification. For example, charitable organizations (those operated exclusively for religious, charitable, scientific, public-safety testing, literary, or educational purposes, or for the prevention of cruelty to children or animals) are described in section 501 (c) (3) of the

Internal Revenue Code and are referred to as 501 (c) (3) organizations. Social welfare organizations, a category which would include civic associations, are referred to as 501 (c) (4) organizations. Social clubs are 501 (c) (7) organizations, while war veterans' organizations are 501 (c) (9) organizations. It is important that a museum director know the correct classification of the museum organization and the consequences of that classification. Rules differ for each classification. For example, a 501 (c) (3) classification provides donors to such organizations with a charitable contributions deduction, whereas a 501 (c) (4) or a 501 (c) (7) classification does not.

A museum organization which is not a governmental agency should seek tax-exempt classification under section 501 (c) (3) as a charitable organization. It would file Form 1023 (see appendix E) to obtain exempt status. Until exempt status has been determined, it should file an information return, Form 990 (or Form 990-PF, should it acknowledge that it is a private foundation. Forms are illustrated in appendixes B and C.) It should indicate on the return that its application for exempt status is pending with the Internal Revenue Service. Once recognition of exemption is established, it is normally effective as of the date of formation of the museum. A museum organization remains exempt as long as its purposes and activities do not change in a manner inconsistent with its exempt status.

Museum as a Charitable Organization

A charitable organization (one operated exclusively for charitable purposes) qualifies for tax-exempt status under section 501 (c) (3) of the Internal Revenue Code. (Contributions to such an organization qualify for deduction as charitable contributions. See chapter 5 for a discussion of valuation of gifts to museums for purposes of deduction as charitable contributions). Charitable purposes include the religious, scientific, literary, and educational as well as those relating to public charities. The Code sets certain limitations on all charitable organizations. No part of the net earnings of such an organization may inure to the benefit of a private shareholder or individual. Further, unless the organization elects to come under the lobbying provisions added by the Tax Reform Act of 1976 (discussed below), no substantial part of its activities may include carrying on propaganda or otherwise attempting to influence legislation or participating in any political campaign on behalf of any candidate for public office.

In order to be exempt under section 501 (c) (3), a museum must be both organized and operated exclusively for a charitable purpose. Consequently, two tests must be met: an organizational test and an operational test.

Organizational Test

The organizational test is determined by a museum's charter or articles of incorporation.[2] Its articles must limit the purposes of the museum to one or more that are considered exempt. If the articles empower the museum to engage in activities which are not in furtherance of its exempt purposes (unless those activities are insubstantial), it cannot qualify under section 501 (c) (3). The articles of incorporation can be broad in stating the purpose of the organization as long as it is charitable. For example, the articles can simply state that the museum is being formed for educational purposes. The articles cannot be broader than the Code itself, however. If the articles state the purposes to be "educational, philanthropic, and benevolent." the IRS is of the opinion that the organizational requirement is not met, in that the terms "philanthropic" and "benevolent" have no legal meaning. Should the purposes for which the museum is created be stated more broadly than those specified in section 501 (c) (3), the museum will not be tax-exempt. The fact that the actual operations have been exclusively in furtherance of exempt purposes is not sufficient to meet the organizational test. Statements, bylaws, or other evidence that the members intend to operate only in furtherance of the exempt purposes are also not material. The articles must state the exempt purposes and must not permit activities that do not promote those purposes (unless the activities are an inconsequential part of the total activities of the organization).

A museum also fails to meet the organization test if its assets are not dedicated to an exempt purpose; upon dissolution the assets must, by reason of a provision in the articles or by operation of law, be distributed for an exempt purpose or be distributed to the federal government or to a state or local government for a public purpose. A museum organization fails to meet the organizational test if its articles provide that its assets will be distributed to its members or shareholders upon dissolution.

Exempt purposes include the charitable, the scientific, and the educational. A museum, depending on the type, could qualify under one of these purposes. The term "charitable" is defined by Treasury Regulations[3] to include erection or maintenance of public buildings, monuments, or works; combating community deterioration and juvenile delinquency; and advancement of education or science. The term "scientific" means the carrying on of scientific research in the public (rather than a private) interest.[4] Scientific research is regarded as serving the public if the results of the research are made available on a nondiscriminatory basis, if the research is performed for a governmental agency, or if the research is directed toward benefiting the public. Scientific research performed to aid in the scientific education of college students, to obtain scientific information for publication, to discover a cure for disease, or to aid a community or area in attracting new industry or the development of industry is regarded as serving the public interest regardless of any agreement granting the sponsor the right to ownership of any patents, processes, or formulas resulting from the research. In other cases, patents and/or processes of formulas must be available to the public. An organization which carries on research only for its creators is not tax-exempt. The term "educational" is defined by the Treasury Regulations[5] as the instruction or training of an individual for the purpose of improving or developing his capabilities or "the instruction of the public on subjects useful to the individual and beneficial to the community." The regulations cite a museum as an example of an educational organization which would qualify as an exempt organization under section 501 (c) (3).

Operational Test

An exempt charitable museum must meet an operational test which requires that the museum engage primarily in activities which accomplish one or more of its exempt purposes. Should more than an insubstantial part of the organization's activities not be in furtherance of its exempt purposes, or should the organization's net earnings inure in whole or in part to the benefit of "private shareholders or individuals," it is not operated exclusively for one or more exempt purposes, and it cannot be a 501 (c) (3) organization. A museum could operate a trade or business and still meet the requirements of 501 (c) (3) if the operation of the business is in furtherance of the museum's exempt purpose and if the museum is not organized for the primary purpose of carrying on the business. In determining the primary purpose of the museum, all the circumstances must be considered, such as size and extent of the business as compared with the size and extent of the activities which are in furtherance of the exempt purposes.

If a substantial part of an organization's activities involves attempting to influence legislation by propaganda or otherwise, it is deemed an "action" organization and, unless it complies with section 501 (h) of the Internal Revenue Code, will not qualify as a 501 (c) (3) organization. Section 501 (h) was added to the Internal Revenue Code by the Tax Reform Act of 1976. It permits 501 (c) (3) organizations to have some lobbying expenditures without losing tax-exempt status. This provision replaces the "substantial part of activities" test with a prescribed limit on the amount of expenditures which can be made to influence legislation and not cause disqualification of 501 (c) (3) status. The basic permitted level of lobbying expenditures for a year is 20 percent of the first $500,000 of the organization's exempt purpose expenditures plus 15 percent of the second $500,000, 10 percent of the third $500,000, and 5 percent of any additional expenditures. In no event may the permitted level exceed $1,000,000 for any one year. Within these limits is a separate restriction on "grass-roots lobbying" (attempts to influence the general public on legislative matters). The grass-roots lobbying nontaxable amount is one-fourth of the total lobbying nontaxable amount. Section 501 (h) is only applicable to electing organizations. (To elect, an organization must file Form 5768. See appendix E.) The election is effective until revoked. If an electing organization exceeds either the general limitation or the grass-roots limitation in a taxable year, it will be subject to an excise tax of 25 percent of its excess lobbying expenditures. Further, if an electing organization's lobbying expenditures over a four-year period exceed 150 percent of the limitations, the organization will lose its 501 (c) (3) status. A private foundation cannot come under the elective lobbying provisions.

Public Charity

A charitable organization under section 501 (c) (3) is deemed to be a private foundation until timely notice is given the Internal Revenue Service that the organization is, in fact, not a private foundation. When a museum applies for exempt status as a charitable organization under 501 (c) (3), it must give such notice on its application Form 1023. This notification should be filed within fifteen months from the end of the month in which the museum was organized.

All charitable organizations under 501 (c) (3) are either public charities or private foundations. Public charities are responsive to the general public, whereas private foundations are supposedly responsive to private groups—the founders or contributors. Consequently, private foundations are subject to much stricter supervision by the Internal Revenue Service and often to substantial penalties. Public charities are less restricted, and contributors to public charities receive more favorable tax treatment on their contributions. Contributions to a 501 (c) (3) public charity can be deducted to as much as 50 percent of an individual donor's adjusted gross income (or 30 percent if he is deducting the fair market value of certain appreciated property). Contributions to private foundations are limited to 20 percent of an individual's adjusted gross income. The remainder of the gift cannot be deducted in the future, whereas there is a five-year carryover of gifts to public charities above the 50 percent (or 30 percent) limitation. Gifts of appreciated property to private foundations that would be treated as long-term capital gains if they were sold can be deducted only to the extent of the cost of the property plus 60 percent of the appreciation (subject to the 20 percent limitation). If such property is donated to a public charity, the deduction (subject to the 30 percent limitation) is the fair market value of the property. If a museum is a private foundation for tax purposes, it will undoubtedly qualify as an operating foundation. Donors to private operating foundations receive the more favorable tax treatment allowed public charities. (See discussion below relating to private operating foundations. See chapter 5 for a more detailed discussion of the tax problems related to contributions of appreciated properties to charities, such as museums).

Section 509 of the Internal Revenue Code is the pertinent statute in regard to public versus private status. Section 509 defines a private foundation by describing what it is not. A private foundation is defined to be any 501 (c) (3) organization except those described in section 509 (a) (1), (2), (3), or (4). This complicated language simply means that "public" charities are either 509 (a) (1), (2), (3), or (4) organizations. All other 501 (c) (3) organizations are private foundations. Inasmuch as Form 1023 requires that each public charity be classified as a 509 (a) (1), (2), (3), or (4) organization, it becomes necessary that the museum director know the meaning of these provisions as they apply to a museum. A museum organization would attempt public charity classification under either 509 (a) (1) or 509 (a) (2).

509 (a) (1) Museums. It is best that a museum qualify under 509 (a) (1). 509 (a) (1) organizations are generally churches, schools, or hospitals. Organizations which normally receive a substantial part of their support from governmental units or from the general public also qualify, however. These organizations are called 170 (b) (1) (A) (vi) organizations, indicating the section of the Internal Revenue Code under which they qualify. A museum of history, art, or science can be classified as a public charity under this provision if it can meet one of two tests: a one-third percent-of-support test or a facts-and-circumstances test.

The one-third percent-of-support test requires that at least one-third of an organization's support (computed for a four-year period immediately preceding the current year) be from the general public or from governmental units. Amounts received by an organization for services rendered, i.e., "gross receipts," are excluded from both the numerator and the denominator of the fraction. Should an organization depend primarily on gross receipts, however, it cannot qualify as a 509 (a) (1) organization. Support from governmental units will be deemed gross receipts if such support constitutes amounts received by the museum from the exercise of its exempt functions.

In order to assure that contributions are from the general public rather than from a few donors, contributions by any one individual, trust, or corporation can be taken into account in the numerator of the fraction only to the extent of 2 percent of the organization's total support for that period. Such contributions will be counted in full in the denominator, however. (When the 2 percent limitation is applied to contributions, any contributions made by a donor and by any of the following persons or entities are considered to have been made by one person: (a) corporation, partnership, trust, or estate in which the donor has more than a 35 percent interest; (b) the family of the donor [spouse, ancestors, lineal descendants, and spouses of lineal descendants]; and (c) a corporation, partnership, or trust in which the donor owns more than a 20 percent interest if the entity has contributed more than $5,000 to the organization, provided that that amount is more than 20 percent of total contributions received by the organization during the current year.)[6] This restriction presents a real problem if the museum is offered a substantial contribution by one individual. Certainly the museum director would want to accept the contribution; however, there is a possibility that acceptance could cause the museum to lose its status as a public charity. (Example 3 below illustrates this problem.)

Some contributions may be excluded from both the numerator and the denominator, thereby substantially lessening the adverse effect of such contributions. This exclusion applies to substantial contributions or bequests which are attracted by the publicly supported nature of the organization, are unusual or unexpected with respect to the amount, and would, by reason of size, adversely affect the status of the organization as normally supported by the public. These unusual grants are most likely excluded if they are bequests, if the organization has met the one-third support test or the 10 percent-of-support limitation (described below) before the year of contribution, if the organization will not place continued reliance on unusual grants to fund its current operating expenses, if the contributor does not exercise control over the organization, and if the organization has been able to attract a significant amount of public support. A grantee organization may request a ruling from the Internal Revenue Service as to whether a grant or contribution may be excluded.

Example 1. Museum X received $300,000 during the four immediately preceding years from operations. The only other support it received was small contributions amounting to $10,000. X received only 3.3 percent of its total support from sources other than gross receipts. It will not qualify as a 509 (a) (1) organization even though the $300,000 is excluded from both the numerator and the denominator in computing the one-third support test. (Museum X may qualify as a public charity under 509 (a) (2), however. (See the discussion of a 509 (a) (2) public charity below.)

Example 2. Assume that Museum X received support from the following sources for the four years preceding the current taxable year:

Contributions	$200,000
Governmental unit	10,000
Investment income	50,000
Receipts from operations	60,000
Total support	$320,000
Excluded support (receipts from operations)	60,000
Qualified support	$260,000

Gross receipts from operations would be excluded from both the numerator and denominator of the fraction. Thus, one-third of total qualified support would be $86,667 (one-third of $260,000). Support from governmental units and from contributions from the general public (above the 2 percent limitation) must total at least $86,667. For these purposes, the following qualify:

Governmental unit	$10,000
Various donors (no one having made contributions in excess of $5,200—2 percent of qualified support	50,000
Six contributions in excess of 2 percent of qualified support (only $5,200 of each contribution qualifies), 6 × $5,200	31,200
	$91,200

Because the amount of Museum *X*'s support from governmental units and from the general public exceeds one-third of its total support ($86,667), the museum qualifies as a publicly supported charity under 509 (a) (1) for the current taxable year and for its succeeding taxable year.

Example 3. Suppose *A*, an individual, gave $400,000 to Museum *X* in Example 2 above. Qualified support would then total $660,000. This figure would be the denominator of the support fraction. Support from the general public would be $152,400 [$10,000 + $50,000 + ($13,200 × 7)] (there would then be seven contributors in excess of 2 percent of qualified support, 2 percent being $13,200 if qualified support is $660,000). The fraction $152,400/660,000 is less than one-third. What alternatives are available to the museum to enable it to accept the gift and yet not lose its status as a public charity? Recall that the one-third support test is computed for a four-year period. The museum may be able to qualify as a public charity over a four-year period in spite of the large gift in one year. The other alternative is to attempt complete exclusion of the gift from both the numerator and the denominator of the fraction, on the ground that it is an unusual and unexpected gift under the criteria noted above. It may be necessary to request a ruling from the Internal Revenue Service as to whether or not the gift will qualify as unusual and unexpected.

Example 4. Museum *X* received support from the following sources for the four immediately preceding tax years:

Contributions	$300,000
Gross receipts from operations	100,000
Total support	$400,000
Excluded support (gross receipts)	100,000
Qualified support	$300,000

One-third of qualified support would be $100,000. Support from governmental units and the general public is as follows:

Governmental units	$30,000
Contributions of less than $6,000 per donor	10,000
Two contributions in excess of $6,000 (only $6,000 per donor qualifies) 2 × $6,000	12,000
	$52,000

Museum X's support from the general public and from governmental units does not meet the one-third test. Because its support from these organizations exceeds 10 percent of its total support, however, it may meet the second test, discussed below.

A second facts-and-circumstances test may be used if the organization fails to meet the one-third support test. Two requirements must be met to satisfy this test. (a) The percentage of support normally received by the organization from governmental units and/or the general public must be at least 10 percent of the total support normally received by such organization. ("Normally" means support computed using the four-year period immediately preceding the current year). (b) The organization must be so organized and operated as to attract new and additional public or governmental support on a continuous basis. The organization will be considered to have met this requirement if it maintains a continuous and bona fide program for solicitation of funds from the general public, community, or membership group involved or if it carries on activities designed to attract support from governmental units or other charitable organizations. Consideration is given to the scope of its fund-rasing activities. Factors taken into consideration in meeting the second requirement include the following. (a) The percentage of support received by an organization from public or governmental sources: The higher the percentage of support above the 10 percent requirement, the less the burden of establishing the publicly supported nature of the organization in other ways. If the percentage is low, the source of endowment funds will be noted. If such funds were originally contributed by a few individuals or members of their families, the burden on the organization of establishing compliance with other factors will increase. (b) The sources of support: A determination will be made as to whether support is from a representative number of persons or almost all from members of a single family. (c) A representative governing body: The fact that an organization has a governing body which represents the broad interest of the public, rather than the personal or private interests of a limited number of donors, is considered in determining whether the organization is "publicly supported." An organization meets this requirement if it has a governing body comprised of public officials acting in their capacities as such, persons having special knowledge or expertise in the particular field or discipline in which the organization is operating, community leaders, or individuals elected pursuant to the governing instrument by a broadly based membership. (d) Facilities available to the public or programs or policies in which the public may participate: The fact that an organization is of the type which generally provides facilities or services directly for the benefit of the general public on a continuing basis, such as a museum, is evidence that the organization is "publicly supported." (e) Additional factors to be considered are whether the solicitation for dues is designed to enroll a substantial number of persons in the community or in a particular field of interest, whether dues for individual members have been fixed at rates designed to make membership available to a broad cross section of the public rather than to restrict membership to a limited number of persons, and whether the activities of the organization will appeal to persons having some broad common interest or purpose.

The 10 percent test applies the same requirements for support as the one-third support test (i.e., contributions from an individual, trust, or corporation are taken into account in the numerator of the fraction only to the extent that the contributions do not exceed 2 percent of the organization's total support, while amounts received for the performance of service are excluded from both the numerator and the denominator).

Grantors and contributors to a public charity under 509 (a) (1) can rely on its status as a publicly supported organization until notice of change of status is made to the public by publication in the Internal Revenue *Bulletin*. This does not apply, however, if the contributor was responsible for, or was aware of, the substantial and material change that caused the organization to cease to be a publicly supported organization. This presents a problem in that a substantial donation by one person could cause the organization to lose its status, as noted above. For their own protection grantors should obtain a written statement from the grantee organization that the grant will not result in the loss of the organization's classification as a publicly supported organization. Such a statement should include a summary of the pertinent financial data for the four preceding years.

If a museum has been in existence for at least one taxable year consisting of at least eight months but for fewer than five taxable years, the number of years for which the organization has been in existence immediately preceding the current taxable year being tested will be substituted for the four-year period.

509 (a) (2) Museums. If a museum receives the majority of its support from activities related to its exempt functions, it may not qualify under 509 (a) (1). It is possible, however, that such a museum, one with large receipts for services in relationship to other support, can qualify as a 509 (a) (2) organization. A museum that provides facilities and charges admission fees would be in this category. To qualify as a 509 (a) (2) organization, two tests must be met, a one-third support test and a one-third gross investment income test. Both of these tests are designed to assure that the organization is responsive to the general public and not to a private interest group or donor.

The one-third support test requires that the museum receive more than one-third of its support from (a) gifts, grants, contributions, or membership fees and (b) gross receipts from admissions, sales, performance of services, or furnishing of facilities, in an activity which is not an unrelated trade or business (discussed below). Funds received from governmental units, from 509 (a) (1) organizations, and from persons *other than disqualified persons* are permitted sources for this test. Disqualified persons include substantial contributors (any person who contributed an aggregate amount of more than $5,000 if the amount is more than 2 percent of the total contributions received by the organization before the close of the taxable year in which the contribution is received), a museum manager (officer, director, or trustee of the museum), an owner of more than 20 percent of a corporation, partnership, or the beneficial interest of a trust which is a substantial contributor, a member of the family of any of the above individuals (spouse, ancestor, lineal descendants, and spouses of lineal descendants), or a corporation, partnership, or trust in which any of the above persons own more than 35 percent. Recall that support from disqualified persons can be added to the numerator of a 509 (a) (1) organization to as much as 2 percent of total support; however, it cannot be counted at all for a 509 (a) (2) organization. Such support is added to the denominator of a 509 (a) (2) museum, but it is not added to the numerator.

In computing the amount of support from gross receipts, those receipts from a "qualified" person or from an agency of a governmental unit are included in the numerator of the support test only to the extent of $5,000 or 1 percent of the organization's support for the year, whichever is greater. Gifts, grants, and membership fees are counted in full. If a governmental unit makes a grant to a 509 (a) (2) museum, it is counted in full; if it is a payment for services rendered, it is subject to the limitation of $5,000 or 1 percent. A payment made to a museum in order to receive a specific service or product to serve the immediate needs of the payor, rather than one made primarily to confer a direct benefit upon the general public, is a gross receipt rather than a grant and is limited to $5,000 or 1 percent. If a donor earmarks a contribution to a charity, and that charity, in turn, makes a contribution to a 509 (a) (2) organization, the contribution is deemed an indirect contribution from the donor and will be excluded from the numerator of the fraction altogether if the donor is a disqualified person.

Example 5. Museum X received $600,000 during the current year from the following sources:

State department for services rendered by X	$15,000
A, an individual, for services rendered by X	20,000
General public (gross receipts)	300,000
Gross investment income	50,000
Contributions from disqualified persons	215,000
	$600,000

Because the $15,000 received from state department and the $20,000 received from A are more than $5,000, each amount is counted in the numerator only to the greater of $5,000 or 1 percent of total support. One percent of support is $6,000; hence, these two amounts are limited to $6,000 each. Contributions of $215,000 from disqualified persons cannot be counted in the numerator at all. In computing for the one-third support test, support received is taken into account as follows:

State department	$6,000
A, an individual	6,000
General public	300,000
	$312,000

The fraction becomes $312,000/$600,000. It is more than one-third; consequently, Museum X meets the one-third support test.

Example 6. Assume that Museum X is a 509 (a) (1) organization under section 170 (b) (1) (A) (vi). Support representing gross receipts for services rendered would be excluded from both the numerator and the denominator of the fraction; consequently, total support would be $265,000 ($50,000 gross investment income and $215,000 contributions from disqualified persons). The $215,000 contributions from disqualified persons could be counted to a maximum of 2 percent of total support of $265,000 or $5,300, for each contribution. Whether Museum X would qualify as a 509 (a) (1) organization would depend upon how many contributors it had. The contribution of each would be limited to $5,300 in determining the numerator of the fraction. If it could not satisfy the one-third support test, it could attempt to satisfy the facts-and-circumstances test. The fact that more than half the museum's income is from receipts from activities of its exempt function probably would not disqualify it as a 509 (a) (1) organization. What percentage disqualifies an organization is not stated in the regulations. (Regulation 1.170A-9 (e) (7) (ii) simply states that an organization which receives almost all its support from gross receipts from related activities and an insignificant amount from governmental units and contributions from the general public will not qualify as a 509 (a) (1) organization.)

A 509 (a) (2) organization must also meet a one-third gross investment test. This test requires that such an organization normally receive no more than one-third of its support in each year from gross investment income. If an organization performs services relating to its exempt function which produce income generally considered to be passive income, such receipts are considered gross receipts and not investment income. Rent on its facilities, for example, could under certain circumstances qualify as gross receipts; however, if the organization rents part of its facilities to persons having no relationship to its exempt purpose, the rental is regarded as gross investment income. Gross investment income does not include net capital gains.

As for a 509 (a) (1) organization, a 509 (a) (2) organization computes the one-third support test (and the gross investment income test) over a four-year period. For purposes of the four-year test, contributions that are substantial and unusual or unexpected may, as in a 509 (a) (1) organization, be excluded from the numerator and from the denominator. A 509 (a) (2) organization must meet the same requirements as a 509 (a) (1) organization in determining whether contributions qualify as unusual or unexpected.

509 (a) (3) and 509 (a) (4) Organizations. An organization which receives little, if any, support from the general public can still qualify as a public charity if it supports other qualified public charities. Section 509 (a) (3) gives public charity status to so-called supporting organizations, those operated exclusively for the benefit of 509 (a) (1) and (2) organizations and controlled by such organizations. Section 509 (a) (3) organizations cannot be controlled by disqualified persons. To qualify for 509 (a) (3) status, certain tests as to organization, operation, and relationship with public charities must be met. Organizations whose purpose is testing for public safety qualify as 509 (a) (4) organizations. It is rather unlikely that a museum would qualify for 509 (a) (3) status, and it definitely would not for 509 (a) (4) status.

Private Foundation

If a museum cannot meet the requirements of either 509 (a) (1) or 509 (a) (2), it will be deemed a private foundation and will be subject to substantial restrictions and reporting requirements. A private foundation will be exempt from federal income taxation only if its governing instrument includes provisions that require distributions of income, prohibit it from engaging in acts of self-dealing, prohibit it from retaining excess business holdings, prevent it from making so-called taxable expenditures, and prohibit it from making certain investments.[7] (This requirement is waived if state law treats these required provisions as being contained in a private foundation's governing instrument.) Gifts to private foundations which have not complied with filing requirements or requirements as to their governing instruments are not tax deductible.

Private foundations must file Form 990-PF on or before the fifteenth day of the fifth month following the close of its accounting period. The information on this return will be made available for public inspection by the Internal Revenue Service. If a private foundation has unrelated business taxable income (discussed below) in excess of $1,000, it must also file Form 990-T. This form must also be filed on or before the fifteenth day of the fifth month following the close of its taxable year. All private foundations having at least $5,000 of assets at any time during a taxable year must file an annual report on Form 990-AR. The annual report must be made available by the foundation manager for public inspection; notice of its availability must be published by the foundation; and a copy of it must be furnished to state officers. (These forms are illustrated in appendixes B and D.)

Private foundations are subject to a 2 percent tax on net investment income and to penalty taxes for engaging in certain prohibited acts. The prohibited acts, sections 4941 through 4945 of the Internal Revenue Code, are: self-dealing, engaging in so-called jeopardizing investments, having "excess business holdings," and making improper expenditures. A private foundation other than an operating foundation is also penalized if it fails to distribute its current income by the close of the following tax year. These prohibited acts, or failures to act, are discussed briefly to alert the reader to the law's provisions and to define areas which may present conflicts of interest for museum directors even if the museum is not a private foundation for tax purposes. I will not discuss planned avoidance of certain tax traps in the Code provisions or attempt to explore the many ramifications of the Code provisions.

Self-Dealing. Section 4941 of the Internal Revenue Code imposes an excise tax on each act of self-dealing between a disqualified person and a private foundation. This tax is imposed on the disqualified person even though he may have had no knowledge that the act constituted self-dealing. The tax on self-dealing is initially 5 percent of the amount involved for each year and is paid by the disqualified person who participates in the act. The foundation manager is subject to a penalty tax of 2½ percent of the amount involved (maximum of $10,000) for each year if he knows the act could be described as self-dealing and he willfully participates. If the foundation manager is also acting as a self-dealer, he may be subject to both the 5 percent penalty and the 2½ percent penalty. Should the act of self-dealing not be corrected within ninety days after the date of mailing of a notice of deficiency for the penalty tax, an additional tax of 200 percent of the amount involved will be due from the disqualified person who participated in the act. An additional tax is also imposed on the foundation manager in the amount of 50 percent of the amount involved (maximum of $10,000) if he refuses to agree to part or all of the correction of the self-dealing act.

The term "self-dealing" includes transactions between a private foundation and a disqualified person which are either direct or indirect. It is immaterial whether the transaction results in a benefit or a detriment to the private foundation.[8] Specific acts of self-dealing include: (a) the sale or exchange of property between a private foundation and a disqualified person. (b) the leasing of property between a disqualified person and a private foundation. (The leasing of property without charge by a disqualified person to a private foundation is not an act of self-dealing.) (c) The lending of money or other extension of credit between a private foundation and a disqualified person. (The lending of money by a disqualified person to a private foundation is not an act of self-dealing if the loan is without interest or other charge.) (d) The furnishing of goods, services, or facilities between a private foundation and a disqualified person. (The furnishing of goods, services, or facilities by a disqualified person to a private foundation is not an act of self-dealing if they are furnished without charge. (e) Payment of compensation (or reimbursement of expenses) by a private foundation to a disqualified person (unless the payment is for performance of personal services which are reasonable and necessary to carry out the exempt purpose of the foundation.) (f) The transfer of the income or assets of a private foundation to, or for the use by, or the benefit of, a disqualified person. (This does not include certain incidental or tenuous benefits from the use by a foundation of its income or assets, such as the public recognition a disqualified person may receive from the charitable activities of the foundation.)

The transfer of real or personal property by a disqualified person to a private foundation is treated as a sale or exchange and thus is an act of self-dealing if the foundation assumes a mortgage or other lien placed on the property prior to the transfer or takes subject to a mortgage placed on the property within a ten-year period ending on the date of transfer. If a private foundation indemnifies or guarantees a loan to a disqualified person, it is an act of self-dealing. Further, if a private foundation satisfies the legal obligation of a disqualified person, it is an act of self-dealing. The furnishing of goods, services, or facilities by a private foundation to a disqualified person is not an act of self-dealing if the goods, services, or facilities are made available to the general public on at least as favorable a basis as they are to disqualified persons. This exception, however, applies only if the goods, services, or facilities are functionally related to the exempt purposes of the private foundation.

The "amount involved" in an act of self-dealing (subject to the 5 percent initial penalty and the 200 percent penalty for failure to correct) is the greater of the amount of money and fair value of property received or the amount of money and fair value of property given. In cases of compensation, only the excess compensation is the amount involved. Should property be leased by a private foundation to a disqualified person, the amount involved is the greater of the amount of rent received from the disqualified person or the fair rental value of the property for the period of use. If an act of self-dealing would not have occurred had the private foundation received fair market value, the amount involved is the excess of the fair market value of the property transferred over the amount which the foundation receives. Correction of an act of self-dealing is generally accomplished by undoing the transaction to the extent possible, but in no case shall the financial position of the foundation be worse than it would have been had the disqualified person acted under the highest standards. For example, in the sale of property by a disqualified person for cash, undoing the transaction includes rescission of the sale. The amount returned to the disqualified person is the lesser of the cash received by the private foundation or the fair market value of the property. The disqualified person must also pay the foundation any income derived by him from the time of the sale, to the extent that it exceeds income earned by the foundation on the cash it received for the sale. In instances of excessive compensation, correction requires the disqualified person to pay the foundation the amount deemed excessive. The correction period begins on the date when the act of self-dealing occurred and ends ninety days after the date of the mailing of a notice of tax deficiency.

Failure to Distribute Income. Section 4942 of the Internal Revenue Code imposes a 15 percent tax on undistributed income of a private foundation (other than an operating foundation), with an additional tax of 100 percent on any undistributed income remaining at the end of ninety days after the mailing of a notice of tax deficiency. Undistributed income is the distributable amount of income reduced by qualifying distributions.

Distributable amount of income is an amount equal to the minimum investment return reduced by taxes imposed upon the foundation.[9] For tax years prior to 1982, it was the greater of minimum investment return or adjusted net income. The minimum investment return is computed by multiplying by 5 percent (for tax years beginning in 1976) the excess of the aggregate fair market value of foundation assets not used to perform its exempt functions over the amount of the acquisition indebtedness on such assets. In computing the fair market value of the foundation's assets, any assets used directly in carrying out the foundation's exempt purposes are excluded. The adjusted net income is the excess of the gross income for the year (including gross income from an unrelated trade or business) over the deductions for the year. Tax-exempt income is included for these purposes as well as short-term capital gains (long-term gains are not). Gross income does not include gifts, grants, or contributions. Gross income includes amounts received that were previously treated as qualifying distributions. Deductions from gross income include all ordinary and necessary expenses incurred for the production or collection of gross income or for the management, conservation, or maintenance of property held for the production of income. Straight-line depreciation is an allowable deduction. Where part of property involved is used for exempt purposes of the foundation, the deductions are apportioned between the exempt and nonexempt uses.

Qualifying distributions are those made for charitable purposes. They include program-related investments and reasonable and necessary administrative expenses. If a private foundation purchased an additional building to carry on its exempt purposes, for example, such purchase would be a qualifying distribution. If an asset not used for exempt purposes is converted to a charitable use, the conversion is a qualifying distribution. A private foundation can set aside amounts for a specific project and have those amounts treated as qualifying distributions if the project will be completed within five years and the project is one which can be better accomplished by set-aside funds than by the immediate payments of funds.

To avoid tax on undistributed income, income must be distributed in the form of qualified distributions no later than the close of the following tax year. Qualifying distributions are first deemed to have been made from undistributed income of the immediately preceding taxable year, then from undistributed income of the current year, and finally from corpus. If qualifying distributions exceed the "distributable amount," the excess can be carried over for five years.

Excess Business Holdings. Section 4943 of the Internal Revenue Code imposes a penalty tax of 5 percent on the value of excess business holdings of a private foundation. There is an additional tax of 200 percent of the excess holdings if they are not disposed of within ninety days after the mailing of a tax deficiency notice. "Excess business holdings" are those that exceed so-called permitted holdings. A private foundation is permitted holdings in a corporation of not more than 20 percent of the voting stock, reduced by the percentage of voting stock owned by disqualified persons, and a 20 percent interest in a partnership. If effective control of the corporation is held by persons who are not disqualified persons, permitted holding can be 35 percent. Nonvoting stock cannot be held by a private foundation unless all disqualified persons own less than 20 percent of the voting stock. Should a disqualified person acquire an interest in a corporation, causing the private foundation to have excess holdings, the foundation can dispose of its own stock, which represents the excess interest, within ninety days from the date the foundation knows, or has reason to know, of the acquisition by the disqualified person, and it will not be liable for the penalty tax on excess holdings.[10] If a private foundation acquires excess business holdings because of a gift or bequest, it has five years to dispose of such holdings before it will become liable for a penalty tax.[11] When excess business holdings are purchased, there is no grace period. Should excess business holdings be sold to disqualified persons, such sale constitutes an act of self-dealing.

Jeopardizing Investments. Section 4944 prescribes a penalty of 5 percent on speculative investments. In addition, if the foundation manager participates in the investment, knowing that he is jeopardizing the performing of the foundation's exempt purpose, a 5 percent penalty of the amount so invested (to a maximum of $5,000) is imposed upon him. His participation must be willful and not due to reasonable cause. If the investment is not removed from jeopardy within ninety days after the mailing of a tax deficiency notice, an additional penalty of 25 percent of the amount of the investment (to a maximum of $10,000) is imposed. There is an additional tax of 5 percent on the manager (to a maximum of $10,000) if he refuses to agree to the removal of part or all of the investment from jeopardy.

The jeopardizing effect of each investment is made on an individual basis, taking into account the foundation's portfolio as a whole. No category of investments is treated as jeopardizing per se. Certain investments are closely scrutinized, however. Trading in securities on margin, trading in commodity futures, investment in working interests in oil and gas wells, purchase of "puts" and "calls," purchase of warrants, and selling short are all mentioned by the regulations as being possible speculative investments.[12] The determination as to whether an investment is speculative is made at the time of the investment and not subsequently on the basis of hindsight.

Taxable Expenditures. Section 4945 of the Code imposes a penalty tax of 10 percent of the amount of so-called taxable expenditures. If a foundation manager agrees to the expenditure knowing that it is taxable and if his action is willful and without reasonable cause, he is subject to a tax at the rate of 2½ percent of the amount of each expenditure (to a maximum of $5,000). Should the expenditure not be corrected within ninety days after the mailing of a deficiency notice, an additional tax of 100 percent of the amount of each taxable expenditure is imposed upon the private foundation. If the foundation manager has refused to agree to part or all of the correction, an additional tax of 50 percent of the expenditure is imposed upon him (to a maximum of $10,000).

Taxable expenditures include amounts paid or incurred by a private foundation to carry on propaganda or otherwise to attempt to influence legislation. "Legislation" includes action by Congress, by any state legislature, by any local council or similar governing body, or by the public in a referendum initiative, constitutional amendment, or similar procedure. It does not include actions by executive, judicial, or administrative bodies. Engaging in nonpartisan analysis, study, or research and making the result available to the general public or to governmental bodies, is not considered the carrying on of propaganda to influence legislation. Any amount paid by a private foundation to influence the outcome of a public election or to carry on a voter registration drive is a taxable expenditure.

Grants in the form of scholarships, prizes, internships, and awards to an individual for travel, study, or other similar purposes are taxable expenditures unless certain conditions are met.[13] A grant must be awarded on an objective and nondiscriminatory basis. The grant must be made pursuant to a procedure approved in advance by the Internal Revenue Service. Further, the grant must be a nontaxable scholarship to be utilized for study at an educational institution, a tax-free prize or award, or a grant whose purpose is to achieve a specific objective, produce a report or other similar product, or improve a literary, artistic, musical, scientific, teaching, or other similar capacity, skill, or talent of the grantee.[14]

Grants to organizations other than 509 (a) (1), (2), or (3) organizations are taxable expenditures unless the private foundation exercises "expenditure responsibility." To exercise expenditure responsibility, the foundation must exert all reasonable efforts, and establish adequate procedures, to determine that the grant is spent solely for the purpose for which it is made. It must obtain full and complete reports from the grantee as to how funds were spent. The foundation should make a pregrant inquiry concerning the potential grantee, should require that the organization repay any portion of the grant not used for its specified purposes, and must require full and complete annual reports on the manner in which the funds were expended.

Any amounts paid by a private foundation for a noncharitable purpose are taxable expenditures. Expenses for unreasonable administrative expenses, including compensation and consultant fees, will ordinarily be taxable expenditures.

Private Operating Foundations

An operating foundation is a private foundation which spends substantially all of its net income directly for the active conduct of the activities constituting the purpose for which it was organized and which meets either an assets test, an endowment test, or a support test.[15] Operating foundations receive the same treatment as public charities as far as charitable contributions deductions to donors are concerned. Further, operating foundations are not subject to the excise tax on undistributed income. Such foundations are subject to the 2 percent tax on net investment income and to the penalty taxes on self-dealing, excess business holdings, speculative investments, and taxable expenditures. If a museum is classified as a private foundation, it should seek operating foundation status. (See illustration of private operating foundation under "Application for Exempt Status.")

Termination of Private Foundation Status

If a museum is a private foundation and finds such status onerous, it can voluntarily terminate as a private foundation pursuant to section 507 of the Internal Revenue Code. Still, unless it transfers all its assets to one or more public charities organized under 509 (a) (1) which have been in existence and so classified for at least sixty months, or itself converts to public charity status under 509 (a) (1) or (2), substantial taxes are imposed upon termination. The taxes imposed are the lesser of (a) the total amounts of all tax benefits (income, estate, and gift) derived by all substantial contributors to the foundation, plus the increased income tax that would have been imposed on the private foundation if it had not been tax-exempt (and interest on such tax liability) or (b) the value of the net assets of the organization.

A museum would terminate private foundation status by itself converting to public charity status. This is accomplished by meeting the requirements of section 509 (a) (1) or 509 (a) (2) for a continuous sixty-month period beginning on the first day of a tax year after it notifies the Internal Revenue Service of its intent to operate as a public charity. The notice must be given the IRS before the beginning of the sixty-month period and must indicate which classification the foundation seeks. If 509 (a) (1) is applicable, the notice should state that the museum seeks 170 (b) (1) (A) (vi) classification and should indicate the date when the museum's regular tax year and the sixty-month period begin. A museum choosing to convert to public charity status under the sixty-month termination should apply for an advance ruling so that contributors can be assured about that status. The decision to grant a favorable ruling will be based on facts and circumstances considering organizational structure, proposed programs and activities, intended methods of operation, and projected sources of support.

A private foundation will be involuntarily terminated if it commits at least two willful acts, or failures to act, giving rise to penalty taxes discussed above. If such acts occur, the foundation cannot terminate under provisions that permit it to transfer its assets to public charities or to go public itself.

Application for Exempt Status

As noted above, application for exempt status is made by filing Form 1023 (appendix E). This form serves both as an application for a ruling letter recognizing the exempt status of the organization and as the required notification that the organization is not a private foundation. (If a particular museum is not a private foundation and has annual gross receipts normally not exceeding $5,000, it need not file Form 1023.)

Form 1023 has eight parts and six schedules. An organization only completes those parts which pertain to that particular type of organization. For example, a museum would eliminate all the schedules. It would complete Parts I (identification); II (information on organizational documents), attaching its articles of incorporation and bylaws, or its trust indenture; III (activities and operation information); IV (statement as to private foundation status); and V (financial data). If it is not a private foundation, it would complete Part VII (basis for nonprivate foundation status). If it is a private operating foundation, it would complete Part VIII (basis for status as a private operating foundation). If an organization fails to give notice that it is not a private foundation within fifteen months from the end of the first month in which it was created, it will not qualify for exempt status during the period prior to the date of the actual notice. Form 1023 and all supporting documents are open to public inspection.

A new organization may apply for an advance ruling as to its status as a publicly supported organization if it has not been in existence for one taxable year consisting of at least eight months. If such a newly created organization can reasonably be expected to meet either the one-third support test or the facts-and-circumstances test for 509 (a) (1) organizations [under section 170 (b) (1) (A) (vi)], or the support and investment tests for 509 (a) (2) organizations, discussed above, it may be issued an advance determination letter that it will be treated as a publicly supported organization under 509 (a) (1) or (2) for its first two taxable years (or its first three taxable years if its first taxable year consists of less than eight months). The basic consideration in determining whether an organization can reasonably be expected to meet the support requirement is whether its organizational structure, proposed programs or activities, and intended method of operation are such as to attract the type of broadly based support from the general public, public charities, and governmental units necessary to meet such tests. Grantors and contributors may rely on the public status of newly created organizations which have received advance determination letters until that ruling letter is terminated and notice of change of status is made to the public by publication in the Internal Revenue *Bulletin*. (This does not apply if the contributor was responsible for, or aware of, the act or failure to act which resulted in the organization's loss of status.) An advance ruling period can be extended for three taxable years after the close of the original advance ruling period if the organization so requests. Still, such a request must include a consent to the extension of the period of limitation of assessment of tax liability by filing Form 872-C (see appendix E). It is doubtful that a museum would receive any contributions until it has received an advance ruling as to its public charity status. It should, therefore, apply for the five-year advance ruling period and should include Form 872-C.

Part VII of Form 1023 is illustrated below. This part is important because the organization completes it in order to classify itself as a public charity. A museum should check either line 7 [section 509 (a) (1) organization under 170 (b) (1) (A (vi)] or line 8 [section 509 (a) (2) organization]. It should check line 8 only if it cannot qualify under line 7. It must then supply information to determine whether it meets the one-third support test or the 10 percent support test for 509 (a) (1) organizations or the one-third support test and the one-third investment income test for 509 (a) (2) organizations. (For these purposes, recall that unusual and unexpected gifts, substantial in amount, which would, by reason of their size, adversely affect the status of the organization in meeting the support tests may be excluded if certain conditions are met.) For purposes of determining support, only the cash method of receipts and disbursements can be used. If a grant is payable over a term of years, it is included in the support fraction only when and to the extent that amounts are received by the grantee organization. For an organization which has been in existence for at least one taxable year consisting of at least eight months but for fewer than five taxable years, the number of years for which the organization has been in existence immediately preceding the current year being tested will be substituted for the four-year period normally used to determine financial support. (If an organization has not been in existence for at least one taxable year consisting of at least eight months, it must apply for an advance ruling. The Internal Revenue Service will use only the information supplied in Part III of Form 1023 to determine if an advance ruling as to public charity status will be issued. In this case Parts V and VII are not completed.)

Operating Foundations. If a museum is a private foundation, it should attempt to qualify as an operating foundation. Part VIII of Form 1023 is completed for this purpose. The museum would list its adjusted net income and qualifying distributions (qualifying distributions had to be at least 85 percent of the adjusted net income. For tax years beginning after 1981, they may be the lesser of adjusted net income or minimum investment return; however, if minimum investment return is less than adjusted net income, substantially all the qualifying distributions must be made directly for the active conduct of the foundation's exempt purposes.) Adjusted net income is the excess of gross income (including gross income from an unrelated trade or business and tax-exempt income) over certain deductions. These deductions include those directly

Part VII.—Non-Private Foundation Status (Definitive ruling only)

A.—Basis for Non-Private Foundation Status

The organization is not a private foundation because it qualifies as:

✓	Kind of organization	Within the meaning of	Complete
1	a church	Sections 509(a)(1) and 170(b)(1)(A)(i)	/////
2	a school	Sections 509(a)(1) and 170(b)(1)(A)(ii)	/////
3	a hospital	Sections 509(a)(1) and 170(b)(1)(A)(iii)	/////
4	a medical research organization operated in conjunction with a hospital	Sections 509(a)(1) and 170(b)(1)(A)(iii)	/////
5	being organized and operated exclusively for testing for public safety	Section 509(a)(4)	/////
6	being operated for the benefit of a college or university which is owned or operated by a governmental unit	Sections 509(a)(1) and 170(b)(1)(A)(iv)	Part VII.–B
7 X	normally receiving a substantial part of its support from a governmental unit or from the general public	Sections 509(a)(1) and 170(b)(1)(A)(vi)	Part VII.–B
8	normally receiving not more than one-third of its support from gross investment income and more than one-third of its support from contributions, membership fees, and gross receipts from activities related to its exempt functions (subject to certain exceptions)	Section 509(a)(2)	Part VII.–B
9	being operated solely for the benefit of or in connection with one or more of the organizations described in 1 through 4, or 6, 7, and 8 above	Section 509(a)(3)	Part VII.–C

B.—Analysis of Financial Support

	(a) Most recent tax year 19........	(b) 19........	(c) 19........	(d) 19........	(e) Total
1 Gifts, grants, and contributions received	40,000	30,000	40,000	40,000	150,000
2 Membership fees received .	10,000	15,000	16,000	18,000	59,000
3 Gross receipts from admissions, sales of merchandise or services, or furnishing of facilities in any activity which is not an unrelated business within the meaning of section 513	100,000	110,000	120,000	200,000	530,000
4 Gross investment income (see instructions for definition)	5,000	6,000	4,000	8,000	23,000
5 Net income from organization's unrelated business activities not included on line 4					
6 Tax revenues levied for and either paid to or spent on behalf of the organization . .					
7 Value of services or facilities furnished by a governmental unit to the organization without charge (not including the value of services or facilities generally furnished the public without charge)					
8 Other income (not including gain or loss from sale of capital assets)—attach schedule.					
9 Total of lines 1 through 8 .	155,000	161,000	180,000	266,000	762,000
10 Line 9 minus line 3 . . .	55,000	51,000	60,000	66,000	232,000
11 Enter 2% of line 10, column (e) only					4,640

12 If the organization has received any unusual grants during any of the above tax years, attach a list for each year showing the name of the contributor, the date and amount of grant, and a brief description of the nature of such grant. Do not include such grants on line 1 above—(See instructions).

Example 7. Museum X received the dollar amounts shown in the table below for the past four years.

	Year				
	1	2	3	4	Total
Gifts, grants, and contributions	40,000	30,000	40,000	40,000	150,000
Membership fees	10,000	15,000	16,000	18,000	59,000
Gross receipts	100,000	110,000	120,000	200,000	530,000
Rents and interest	5,000	6,000	4,000	8,000	23,000
Total	155,000	161,000	180,000	266,000	762,000

Of its gifts, $15,000 was received from disqualified donors ($8,000 from John Doe and Mary, his spouse, and $7,000 from Richard Roe). Total qualified support is $232,000 ($762,000 less $530,000 from gross receipts). Two percent of total qualified support is $4,640 (2 percent × $232,000). Hence, only $4,640 of John Doe's gift (his spouse is considered as the same person) and $4,640 of Roe's gift qualify. The numerator of the fraction would then be $226,280 [$232,000 − $5,720 [$15,000 − ($4,640 × 2)]], and the denominator would be $232,000. As the fraction exceeds one-third, Museum X qualifies as a public charity under sections 509 (a) (1) and 170 (b) (1) (A) (vi). Part VII of Form 1023 is shown completed on page 33. The statement attached to Part VII, shown below in tabular form, lists names and amounts contributed to Museum X by persons whose gifts for the total period exceeded the amount shown on line 11 of Part VII, B:

	Total contributions ($)	Amount in excess of 2 percent of line 11 ($)
John Doe	5,000	360
Richard Roe	7,000	2,360
Mary Doe (her contribution is considered to have been made by John Doe)	3,000	3,000
Total	15,000	5,720

Example 8. Assume the same facts as in Example 7, but assume that Museum X checked line 8 (it is attempting to qualify as a 509 (a) (2) organization). It must attach a list of all contributions from disqualified persons, who in this instance included the foundation manager as well as those who contributed more than $5,000 (assuming that that amount is more than 2 percent of total contributions received by the foundation from the time of its creation). (All such contributions are eliminated from the numerator of the fraction but are included in the denominator.) In addition, all gross receipts

from one person, or a governmental unit, in excess of $5,000 must be listed. These receipts are included in the numerator only to the extent of $5,000 or 1 percent of total support for the year, whichever is greater. Assume that the foundation manager contributed $3,000. The $15,000 received from John Doe and Richard Roe and the $3,000 from the foundation manager are eliminated from the numerator. Sales to A, an individual, were $10,000 in Year 1, $20,000 in Year 2, $30,000 in Year 3, and $15,000 in Year 4, State department paid the following amounts for services rendered: $80,000 in Year 1, $50,000 in Year 2, $60,000 in Year 3, and $100,000 in Year 4. The amounts excluded from the numerator from these amounts would be $325,000, computed as shown below.

	Excess of greater of $5,000 or 1 percent of annual support (whichever greater)	
	A	*State department*
Year 1. 1% of support is $1,550. Amount in excess of $5,000 is ($)	5,000	75,000
Year 2. 1% of support is $1,610. Amount in excess of $5,000 is ($)	15,000	45,000
Year 3. 1% of support is $1,800. Amount in excess of $5,000 is ($)	25,000	55,000
Year 4. 1% of support is $2,660. Amount in excess of $5,000 is ($)	10,000	95,000
Total	55,000	270,000

The numerator of the fraction is $419,000 [$762,000 − $18,000 − ($55,000 + $270,000)]. The denominator of the fraction is $762,000. As the fraction is greater than one-third, Museum X meets the one-third support test. It must also meet the one-third investment income test. Investment income on line 4 totals $23,000. This does not exceed one-third of total support; consequently, Museum X qualifies as a 509 (a) (2) organization.

connected with any trade or business, straight-line depreciation, cost depletion (on any oil or gas interests), and expenses relating to production or collection of income or the maintenance of income-producing property. Expenses for the general operation of the organization pursuant to its charitable purposes are not deductions for these purposes. They are qualifying distributions. In computing gross income, only short-term capital gains are counted; long-term capital gains are excluded. Repayments of prior qualifying distributions, amounts formerly set aside for specific charitable purposes no longer necessary for that purpose, and gross receipts from the sale of assets to the extent that the prior acquisition of such property was a qualifying distribution are all included in the computation of gross income.

A qualifying distribution is one made for a charitable purpose. It includes program-related investments and reasonable and necessary administrative expenses. Assume that the foundation purchased an additional building to carry on its exempt purpose. Such a purchase would be a qualifying distribution. When an asset not used for exempt purposes is converted to charitable use, such conversion is a qualifying distribution. A foundation can set aside amounts for a specific project and can have those amounts treated as qualifying distributions if the project will be completed in five years and is better accomplished by set-aside funds than by the immediate payments of funds.

An operating foundation must also meet one of three tests: an assets test, an endowment test, or a support test. The assets test is met if 65 percent or more of the assets of the foundation are devoted directly to the active conduct of activities constituting the foundation's exempt purpose or to functionally related businesses. This is the test a museum should use.

The endowment test requires the foundation to make qualifying distributions directly for the active conduct of activities constituting its exempt purpose in an amount not less than two-thirds of its minimum investment return. Minimum investment return is the excess of the aggregate fair market value of foundation assets not used to carry out its exempt function over the amount of any acquisition indebtedness on such assets, multiplied by 5 percent. This test applies to foundations in which personal services are large as compared with charitable assets.

The support test requires that 85 percent of the foundation's support (other than gross investment income) be received from the general public and from five or more exempt organizations, with not more than 25 percent of its support coming from any one exempt organization and not more than half its support being received from gross investment income. Support from exempt organizations can be counted only if the foundation receives support from no fewer than five exempt organizations. Suppose a foundation normally received 20 percent of its support from each of five exempt organizations. It could qualify even though it receives no support from the general public. Support from the general public can be counted only to the extent that total support received from any individual, trust, or corporation does not exeeed 1 percent of the foundation's total support (other than gross investment income). If a museum can meet this test, it should consider public charity status under 509 (a) (1) and 170 (b) (1) (A) (vi).

Example 9. Museum X was established by one donor. It receives no support from the general public; hence, it cannot qualify as a public charity. It should attempt to be classified as an operating foundation. Assume that its gross income for the year is $100,000. Its expenses relating to production of income total $20,000. Reasonable expenses of managing the museum total $30,000. Museum X purchased new museum objects during the year costing $40,000. The museum building and its contents, and other assets used in activities to directly carry out its exempt purposes, are valued at $1,000,000. Museum X has other assets not related to its exempt purposes valued at $200,000. Museum X would qualify as an operating foundation. Its adjusted net income is $80,000 ($100,000 − $20,000). Qualifying distributions total $70,000 ($30,000 + $40,000). Hence it satisfies the income test. It also satisfies the assets test in that 83.33 percent of its assets ($1,000,000/$1,200,000) are devoted directly to the active conduct of activities constituting the museum's exempt purpose. It would complete Part VIII of Form 1023 as shown on page 38.

Appeal Procedures. An application for exempt status is considered by a district director of the Internal Revenue Service. If the district director issues a proposed adverse determination letter denying exempt status, the organization may appeal to the regional director of appeals within thirty days from the date of the adverse determination letter. After it has exhausted administrative appeals within the IRS, an organization may seek a declaratory judgment from the U.S. Tax Court, the U.S. Court of Claims, or the U.S. District Court for the District of Columbia as to its exempt status. This remedy can be used for adverse determinations regarding section 501 (c) (3) status, section 509 (public charity) determinations, and section 4942 (j) (3) determinations (which conclude that an organization is not a private operating foundation). The declaratory judgment remedy cannot be used until all administrative remedies have been exhausted or 270 days have elapsed since the organization requested a determination as to the issue in question and the organization has taken, in a timely manner, all reasonable steps to

Part VIII.—Basis for Status as a Private Operating Foundation

If the organization—

(a) bases its claim to private operating foundation status on normal and regular operations over a period of years; or

(b) is newly created, set up as a private operating foundation, and has at least one year's experience;

provide the information under the income test and under one of the three supplemental tests (assets, endowment, or support). If the organization does not have at least one year's experience, complete line 21. If the organization's private operating foundation status depends on its normal and regular operations as described in (a) above, attach a schedule similar to the one below showing the data in tabular form for the three years next preceding the most recent tax year.

	Income Test	Most recent tax year
1	Adjusted net income, as defined in section 4942(f)	$80,000
2	Qualifying distributions:	
	(a) Amounts (including administrative expenses) paid directly for the active conduct of the activities for which organized and operated under section 501(c)(3) (attach schedule)	30,000
	(b) Amounts paid to acquire assets to be used (or held for use) directly in carrying out purposes described in sections 170(c)(1) or 170(c)(2)(B) (attach schedule)	40,000
	(c) Amounts set aside for specific projects which are for purposes described in section 170(c)(1) or 170(c)(2)(B) (attach schedule)	
	(d) Total qualifying distributions (add lines 2(a), (b), and (c))	70,000
3	Percentage of qualifying distributions to adjusted net income (divide line 2(d) by line 1—percentage must be at least 85%)	87.5 %
	Assets Test	
4	Value of organization's assets used in activities that directly carry out the exempt purposes. Do not include assets held merely for investment or production of income (attach schedule)	$1,000,000
5	Value of any stock of a corporation that is controlled by applicant organization and carries out its exempt purposes (attach statement describing corporation)	-0-
6	Value of all qualifying assets (add lines 4 and 5)	1,000,000
7	Value of applicant organization's total assets	1,200,000
8	Percentage of qualifying assets to total assets (divide line 6 by line 7—percentage must exceed 65%) .	83.33 %
	Endowment Test	
9	Value of assets not used (or held for use) directly in carrying out exempt purposes:	
	(a) Monthly average of investment securities at fair market value	
	(b) Monthly average of cash balances	
	(c) Fair market value of all other investment property (attach schedule)	
	(d) Total (add lines 9(a), (b), and (c))	
10	Subtract acquisition indebtedness related to line 9 items (attach schedule)	
11	Balance (subtract line 10 from line 9(d))	
12	For years beginning on or after January 1, 1976, multiply line 11 by a factor of 3⅓% (⅔ of the applicable percentage for the minimum investment return computation under section 4942(e)). Line 2(d) above must equal or exceed the result of this computation	
	Support Test	
13	Applicant organization's support as defined in section 509(d)	
14	Subtract amount of gross investment income as defined in section 509(e)	
15	Support for purposes of section 4942(j)(3)(B)(iii) (subtract line 14 from line 13)	
16	Support received from the general public, five or more exempt organizations, or a combination of these sources (attach schedule)	
17	For persons (other than exempt organizations) contributing more than 1% of line 15, enter the total amounts that are more than 1% of line 15	
18	Subtract line 17 from line 16	
19	Percentage of total support (divide line 18 by line 15—must be at least 85%)	%
20	Does line 16 include support from an exempt organization that is more than 25% of the amount on line 15?	☐ Yes ☐ No

21 Newly created organizations with less than one year's experience: Attach a statement explaining how the organization is planning to satisfy the requirements of section 4942(j)(3) for the income test and one of the supplemental tests during its first year's operation. Include a description of plans and arrangements, press clippings, public announcements, solicitations for funds, etc.

secure such a determination. The administrative remedies which must be exhausted are as follows: (a) the filing of application Form 1023 in substantial compliance with the law, (b) the timely submission of all additional information requested to perfect an exemption application, and (c) exhaustion of all administrative appeals available within the IRS. A petition for declaratory judgment must be filed with the appropriate court within ninety days from the date on which the Internal Revenue Service has sent a notice of its determination.

Unrelated Business Taxable Income

A museum, even though exempt, would be subject to income taxation if it engaged in activities of a commercial nature unrelated to its exempt purpose.[16] Taxable income in this context is determined by computing "unrelated business taxable income." The theory underlying a tax on unrelated business taxable income is that such business income distorts the exempt purpose of the organization and is a form of unfair competition to taxable organizations. Exempt organizations which have unrelated business taxable income of $1,000 or more (only net unrelated business income above $1,000 is taxed) must file a return on Form 990-T by the fifteenth day of the fifth month following the close of the taxable year for the organization. Tax liability is computed in the same manner as for a taxable organization. (See Form 990-T in appendix D). There are three types of unrelated business taxable income for an exempt organization: (a) income from an unrelated trade or business, (b) rental income from personal property, and (c) debt-financed income.

Income from an Unrelated Trade or Business

Unrelated business taxable income includes gross income derived from any unrelated trade or business regularly carried on less those deductions directly connected with the carrying on of such trade or business.[17] A trade or business is "regularly carried on" if the activities are frequent and continuous and are pursued in a manner generally similar to comparable commercial activities or nonexempt organizations. (Where income-producing activities are of a kind normally conducted by taxable organizations on a year-round basis, the conduct of such activities by an exempt organization over a period of a few weeks would not constitute the "regular carrying on" of a trade or business, and consequently the income would not be unrelated business income.) If the conduct of a trade or business produces income which is substantially related to the exempt purpose of the organization, the income is not subject to the unrelated business income tax.[18] To be related substantially to the exempt purpose of an organization, the production or distribution of goods or the performance of services must contribute in a significant manner to the accomplishment of the exempt purposes. For example, the IRS has ruled that operation of a parking lot, gift shop, or cafeteria by a hospital is not an unrelated trade or business.[19] It has also ruled that the sale of greeting card reproductions of art works by an art museum is not an unrelated trade or business.[20] The IRS ruled that the sale of these types of greeting cards stimulated and enhanced public awareness, interest, and appreciation of art; a broader segment of the public was conceivably being encouraged to visit the museum to share in its educational functions and programs as a result of seeing the cards. On the other hand, the IRS has ruled that the sale of scientific books and various souvenir items relating to the city in which a museum was located by a museum of folk art did constitute an unrelated trade or business.[21] It also ruled, however, that sales of reproductions of works in the museum's own collection and reproductions of artistic works from the collections of other art museums in the form of cards, slides, metal, wood, and ceramic copies, and instructional literature concerning the history and development of art would not be unrelated business taxable income. Sales must be related to the exempt educational purpose of the particular museum. Sales of scientifific books by a science museum would undoubtedly qualify as being related to its exempt purpose. The IRS has ruled that eating facilities operated by an exempt museum do not constitute an unrelated business, considering the size and methods of operations.[22] The sale of advertising, even though in a journal containing articles which contribute significantly to the accomplishment of the organization's exempt purpose, does constitute unrelated trade or business income.[23]

Section 513 (f) of the Internal Revenue Code provides that proceeds from bingo games will not be unrelated business income if state or local law permits nonprofit organizations to carry on bingo games and if the nonprofit organization does not compete with other, taxable organizations. (This is not the case in a jurisdiction where bingo games are carried on on a commercial basis.) Section 513 (f) only applies to bingo games; other games of chance are not exempt. Further, income from a regularly held lottery does constitute unrelated business income.

Deductions from unrelated business taxable income are those expenses which are generally allowable tax deductions; however, they must be "directly connected with" the conduct of the unrelated business. The expenses must have proximate and primary relationship to the operation of the business. Expenses attributable to facilities or personnel used both to operate exempt functions and to conduct unrelated trade or business must be allocated between the two uses on a reasonable basis. For example, if an employee of an exempt organization earns $12,000 a year and devotes 10 percent of his time to an unrelated business, the organization could deduct $1,200 of his salary in computing its unrelated business income.

The term "unrelated trade or business" does not include four types of activities. These are: (a) a trade or business in which substantially all the work in performing the activities is done without compensation; (b) a trade or business performed primarily for the convenience of members, students, officers, or employees (e.g., a museum operates a snack bar for members and employees); (c) the sale of items of work-related clothes and equipment and items normally sold through vending machines, through food-dispensing facilities, or by snack bars, for the convenience of its members at their usual place of employment; or (d) the selling of merchandise substantially all of which has been received by the organization as gifts or contributions.[24]

Example 10. A museum shop is selling souvenir items relating to the city in which the museum is located. The Internal Revenue Service has ruled that the sale of such items constitutes unrelated business taxable income. (See discussion above.) If museum volunteers perform all the activities of selling the souvenir items, the sales would not be taxable under section 513 of the Internal Revenue Code. In addition, the sale of any items given to the museum shop would not constitute taxable sales.

Investment Income

Unless investment income is from debt-financed property (discussed below), is received from a controlled organization, or is rent from personal property, it generally is not included in the definition of unrelated business taxable income and thus is not subject to taxation.

Rents. Rents, like dividends, interest, royalties, and annuities, are subject to the unrelated business income tax if they are derived from debt-financed property or from controlled organizations. Determination of amounts of taxable income from these sources is discussed below. Other rents are included in unrelated business taxable income only if they are derived from personal property. Rents from real property (buildings) are excluded (assuming that the amount of the rent charged is not based on profits). If personal property (property other than a building or land) is leased with real property and the rents attributable to the personal property are only an incidental amount of total rents received, they are also excluded from unrelated business taxable income. (Rents from personal property are considered to be incidental if they are not more than 10 percent of total rents from the leased property.) If personal property is leased with real property and rents from the personal property exceed 50 percent of total rents, all rents will be considered unrelated business taxable income. Rents from real property will also be unrelated business taxable income if the amount received depends in whole or in part on income or profits earned by the lessee (other than an amount based on a fixed percentage of the gross receipts or sales).

Example 11. Museum X owns a building which contains printing equipment. X rents the building and the equipment for $20,000 a year. The lease states that $18,000 is for the building and $2,000 is for the equipment. It is determined, however, that $6,000 of the rent is actually attributable to the equipment. During the year, X has $5,000 deductions, all of which are allocated to the land and building. X has unrelated business income of $6,000 attributable to the equipment. Because the rent on the personal property (the equipment) exceeds 10 percent of the total rents, it is counted as unrelated business income. Because the $5,000 deductions relate to the real property, none of the deductions can offset the $6,000 unrelated business income.[25]

Example 12. Museum X executes two leases with A. One is for the rental of equipment, with a stated annual rent of $1,500. The other is for rental of office space in which to use the equipment at a stated rental of $15,000. It is determined that, notwithstanding the terms of the leases, $5,000 (or 33.33 percent) of the rent is actually attributable to the equipment. Consequently, only $11,500 [($1,500 + $15,000) − $5,000] attributable to rental of the office space is excluded from X's unrelated business taxable income. Assume that the next year the rent on the equipment is $9,000 and the rent for the office is $8,000. Now rental on personal property exceeds 50 percent of total rents. The rent on the office space will continue to be excluded from unrelated business taxable income only if there was no modification of the terms of the leases. If the original lease provided that the rent would be increased or decreased, depending upon the prevailing rental value for equipment and office space, the rent for the office space could still be excluded. If a new lease is in effect, however, the rent for the office space will not be excluded because rent for personal property exceeds 50 percent of total rents.

Other Passive Income. Other passive income, such as interest, annuities, and royalties, is not unrelated business income unless such income is derived from a controlled organization. If an exempt organization has control of another organization (stock ownership of at least 80 percent of voting power and 80 percent of all other classes of stock, or control of 80 percent of trustees of a nonstock organization), unrelated business taxable income includes a portion of the passive income derived from the controlled organization. The amount of income received by the controlling organization that is unrelated business income will differ according to whether or not the controlled organization is, itself, an exempt organization. If the controlled organization is also an exempt organization, the amount of unrelated business income is determined by multiplying the total income received from the controlled organization by a fraction the numerator of which is the unrelated business taxable income of the controlled organization and the denominator of which is the greater of (a) the taxable income of the controlled organization, computed as though the controlled organization were not exempt, or (b) the unrelated business taxable income of the controlled organizations.

Example 13. Museum X rents laboratory space to A, an exempt scientific organization, for $20,000 per year. X owns all the stock of A. A's total deductions for the year on the leased property are $5,000 ($3,000 for maintenance and $2,000 for depreciation). If A were not an exempt organization, its total taxable income would be $300,000, disregarding rent paid to X. A's unrelated business taxable income, disregarding rent paid to X, is $100,000. X will have unrelated business taxable income of $5,000 from the rent paid it by A, determined as shown in the following.[26]

A's unrelated business taxable income	$100,000
A's taxable income	300,000
Ratio	⅓
Total rent	20,000
Total deductions	5,000
Difference	$15,000
One-third of net rentals	$ 5,000

If the controlled organization is not an exempt organization, the portion of the interest, annuities, royalties, or rents received from the controlled organization which is unrelated taxable business income is determined by multiplying the total amount received from the controlled organization by a fraction the numerator of which is the "excess taxable income" of the controlled organization and the denominator of which is the greater of (a) the taxable income of the controlled organization or (b) the "excess taxable income" of the controlled organization. "Excess taxable income" means the excess of the controlled organization's taxable income over the amount of its taxable income which would not be unrelated business income if it were an exempt organization.

Example 14. Museum X leases a building to A, a nonexempt organization which X controls, for $20,000. During the taxable year, A has $50,000 of taxable income, disregarding the rent paid to X. X's deductions for the taxable year with respect to the leased property are $5,000. Under these circumstances, X will include $15,000 of the amount paid by A as unrelated business taxable income, computed as shown below.[27]

A's taxable income	$50,000
Taxable income which would not be unrelated business taxable income if A were an exempt organization	
	0
Excess taxable income	$50,000
Ratio	100%
Total rent paid to X	$20,000
Total deductions	5,000
Rental income treated as unrelated business taxable income by X (100% of $15,000)	$15,000

Unrelated Debt-Financed Income

Income from property unrelated to the exempt function of the organization and subject to "average acquisition indebtedness" is also included in unrelated taxable business income. The portion of income from debt-financed properties which is subject to tax is called unrelated debt-financed income. The amount of unrelated debt-financed income from each debt-financed property is determined by multiplying the total gross income from the property by a percentage the numerator of which is the "average acquisition indebtedness" on the property and the denominator of which is the "average adjusted basis" of the property. This percentage is called the debt/basis percentage.

Property which is held to produce income unrelated to the organization's exempt purpose and on which there is an acquisition indebtedness at any time during the year is called debt-financed property.[28] The average acquisition indebtedness with respect to debt-financed property is the average amount of outstanding principal indebtedness for the portion of the year during which the property is held by the organization. Average acquisition indebtedness is computed by determining the amount of the outstanding principal indebtedness on the property on the first day of each calendar month during the year the organization held the property, adding these amounts, and dividing the sum by the total number of months during the year the organization held the property. A fractional part of the month is treated as a full month.[29]

Example 15. Museum X purchased a building which will not be devoted to the museum's exempt purposes on July 1 of the current year for $400,000, using $300,000 of borrowed money. Beginning on July 31, X makes payments of $15,000 per month on the principal. The average acquisition indebtedness for the year would be $262,500, computed as shown below.

	Indebtedness on first day in each calendar month the property is held ($)
July	300,000
August	285,000
September	270,000
October	255,000
November	240,000
December	225,000
Total	1,575,000

Average acquisition indebtedness: $1,575,000/6 = $262,500.

The average adjusted basis of debt-financed property is the average amount of the adjusted basis of the property for that portion of the year during which the property is held by the exempt organization. Adjusted basis is the cost of the property less depreciation allowable from the date of acquisition. The average adjusted basis is the average of the adjusted basis of the property on the first day of the year for which the organization held the property and the adjusted basis of the property on the last day of that year.

Example 16. In Example 15 above, Museum X purchased the building for $400,000. The building has a useful life of forty years; hence, depreciation would be $10,000 per year ($400,000/40). Depreciation for six months would be $5,000. Adjusted basis of the property at the end of the first year would be $395,000 ($400,000 − $5,000 depreciation). Average adjusted basis would be $397,500 [($400,000 adjusted basis at the beginning of the year + $395,000 adjusted basis at the end of the year) ÷ 2].

The debt/basis percent for the building purchased by Museum X would be 66 percent, computed as shown below.

$$\frac{\text{Average acquisition indebtedness}}{\text{Average adjusted basis}} = \frac{\$262,500}{\$397,500} = 66 \text{ percent.}$$

Assume that rentals from the building total $20,000 for Year 1. The unrelated debt-financed income for Museum X in Year 1 would be $13,200 ($20,000 × 66 percent). The same percentage would be applied to the deductions relating to the property. If allowable deductions total $6,000, $3,960 ($6,000 × 66 percent) would be a deduction in computing net unrelated debt-financed income.

Indebtedness incurred before the acquisition or improvement of property is included in acquisition indebtedness if the debt would not have been incurred but for the subsequent acquisition or improvement. Also, indebtedness incurred after the acquisition or improvement of property is included in acquisition indebtedness if it would not have been incurred except for the earlier acquisition or improvement and the incurrence of the indebtedness could reasonably have been foreseen at the time of the acquisition or improvement.[30] If property is acquired subject to a mortgage, the amount of the outstanding principal indebtedness is treated as acquisition indebtedness even though the organization does not assume or agree to pay the indebtedness. This is true whether the property is acquired by purchase, gift, devise, bequest, or other means. Where property subject to a mortgage is acquired by an organization by bequest or devise, the outstanding principal indebtedness is not treated as acquisition indebtedness during the ten-year period following the date of acquisition. For property acquired by gift but subject to a mortgage, the outstanding principal indebtedness is not treated as acquisition indebtedness during the ten-year period following the date of the gift if the mortgage was placed on the property more than five years before the date of the gift, and the property was held by the donor for more than five years before the date of the gift. If the organization agrees to pay all or any part of the indebtedness on property acquired by gift, devise, or bequest, the above exceptions do not apply.

Example 17. Museum X acquires a building by bequest. It is subject to a mortgage but the museum does not agree to pay it. For ten years, the outstanding principal indebtedness is not acquisition indebtedness. After ten years, any remaining outstanding principal indebtedness would be acquisition indebtedness if the building is otherwise treated as debt-financed property. If Museum X agreed to pay the mortgage, the outstanding principal indebtedness would be treated as acquisition indebtedness on the date of acquisition (assuming the building is treated as debt-financed property).[31]

If the use of property is substantially related to the exercise or performance of an organization's exempt purpose (aside from the need for funds), it is not treated as debt-financed property, and any income produced by such property is not unrelated business income. If 85 percent or more of the use of the property is devoted to the organization's exempt purposes, the property is considered substantially related to the performance of the organization's exempt purposes. For property used less than 85 percent for the organization's exempt purposes, the portion of the income that does not pertain to the performance of the organization's exempt purposes will be considered income from debt-financed property.

Should an organization acquire real property for the principal purpose of using the land in the performance of its exempt purpose, beginning such use within ten years from the time of acquisition, the property will not be treated as debt-financed property if the property is in the neighborhood of other property that is owned by the organization and is used in the performance of its exempt purpose and if the organization does not abandon its intent to use the land for its exempt purposes within the ten-year period. Once the organization abandons its intent to use the property for its exempt purpose, it becomes debt-financed property as of that date.

An organization is entitled to reduce its income from debt-financed property by deductions directly connected with the property. Depreciation deduction must be computed by the straight-line method. If the deductions exceed debt-financed income (after the debt/basis percentage has been applied to both), the organization has sustained a net operating loss and may carry it back three years and forward fifteen to offset income in those years.

If receipts are included in the computation of unrelated business taxable income from other sources, such as rents from personal property or interest from controlled organizations, they are not also considered unrelated debt-financed income.

Other Considerations in Computing Unrelated Business Taxable Income

Gains and losses from the sale, exchange, or other disposition of property, except property held primarily for sale to customers, are excluded from unrelated business unless they are gains from the sale or other disposition of debt-financed property. When debt-financed property is sold, unrelated debt-financed income includes a percentage of the gain. The percentage is computed by dividing the highest acquisition indebtedness on the property during the twelve-month period preceding the date of the disposition by the average adjusted basis of the property.

Example 18. Museum X purchased a building for $400,000 using $200,000 of borrowed funds. During the year, depreciation of $10,000 was deducted. In January of the following year the building was sold for $450,000. As of January, the adjusted basis of the building would be $390,000 and the indebtedness $180,000. The average adjusted basis of the property would be $395,000 [($400,000 − $390,000) ÷ 2]. The debt/basis percentage would be 50.6 percent, computed as shown below.

$$\frac{\text{Highest acquisition indebtedness on property during 12-month period preceding disposition}}{\text{Average adjusted basis of property}} = \frac{\$200,000}{\$395,000} = 50.6 \text{ percent}$$

Gain on the sale would be $60,000 ($450,000 selling price less $390,000 adjusted basis on date of sale). Of this amount, $33,360 ($60,000 × 50.6 percent) would be debt-financed income.

Preparation of Returns for Exempt Museums

If a museum is a private foundation, it must file an annual tax return on Form 990-PF on or before the fifteenth day of the fifth month following the close of its taxable year. If the foundation fails to file the return on or before the due date (taking into account any extensions granted), it will be required to pay a penalty of $10 for each day the return is late (not to exceed $5,000), unless it can be shown that the failure was due to reasonable cause. A private foundation is required to attach to its Form 990-PF a list of all states to which the organization reports concerning its organization, assets, or activities, or with which the organization has registered that it is a charitable organization or the holder of property devoted to a charitable purpose. All the information on Form 990-PF, including attachments, is available for public inspection. If the assets of the foundation are at least $5,000 at any time during the tax year, the foundation manager must also file an annual report indicating contributions, income, expenses, assets, liabilities, and net worth for the year. Form 990-AR may be used for these purposes.

At the same time that the reports are filed with the Internal Revenue Service, copies of the annual reports, Forms 990-PF and 990-AR (see appendix B), must be furnished to the attorney general of (a) each state listed on the Form 990-PF, (b) the state in which the principal office of the foundation is located, (c) the state in which the foundation was incorporated, and (d) any other state which requests the forms. The annual report, Form 990-AR, must be made available for inspection at the principal office of the foundation to any citizen upon request made within 180 days after notice of its availability has been published. The notice that the report is available, which must list the foundation's address and the name of its principal manager, must be published in a newspaper having general circulation in the county in which the foundation's principal office is located no later than the day prescribed for filing of the report. A copy of the notice and proof of publication must be filed with the annual report. Income tax returns for private operating foundations and public charities are illustrated in appendixes B and C, respectively (in addition, appendix D shows a tax return for a private operating foundation with unrelated business taxable income).

3

Legal Liability
of Museums

Liability on the part of an organization, such as a museum, is imposed when a legally created right of another party is infringed by that organization. Liability stems from one of two branches of the law—tort or contract. A tort is defined as a wrong independent of contract or a breach of duty that the law, as distinguished from a mere contract, has imposed.[1] A tort, then, is a wrongful act not involving a breach of contract for which a civil action may be maintained.[2] Contract law, on the other hand, imposes duties and obligations and bestows rights upon the parties based upon the terms of the contract. The parties to the contract create their own rights and obligations by mutual agreement and often determine the liability for a breach of the contract.

Tort Law

A tort is distinguished from a breach of contract in that the latter arises under an agreement of the parties, whereas a tort is ordinarily a violation of duty fixed by law independent of a contract, though it may sometimes have relation to obligations growing out of or coincident with a contract.[3] Liability from a tort violation depends upon a legal right possessed by a party, called the plaintiff, a corresponding duty or obligation on the part of another party, called the defendant, and a breach of or failure to perform the duty or discharge the obligation by the defendant. A legal right is "something with which the law invests one person and in respect to which, for his benefit, another, or perhaps all others, are required by law to do or perform acts or to forbear or abstain from acts."[4] The general area of torts is divided into three parts:

(a) intent to interfere with plaintiff's interest, (b) negligence, and (c) strict liability, where the defendant is held liable in the absence of intent or negligence, very often for policy reasons.[5] Those torts involving intent (to interfere with plaintiff's interest) include, among others, assault and battery, libel and slander, malicious prosecution, false arrest, and trespass.

Negligence

Liability would be most likely imposed upon a museum because of negligence, or fault, on the part of its officials or employees. Negligence is conduct which falls below a standard established by law for the protection of others. It is composed of the following elements:[6] (a) a duty, or obligation, recognized by the law, requiring the individual or organization to conform to a certain standard of conduct, for the protection of others against unreasonable risks, (b) a failure on the part of the individual or organization to conform to the standard required, (c) a reasonably close causal connection between the conduct and the resulting injury, called "proximate cause," and (d) actual loss or damage resulting to the interest of another. The standard of conduct required is an external one; it is the care or conduct of a so-called "reasonably prudent person under the same or similar circumstances." The actor is required to do what such a prudent person would have done had he, the prudent person, been in the actor's place. Professional persons and those who are engaged in occupations requiring special skills, are required not only to exercise reasonable care in what they do but also to possess a standard minimum of special knowledge and ability.[7] A physician, for example, is required to exercise that care and/or skill which an ordinarily prudent physician would exercise under the same or similar circumstances. If the physician is a specialist, the level of care or skill required would increase; his conduct would then be measured against a reasonably prudent specialist. A museum director would be held to that care or skill which an ordinarily prudent museum director would exercise under similar circumstances. If his conduct does not meet this standard, he has been negligent.

Example 1. A visitor to Museum X falls on a stairway because some chewing gum was lodged on a step. The museum will be liable for injuries to the visitor if museum personnel knew or should have known of the condition and failed to act within a reasonable time to remove the gum. The mere fact that the gum was lodged on one of the steps will not render the museum liable if its employees have not had time to discover its existence.

Example 2. A visitor to Museum X slips and falls on the sidewalk outside the museum because it was covered with snow and ice. Museum personnel have the duty to use reasonable care to maintain areas over which the museum has control. The sidewalk leading into the museum must be cleared; however, the mere accumulation of snow does not make the museum immediately liable. Its personnel must be given a reasonable time after the storm has ceased to remove the accumulation of snow or ice or to take such measures as will make the area reasonably safe from hazards arising from such a condition.

There are degrees of negligence. For example, if danger from a particular event is present, an actor is required to exert more caution. The degree of care required would increase as the danger increased. Further, one's actions may be deemed "gross negligence," the want of even scant care. There is also a "willful, wanton, or reckless" action which differs in quality rather than in degree from ordinary lack of care. There is no clear distinction between such conduct and gross negligence, however. Sometimes a statute prescribes a standard of conduct, deviation from which is negligence.

To be awarded damages for negligence on the part of a defendant, a plaintiff must convince a judge or jury by a preponderance of the evidence that the defendant was negligent. This means that the burden of proof is on the plaintiff. The plaintiff is asking the court for relief; hence, he must show by the greater weight of the evidence that the defendant was negligent. Negligence must be proved and will not be presumed.[8] The mere fact that an accident has occurred does not establish negligence on the part of anyone. Negligence may be proved by circumstantial evidence, however.

One type of circumstantial evidence is called "res ipsa loquitur," the thing speaks for itself. This doctrine assumes, in certain situations, that the defendant must have performed an act and that his conduct may be deemed negligent. This is because the object causing injury was in the exclusive control of the defendant and the accident would not normally occur in the absence of negligence. Three conditions are necessary for the application of the doctrine—the event must be of a kind which does not ordinarily occur without negligence, it must be caused by an agency or instrumentality within the exclusive control of the defendant, and it must not have been due to any voluntary action or contribution on the part of the plaintiff.[9]

Example 3. An explosion rips through Museum X at a time when visitors are on the premis The explosion causes injury to several of the visitors. Causation of the explosion cannot be determined; consequently, those injured cannot prove that museum personnel were negligent. The doctrine of res ipsa loquitur may apply, leading to a presumption of negligence on the part of museum personnel.

Example 4. A visitor to Museum X enters its elevator. The elevator falls and injures the visitor. Such an accident does not ordinarily occur without negligence; consequently, negligence of those in control can be inferred from a mere showing that accident occurred. The doctrine of res ipsa loquitur is applicable.

Vicarious Liability. A museum organization becomes liable for tortious acts of its officials or employees through vicarious liability, imposition of this doctrine being based on an agency theory. One party, the agent, is authorized to act for another party, the principal. When a person acts through an agent, the agent is a representative of the principal for conduct of the transaction. Acts performed by the agent, whenever they are within the scope of his actual or apparent authority, are binding on the principal. A principal will be held liable in damages for all tortious acts committed by his agent when such agent is acting in the course of the principal's business and in furtherance of the principal's interest. Still, if the agent's tort is committed during the pursuit of his own interests and not in furtherance of the principal's business, the principal will not be held responsible.

An employee is a particular kind of agent. Vicarious liability for an employee's tortious acts has also been imposed upon an employer, however, under the doctrine of "respondeat superior." This ancient doctrine means that a master is liable for the torts of his servant in the course of employment. The losses caused by the torts of employees, which as a practical matter are certain to occur in the conduct of a business, are placed upon that organization as a required cost of doing business. The theory is that by placing the loss upon the employer, rather than upon the innocent injured plaintiff, he, the employer, will distribute such loss through prices, rates, or liability insurance, to the public, and so will shift them to society, or the community at large.[10]

Further, the employer is supposed to instruct and supervise his servants to see that his enterprise is conducted safely.

Once it is determined that an employer-employee relationship exists, the employer becomes subject to vicarious liability for the employee's torts. Vicarious liability only extends to conduct "within the course of employment," however. Many factors determine what occurs "within the course of employment." Among these are: time, place, and purpose of the act; its similarity to authorized conduct; whether it is an act commonly performed by such employees; the extent of departure from normal methods; previous relations between the parties; and whether the employer had reason to expect that such an act would be done. Expressly forbidding an act of the employee does not necessarily remove it from "course of employment."

Example 5. Museum X was presenting a series of lectures on historical objects within the museum to some schoolchildren. A, an employee of Museum X, was instructed to use his car to give several children rides home. After delivering all the children to their homes, A was driving at an excessive rate of speed to his own home. He failed to stop for a red light and collided with another automobile. Several parties in the other automobile were seriously injured. These parties want to bring suit against the museum on the theory that A's reckless conduct occurred during the course of A's employment. The museum's defense would be that A ceased to work for the museum for that day after all the children had been delivered. Given the time, place, and purpose of A's act, i.e., driving himself home, A was not acting within the course of employment.

Example 6. If A had the accident while driving the children home, the museum would probably be vicariously liable (unless it had some defense as discussed below).

If an individual performing services for an organization is an independent contractor, rather than an employee, the employer is ordinarily not vicariously liable for torts of that individual. The reason for this is that the employer has no right to control the manner in which the work is to be done; consequently, the contractor is, in fact, engaged in his own business and should himself be charged with the responsibility of preventing accidents. An independent contractor may be an agent of the employer, however, in which case the employer may or may not become vicariously liable for the contractor's torts. An employer could be individually liable for other reasons even though an independent contractor is performing the service. The employer is required to exercise reasonable care in selecting a competent and careful contractor and is required to keep the premises safe.

Defenses. A defendant can defeat a plaintiff's claim based on negligence by demonstrating that the plaintiff has not shown a duty to act, that the plaintiff has not shown a proximate cause between the defendant's act, or failure to act, and the harm to the plaintiff, or that the plaintiff could not show that the defendant failed to meet the required standard of care. There are also affirmative defenses which can defeat plaintiff's claim. These include contributory negligence and/or assumption of the risk as well as governmental or charitable immunity.

In some cases, a negligent defendant is excused from liability if the plaintiff was also negligent and the plaintiff's negligence was a proximate cause of plaintiff's injury. Plaintiff must also act as a reasonably prudent person, though the defendant has a greater duty toward the plaintiff than the plaintiff has toward himself. Further, some states have abolished the contributory negligence rule and have adopted a comparative negligence theory. Comparative negligence can mean that a plaintiff may recover regardless of his own negligence but only as to the defendant's negligence. Assume that the plaintiff is 60 percent at fault in an accident and that the defendant is 40 percent at fault. Under this theory, the plaintiff can recover 40 percent of his damages. Some states use comparative negligence to mean that the plaintiff can recover even though he, too, is negligent, as long as he is not as negligent as the defendant. Under this application of the comparative negligence theory, the plaintiff could not recover if his negligence was at least 50 percent.

Assumption of the risk is another defense to the defendant's action. If the plaintiff assumes the risk of the defendant's negligence, the defendant is relieved from liability. Assumption of the risk is a form of consent on the part of the plaintiff, while contributory negligence involves conduct of the plaintiff. An assumption by the plaintiff of the risk of the defendant's negligence may be express or implied. Express assumption occurs in the form of a release, or agreement to hold harmless. (See appendix F.) Such releases may or may not be accepted by a court. A release must be voluntarily made. It will not be enforced in the event of gross negligence or willful negligence, nor will it be enforced if the party executing such an agreement is at an obvious disadvantage. Assumption of the risk may be implied if the plaintiff understood the risk that he was incurring and if his choice to do so is entirely free and voluntary.[11]

Example 7. Museum X has arranged a tour of several historical sites. It required all participants to sign a release holding the museum harmless from any injury which might occur to the participants. In exploring some dangerous caverns, one of the participants falls into a pit and is seriously injured. If the tour guide is held to have been grossly negligent in supervising the exploration in the dangerous area, a court may hold that the release is ineffective to release the museum from liability. A release of this type does not generally prevent liability for gross negligence. Nonetheless, such a release should always be secured from each participant before conducting a tour in that it probably will provide the defense of assumption of the risk for ordinary negligence and may also deter an injured party from bringing suit.

The doctrine of assumption of the risk has been abolished in some states, and it has little application in a state which has adopted the doctrine of comparative negligence. In states adopting the doctrine of comparative negligence, however, assumption of the risk may still be applicable to strict liability suits and to cases in which the plaintiff knowingly consents, either orally or in writing, to a dangerous activity or condition.

Immunity. Recall that vicarious liability of an employer for the torts of his employees is based on the concept that losses of this type should be borne by the business, as a cost of business, rather than by the injured plaintiff. Theoretically this concept should not apply to an organization which is not operating a business for profit. As a result, immunity from tort liability evolved for certain governmental and charitable organizations. These organizations have historically been given special protection at the expense of the injured plaintiff in the form of an immunity from liability. An immunity assumes that a wrong has been committed but provides a defense for the protected group.

The concept of governmental immunity is predicated on the theory "the King can do no wrong." Originally, consent to sue the United States had to be secured before a suit could be brought. Nevertheless, the United States waived its immunity from liability in tort in 1946 when Congress passed the Federal Tort Claims Act.[12] This act makes the United States government liable for tortious acts of federal employees acting within the scope of their employment. There are some exceptions to tort liability on the part of the federal government, however. It is not liable for assault or battery, false imprisonment, false arrest, malicious prosecution, abuse of process, libel, slander, misrepresentation, deceit, or interference with contract rights.[13] In addition, the federal government is not liable for acts done with due care in the execution of a statute or regulation, even though the state is invalid, nor is it liable for acts, or omissions to act, within the "discretionary function or duty of any federal agency or employee."[14] Most states have a tort claims act similar to the Federal Torts Claims Act, waiving immunity from liability for most torts. The extent of waiver of immunity varies from state to state. Some states still preserve governmental immunity, whereas some do not. As to suits in federal courts, the Eleventh Amendment to the federal Constitution grants immunity to a state from suit by a private citizen. If a museum is either an agency of the federal government or of a state government, it may have some governmental immunity for the torts of its employees or officials.

Political subdivisions of the state, such as cities and counties, are treated differently from states for purposes of immunity. These entities have a dual character. They are both governmental units and proprietary units in that they provide both governmental services and private services. The law has attempted to distinguish between the two functions and to hold that insofar as they represent the state in their "governmental" capacity, they share its immunity from tort liability, while in their "proprietary" character, they may be liable.[15]

Charities also share in the defense of immunity from liability. The doctrine of "charitable immunity" evolved from an old English case which held that trust funds in the hands of a charity could not be subjected to the payment of tort claims because the funds would thus be diverted from the purpose intended by the donor.[16] Currently, the doctrine has limited application. Some courts have held that a charity is liable for damages in the exercise of a nondelegable duty, as distinguished from employee negligence,[17] but that it cannot be liable for the negligence of its employees as long as it is not negligent in the hiring or retention of its employees. The doctrine has been completely abrogated in some states.

Strict Liability

In some instances a defendant may be held liable when there has
been no departure from a standard of care. Strict liability is imposed in
instances wherein there are abnormally dangerous conditions or activities, and the defendant has voluntarily engaged in or permitted such
conditions or activities. In these cases the defendant acts "at his peril"
and is an insurer against the consequences of his conduct.[18] The keeping of vicious animals is an example of an instance when this doctrine
may be applied. (If such animals should attack or otherwise harm
someone, the person in charge of such animals may be liable even if he
was not negligent.) Vicarious liability is a form of strict liability.

Example 8. Museum X has vicious animals on its premises as part of a
display. Though properly caged, one of the animals injured a visitor to the
museum who placed his hand in the cage. The museum may be liable even
though it was not negligent under the doctrine of strict liability. "Assumption of the risk" may be a good defense in this case, however.

In a number of states, the manufacturer of food and drink is held
strictly liable to the consumer for defective food or drink. Strict liability
also applies to the manufacturer of other products, and in some states it
applies to the retail sellers as well. In nearly all states, the supplier of a
product that was defective and unreasonably dangerous at the time
possession was surrendered can incur liability without proof of negligence for all those whose injuries were likely to result from the kind of
defect established.[19] For liability to attach, the product must be found
to have been defective as marketed. It may be defective as marketed if
there is a flaw in the product, if there is a failure to warn adequately of a
risk or hazard related to the way the product was designed, or if there is
a defective design.[20] The mere occurrence of injury by an unreasonably
dangerous product does not cause liability, however. The defective
condition must exist when the manufacturer surrenders control (unless
change can occur with respect to the product, creating a dangerous
condition).

Example 9. A visitor buys a soft drink from a vending machine in the
museum. The bottle explodes, causing injury to the visitor. Should the
visitor sue the manufacturer, alleging strict liability on the part of the manufacturer, the visitor must show that the bottle was defective when it left the

manufacturer's possession and control. A defect in the product at the time of the accident is not by itself sufficient to render the manufacturer strictly liable.

Example 10. The visitor in Example 9 above discovers an insect in the soft drink. The manufacturer will undoubtedly be held liable in that he breached his duty to prevent injurious foreign substances in the product.

As to a user of a dangerous product, the defense of assumption of the risk may apply.

The principal statutory application of the doctrine of strict liability is workmen's compensation acts,[21] which are based upon the theory that the burden of industrial accidents should fall upon the employer, inasmuch as the employer is in a better position, through insurance, to pay. The employer is liable for injuries caused by pure unavoidable accident or by the negligence of the employee himself. When an employee is covered by workmen's compensation, the statutory compensation is normally the only remedy, and any recovery at common law is barred. The remedy is in the nature of a compromise by which the employee accepts a limited compensation in return for an extended liability of the employer, and an assurance that he will be paid.[22] If an employee is injured while at work, his injury is compensated according to a fixed schedule of benefits ordinarily payable weekly for a fixed number of weeks. Compensable injuries include temporary and permanent disability, fracture, disfigurement, and total or partial loss of parts of the body. The employee files a claim with an administrative agency which determines the award. Judicial review is available. Whether or not an organization is required to carry workmen's compensation insurance depends upon state requirements. Some of the acts are compulsory for some employers and elective for others. Some are compulsory for all employers employing more than a stated number of employees and elective for those employing fewer.

Example 11. Museum X has twenty employees. It is required by law to carry workmen's compensation insurance because of the number of its employees; however, it does not do so. One of its employees is injured while working in the museum. Even though the employee was negligent in causing his own injury and the museum was not negligent, the museum will be liable for the employee's injuries. Further, because it failed to carry workmen's compensation, it will be liable for full damages. It has no defenses such as contributory negligence or assumption of the risk.

Special Liability Rules

Owners and Occupiers of Land. A museum director must be aware of certain laws pertaining to owners and occupiers of land. As the possessor of land, a museum is required to exercise reasonable care with regard to any activities which are carried on and must also use care to determine that the premises are safe for persons who are on the property. Liability for a breach of these obligations may fall into one of three categories: it may rest upon intent, it may be based upon negligence in the creation of an unreasonable risk, or there may be strict liability, as when vicious animals are kept on the premises.[23]

The concept of duty becomes especially relevant in the area of liability to persons who are on the premises. Those who enter upon land are divided into three fixed categories: trespassers, licensees, and invitees.[24] A trespasser is one who enters another's property without that person's consent. An owner of property owes no duty to a trespasser except to make the premises reasonably safe and not to engage in activities on the premises that might endanger a trespasser. A trespasser cannot expect ordinary care for his safety. Most states require that a possessor of land exercise care with respect to trespassing children, however. In some jurisdictions, a doctrine termed "attractive nuisance" exists. Under this doctrine, a possessor of land who has an artificial condition upon his land is liable to children trespassing upon his land if the condition is such that the possessor knows, or has reason to know, that children are likely to trespass[25] and if he knows, or has reason to know, that the condition will involve an unreasonable risk of death or serious bodily harm to children.[26] The possessor need not have created the condition; he can be liable if he maintains it or permits it to exist. Normally, however, the doctrine only applies to artificial conditions such as swimming pools, equipment, or excavations, and not to natural formations. There is no duty to inspect the premises, but the possessor is charged with facts he actually knows or should know.

Example 12. Museum X has a reflector pool in the front of the museum. It also has several sculptures in an outdoor court. One is a sculpture of an animal. These are located on a rock surface. A young child climbs on the animal for "a ride"; he falls from the animal onto the rock surface and suffers head injuries. Another child falls into the pool and suffers injuries. The children were not supposed to be on the premises unless supervised by parents. Even though the children were trespassers, the museum may be liable under the "attractive nuisance" doctrine.

A licensee is one who has a privilege to enter upon land. An invitee is a licensee, but an invitee is in a special category because he has been invited by the possessor of the land to enter or remain upon the land for a particular purpose. A customer in a gift shop on museum premises would be an invitee. In most states, a visitor to museum displays would also be an invitee. Employees and independent contractors are invitees. Those who enter for some other purpose are licensees. The duty owed a licensee is like that owed a trespasser. There is no general duty to exercise ordinary care. The premises must be reasonably safe and without dangerous traps, but there is no express or implied duty to a licensee except for active operations of the landowner. With respect to an invitee, however, the possessor of land owes a duty to exercise reasonable care for his safety.[27] The premises must be in reasonably safe condition, and the invitee must be given adequate and timely notice of concealed or latent perils known to the possessor. The possessor is not a guarantor of the invitee's safety, however.

If land is leased, the law of property regards the lease as equivalent to a sale of the premises for the term,[28] and the lessee becomes responsible for the premises. If land is leased for a purpose which involves the admission of the public, however, the lessor remains under an affirmative duty to exercise reasonable care to inspect and repair the premises before possession is transferred so as to prevent any unreasonable risk of harm to the public who may enter.[29] A museum director would most often be in the latter category. If portions of the museum building are leased for special functions, the museum director should inspect the premises to make certain that there are no areas in need of repair and that no hidden defects exist. He should require, in the rental agreement, that the land not be opened to the public until certain repairs have been made. The lessor's liability extends only to those parts of the premises which are in fact open to the public and to those invitees who enter for the purpose for which the premises were leased.[30] The lessor is not liable for the negligence of the lessee in maintaining the premises, once he, the lessor, transfers the property in good condition; further he is not liable if the land is used for a public purpose not contemplated by the lease.[31]

Some states have abolished the distinctions between trespasser, licensee, and invitees and hold that liability on the part of the possessor of land is determined by the ordinary rules of negligence and that ordinary care is owed to all three categories of persons who enter upon one's land.

Volunteers. In examining the relationship of an unpaid docent to a museum, courts in states not adhering to either the general charitable immunity doctrine or the doctrine finding respondeat superior inapplicable would first determine whether the volunteer was in fact a servant of the charity and, if so, whether as a servant the volunteer was acting within the scope of his "employment," so as to make the charity liable for his torts.[32] Courts which do not adhere to the immunity doctrine have taken the position that one who volunteers services without an agreement for or expectation of reward may nonetheless be a servant of the one accepting the services. Consent of the master is a requisite for the relationship to exist. Generally, it has been held that a charity must have the right to control the activities of the volunteer before the charity will be liable for the volunteer's torts. Various factors will be considered to determine if a requisite right of control exists. The degree to which the organization controls the specific actions of the volunteer and the degree of contact between the organization and the volunteer, both before and after a tort is committed, are the most crucial factors. The structure of the organization may be viewed to determine whether the volunteer is a servant. Where a volunteer regularly offers his services, his relationship to the organizational structure may be seen as evidence of a right of control.[33]

If practical, given the particular circumstances involving the use of docents, some general rules can be instituted to assure that a master servant or an agency relationship does not exist. The museum organization should not solicit performance by volunteers; it should not have a right of control over the mode of performance of a volunteer's work; and it should not keep lists of volunteers or other documentation indicating a quasi-employee status for the volunteers. The museum should not certify or otherwise accredit volunteer help, indicating an investigation of the qualifications of the volunteer and a desire to control or direct the volunteer in the performance of his duties. Instructions should not be issued to the volunteer as to how to perform his duties. Still, if a volunteer is placed in a situation requiring skills beyond his ability and the organization fails to supervise the volunteer properly, it may find that it is liable for failure to supervise. Volunteers should not be placed in situations requiring skills beyond their capabilities nor be asked to perform duties that are somewhat risky. Because docents can be an integral, almost required, part of the museum's operations, it may not be possible to limit the museum's liability for their actions. If such be the case, supervision of the docents becomes a necessity.

If volunteers are themselves injured, liability to the volunteer would undoubtedly be based on that of a possessor of land to an invitee. Workmen's compensation statutes normally would not apply, inasmuch as volunteers are not paid employees.

Other Torts

Libel and Slander. Defamation is made up of the twin torts of libel and slander—libel being written defamation, while slander is oral. In either form, defamation is an invasion of another's reputation and good name.[34] Defamation requires that something be communicated to a third person that may affect that person's opinion. Derogatory words and insults directed to the plaintiff himself are not defamation.[35] A defamatory communication is one which tends to expose the plaintiff to hatred, contempt, or ridicule or to cause him to be shunned or avoided. Defamation tends to injure reputation or to diminish esteem, respect, goodwill, or confidence in the plaintiff.[36]

A plaintiff's case for libel or slander is made when he establishes a publication to a third person for which the defendant was responsible, the recipient's understanding of the defamatory meaning, and its actionable character.[37] The defendant has a defense of privilege or truth, either of which is a complete defense. The defense of "privilege" is available in judicial proceedings (to the judge, the witnesses, parties in the case, and counsel for the parties). It is available in legislative proceedings, executive communications, and political broadcasts. Publishers have qualified privileges. "Truth" is a complete defense; however, it may prove a hazardous venture for the defendant if he fails to convince the court of the truth of his statements.

It has been held that there can be no defamation of one who is dead unless there is a reflection upon those still living. The theory is that while there may be liability to those living who are themselves defamed, to provide the deceased person with a right of action would interfere with historical research.

Invasion of Privacy. The right of privacy is the right to be free from intrusion upon one's physical solitude or seclusion. Such intrusion includes eavesdropping upon private conversations by means of wire-

tapping, persistent and unwanted telephone calls, compulsory blood
tests, an illegal search of a shopping bag in a store, or the taking of a
photograph when the plaintiff is in a hospital or within the seclusion of
his home.[38] A public disclosure of private information about the plaintiff, even though it is true and thus would not support an action for
libel, may be an invasion of privacy. The facts disclosed to the public
must be private facts and not public ones, for a person cannot complain
when an occupation in which he publicly engages is called to public
attention or when publicity is given to matters concerning him which
are matters of public record and open to public inspection. To be an
invasion of privacy, the matter made public must be that which would
be offensive and objectionable to a reasonable man of ordinary
sensibilities.[39] Publicity which places the plaintiff in a false light in the
public eye is an invasion of privacy.[40] An appropriation of the plaintiff's name or likeness for the defendant's benefit or advantage is an
invasion of privacy.[41] Public figures are held to have lost, to some
extent, their right of privacy. The loss is only a limited one, however.
The private letters of famous persons cannot generally be published
without their consent. Still, courts sometimes balance this right against
the public interest in disclosure and thereby protect the media. The
right of privacy is a personal one; it does not extend to members of the
plaintiff's family unless their own privacy is invaded along with that of
plaintiff. The right is not assignable and does not survive death.

Right of Publicity. As noted above, an appropriation of a person's
name for another's benefit constitutes a violation of one's right of privacy. This also constitutes a newer cause of action recognized in some
states as the "right of publicity." This right of action differs from the
right of privacy in that it centers on loss of economic benefit to the
injured party. Further, the right of privacy, like an action in libel or
slander, is personal and nonassignable. It does not survive death. The
right of publicity, on the other hand, has been held to survive death, it
being a valid, transferable property right.[42]

Example 13. X, a historical museum, wants to display the letters of a
famous person to his mistress. If the famous person is still living, the
museum should not display the letters without that person's consent unless
his status as a public figure makes disclosure in the public interest. The
museum might also be subject to possible liability if it failed to secure the

consent of the mistress. If the persons are no longer living, there can be no invasion of privacy action as that cause of action does not survive death. It has been held there can be no defamation of one who is dead; consequently, defamation of character would not be applicable. The right of publicity, which is inheritable, would probably not apply because the museum would not be appropriating a person's name for economic gain. Thus, it would seem that the museum would be protected once the persons are no longer living and as long as the rights or privacy of living persons are not invaded.

False Imprisonment. A plaintiff can recover against a defendant who restrains his movement. The tort occurs when plaintiff is restrained by means of physical barriers or by threats of force which intimidate the plaintiff into compliance with orders. The restraint must be against the plaintiff's will. A false arrest is false imprisonment, as is the groundless institution of criminal proceedings against the plaintiff. In addition, simply confining the plaintiff against his will can be false imprisonment.

A person is not liable for the detention of another in circumstances where the detention is authorized by law. As a general rule, any person may arrest an offender who commits a felony (a crime punishable by imprisonment in the penitentiary) within that person's presence. In addition, a peace officer may arrest an offender without a warrant when he believes, on reasonable grounds, that the person to be arrested has committed or is committing a felony. Generally, the officer may justify the arrest and is not liable for false imprisonment upon a showing of satisfactory proof that a felony crime has been committed and that the offender is about to escape so that there is no time to procure a warrant. In other cases an arrest by either a peace officer or a private citizen renders the arrester liable for false imprisonment. Ordinarily, neither a police officer nor a private person may make an arrest without a warrant for a misdemeanor (a crime of a lesser degree than a felony, it being punishable by fine or imprisonment in a jail). It has been held, however, that the doctrine of reasonable cause is a good defense in an action for false arrest or false imprisonment where the act was actually committed in the officer's presence and where the offender's conduct was such as to cause a reasonable person to conclude that a public offense was being committed.

Although a detention may originally have been lawful, circumstances may be such that a continued detention becomes unlawful. When an officer rightfully makes an arrest without a warrant, it is his duty to take the arrested person immediately to a magistrate for examination. Some states have statutes allowing the temporary detention of a person believed to have stolen property by bringing the suspected party and the stolen property before a magistrate for examination, provided that there are reasonable grounds for supposing the property to be stolen, that the seizure is openly made, and that the proceedings are had without delay. If a person voluntarily accompanies another, there is no detention and consequently no false imprisonment. One who voluntarily submits himself to law enforcement officers for questioning concerning a crime is not illegally restrained.

The measure of damages for false imprisonment is the amount that will afford reasonable compensation to the injured party. The plaintiff can be compensated for physical and mental suffering and for injury to his reputation. Because the mental suffering resulting from an unlawful detention depends on the manner in which the detention occurred, great care should be exercised when a museum employee suspects a museum visitor of theft. If an arrest or imprisonment is effected in a reckless or insulting manner or is willful and malicious with a desire to oppress and injure, the plaintiff may recover punitive damages. Should an employee be acting within the line of his duty in exercising the functions of his employment, the employer is generally liable for an action for false arrest or imprisonment. In some states the employer is not liable if the employee is not acting to protect the employer's property or interest but is rather acting to vindicate public justice or to redress an offense against society or to punish an offender for something already done. Some states have held that an employer is not liable for punitive damages unless the employer either authorized or ratified the acts of the employee.

It would be wise to prepare a manual on the authority of a museum's floor supervisor or security guards to detain visitors. State law should be consulted to determine what legal actions a security guard can take to prevent theft. Rules should then be formulated and made a part of the manual. Such a manual should caution the guards about acceptable behavior in this regard.

Example 14. A security guard employed by Museum X believes that a visitor to the museum has one of the museum objects in his possession with the intent of stealing the object. The guard did not see the visitor take the object, however. The guard wants to detain the visitor and question him.

The guard should request that the visitor accompany him into another room outside the presence of other museum visitors and should question him in a tactful manner. If the guard is mistaken in his belief that the visitor has the museum object, the visitor probably has not been damaged under these circumstances (he has not been publicly ridiculed), so that an action for false imprisonment would not render the museum liable.

Unfair Competition. Wrongful or malicious interference with the formation of a contract or the right to pursue a lawful trade has generally been held to constitute a tort.[43] Because everyone has the right to enjoy the results of his own enterprise, industry, and skill and is entitled to full freedom in disposing of his own labor or capital, free from malicious interference or disturbance, the right to pursue one's business or trade (or the reasonable expectancy of a contract) becomes a property right protected by the law from unjustifiable or wrongful interference. A person does not have the right to be protected against competition, however, and if the disturbance or loss is a result of competition, in the absence of some contract right it is not actionable. On the other hand, exploitation of the competitive market should be with lawful means, and should conduct not be in the advancement of competitive interests or should unfair means be used, such conduct is not justified. One who wrongfully or without justification interferes with any contract or causes a party to violate his contract with another is also guilty of an actionable tort. Such interference constitutes an invasion of the property rights of the parties to the contract.

Example 15. False attribution of authorship or the unauthorized disclosure of an author's name could constitute the tort of unfair competition. Presentation of an artist's works in a distorted, "garbled" version can also constitute unfair competition. (See chapter 4 for further discussion.)

Prevention of Liability

A museum director should take certain precautions to avoid liability. The best protection against liability is to obtain adequate insurance. Liability insurance is a form of indemnity whereby the insurer undertakes to indemnify the insured against loss which the insured may sustain by becoming legally liable to a third person. This becomes a matter of contract, the insurance policy, between the insurer and the insured. Governmental and/or charitable immunity has limited application and has been abrogated completely in some states; hence, insurance is normally warranted. Liability on the part of the insurance company is based upon liability on the part of the insured; in the absence of strict liability, if there was no negligence, there will be no liability.

A liability insurance policy not only pays damages to an injured party but also protects the insured against the expense and inconvenience of litigation based on claims of negligence. The investigation of the third person's claim, negotiation with the claimant, defense of the action brought against the insured, and payment of attorney's fees and all other expenses, including payment of medical expenses for the injured person, become the responsibility of the insurer. One caveat: in those states in which charitable immunity is still available, purchase of liability insurance can cause the courts to ignore the doctrine on the ground that liability would no longer deplete trust funds or discourage donors.

A museum director should purchase adequate general comprehensive liability coverage that would cover automobile accidents and defects in the premises. Remember that such coverage may fail if the museum does not give notice of an accident, does not cooperate with the insurance company, or misrepresents the facts. If an accident occurs on the premises of the museum, the director should obtain a report at the time of occurrence. (Further, proper sympathy and concern for anyone injured can lessen the chances that a lawsuit will be instituted.)

If a museum chooses to rent its premises temporarily, it should endorse the lessee onto its insurance policy for the time of the activity or make certain the lessee has adequate insurance and that it covers the particular activity as well as the museum. There should be a written agreement between the museum and the lessee in which any latent defects on the property are pointed out to the lessee. If the museum director is aware of activities of the lessee which might subject others to harm, he should require proper precautions on the part of the lessee.

A museum that has a snack bar or a museum shop may be strictly liable for defective food or products. Again, liability insurance may be needed. If a museum supervises tours, it should provide travel insurance and should particularly check the territorial limitations of such insurance. A travel agency engaged to conduct the tour should supply proper evidence of insurance. The museum director should secure a release from all travelers. (See appendix F.)

Contract Law

The subject, contract law, is voluminous. No attempt will be made here to cover the many ramifications of contract law; however, some of the basic elements are summarized to alert the museum manager to the possible consequences of his agreements. A contract is defined as an agreement which creates obligations. Its essentials are competent parties, subject matter, a legal consideration, mutuality of agreement, and mutuality of obligations.[44] The duty imposed by law on the parties to a contract to perform their agreement constitutes the obligation of the contract. Every obligation is the correlative of a corresponding right. The purpose of the contract is to reduce to writing the conditions on which the minds of the parties have met and to fix their rights and duties with respect to those conditions.

Every agreement, whether written or oral, is the result of an offer and the acceptance of that offer. The offer and acceptance must have the characteristics of a bargain. To be enforceable, the parties to the contract must have the legal capacity and mental competence to contract. Further, a contract must have consideration to be binding. Consideration is the price bargained for and paid for a promise. It can be a benefit to the party promising, or a loss or detriment to the party to whom the promise is made.

An ordinary contract involves only two parties, the offeror and the offeree. Still, some contracts are drafted in a form wherein performance is rendered to a third party, called a third-party beneficiary. Third-party beneficiaries who are donee or creditor beneficiaries normally have enforceable rights under contracts executed by other parties. (Donee beneficiaries are third parties upon whom a gift is conferred by the contract; creditor beneficiaries have a debt discharged by a contract between two other parties.)

Example 16. A, an individual, contracts with B that he, A, will contribute $10,000 to Museum X, B's favorite charity, if B will perform certain tasks enumerated in the contract. B performs his obligations under the contract, but A refuses to pay Museum X. Museum X is a donee beneficiary under the contract between A and B and as such has an enforceable right against A to collect the $10,000.

The duties and rights of parties to a contract are created by, and arise solely from, the contract. (Rights and duties under a contract can be assigned unless the contract prohibits such assignment.) If any essential element of an agreement is absent, it is a bar to the enforceability of the contract. A court cannot write a contract for the parties, and when parties have not, expressly or by implication, agreed on essential terms of a contract, the court cannot supply them. Further, a court cannot relieve a party of the burden of a contract, should the contract prove to be improvident or should one of the parties find it convenient to repudiate his obligations under the contract. Still, the fairness of the transaction and its freedom from any taint of oppression are matters for consideration in weighing the rights of a party to aid a court in enforcing a contract.[45] A contract which offends public morals or which is contrary to public policy will not be enforced. Construction of a contract is determined by the law of the place where the contract was made unless the parties agree otherwise.

Example 17. Museum X is located in Connecticut. It is planning to grant a company located in California a license to reproduce and sell its art objects. The proposed contract specifies that the law of the state of California will apply. This could cause problems for the museum, should questions arise regarding the contract. All provisions will be construed according to California law. The contract may also provide for venue in California (a lawsuit filed to construe the provisions of the contract must be brought in California). The museum director should strike these provisions or require that Connecticut be substituted for California.

Contracts may be express or implied. An express contract is one where the intention of the parties and the terms of the agreement are declared or expressed by the parties, in writing or orally, at the time of the agreement. Implied contracts are those contracts implied in fact or implied in law. Parties may be as firmly bound by implied contracts as by express contracts, aside from requirements of the Statute of Frauds, discussed below, or other control of the forms of contract. Where there is an express contract, however, the law will not imply some other agreement. There must be some act or conduct of a party for an implied contract to arise. The essential elements of an implied contract are a benefit conferred on the defendant by the plaintiff, appreciation by the defendant of the benefit, and acceptance and retention by the defendant of the benefit under circumstances where it would be inequitable for the defendant to retain the benefit without payment of its value. A contract implied in fact is a true contract, the agreement of the parties being inferred from the circumstances, while a contract implied in law is a duty imposed by law and treated as a contract for the purposes of a remedy only.[46]

Some contracts must be in writing to be valid. The so-called Statute of Frauds requires that the following contracts be in writing: (a) an agreement that by its terms cannot be performed within a year from the making of such contract, (b) an agreement to guarantee a debt of another, (c) a sale of real property, (d) an agreement employing an agent to purchase or sell real estate, (e) an agreement by a purchaser of real estate to pay an indebtedness on the property purchased, and (6) a contract for the sale of goods priced at $500 or more. (See chapter 5 for modifications of the Statute of Frauds for sales and purchases of personal property, such as museum objects, provided for by the Uniform Commercial Code.) A written memorandum which contains the essential terms of the agreement, whether made when the agreement was executed or at a later time, is sufficient when signed by the parties who are to be bound. Where a contract has been reduced to writing in a contract intended to be the complete statement of the parties' agreement, statements or understanding made prior to or at the time of execution of the contract may not be used to add to or contradict the written agreement. This is the so-called parol evidence rule. (For sales and purchases of personal property, including museum objects, the Uniform Commercial Code, discussed in chapter 5, permits the parties to prove "extrinsic" facts not a part of the written agreement.)

There are two kinds of contracts—unilateral and bilateral. A bilateral contract is one in which there are reciprocal promises, i.e., both parties to the contract must perform some act. Mutual obligations are a requisite. A unilateral contract is one in which there is a promise on one side only. The offer or promise of the other party does not become binding or enforceable until there is performance by the other party. Contracts can be conditional, in which case performance depends on a condition. There are also so-called contracts of adhesion, whereby the party of superior bargaining strength relegates to the subscribing party only the opportunity to adhere to the contract or to reject it. Whether or not a contract of adhesion is enforceable depends on the law of the particular state.[47]

A contract is breached when a party fails to perform. Still, the duties of the parties to a contract may be discharged. Discharge of performance, in whole or in part, can occur through impossibility of performance or by accord and satisfaction. If a party to a contract enters into a different later agreement with his debtor, the later agreement is called an accord. When the debtor performs the duty under the subsequent agreement, he performs the accord, this being deemed satisfaction. The satisfaction operates as a discharge of the original contract. For example, if a party to a contract is to pay another a certain sum of money but later offers to satisfy the sum by delivering merchandise of the same value as the sum of money owed, and the other party accepts the subsequent agreement, there is accord. Delivery of the merchandise is satisfaction, and the original agreement is discharged.

Bailments

When goods (personal properties) are delivered for a specific purpose to another person, with a contract, express or implied, that such goods will be returned or accounted for by the party to whom such goods are delivered, a bailment occurs. The person who delivers the property to another under circumstances within the definition of the term "bailment" is called the bailor, and the person to whom the personalty is delivered is called the bailee. Bailments are of three types: (a) those for the sole benefit of the bailor, (b) those for the sole benefit of the bailee, and (c) those for the mutual benefit of both parties. Bailments are also classified as gratuitous (without compensation) and lucrative (with compensation, or for hire). Gratuitous bailments are those bailments for the sole benefit of the bailor or the bailee, while lucrative bailments benefit both parties. A constructive bailment can occur, as when a person acquires property other than by mutual contract of bailment and is, by operation of law, treated as a bailee of the property. Such a bailment would occur, for example, when there is delivery of goods which have not been ordered and they are not accepted. A person who finds lost property is a constructive bailee of such property.

Example 18. *A*, an individual, loans Museum *X* a valuable art collection for exhibition. *X* is to display the art collection for a period of one year without compensation to *A*. A bailment for gratuitous use occurs. The bailment would generally be for the sole benefit of the bailee. If the collection becomes more valuable as a result of the display, however, it may become a bailment for the mutual benefit of the parties.

The terms of the contract of bailment determine the rights and duties of the parties to the contract; however, the care to be exercised by a bailee under a general contract of bailment is fixed by law, though the contract can change the duty of care. Any deviation from the terms of the bailment renders the bailee absolutely liable for any damages suffered to the goods while in the bailee's possession. The parties may by special contract diminish the liability of the bailee, however; or they may limit the amount of the bailee's liability to an agreed valuation of the bailed property. An agreement by the bailor to give the bailee the benefit of insurance carried by the bailor does not have the effect of freeing the bailee from responsibility for his negligence but rather merely limits his liability to the extent that the bailor is compensated by insurance.

The particular standard of care imposed by law on a bailee in caring for property entrusted to him, and the liability for loss or damage to such property, generally depends on the nature of the bailment. Where the bailment is for the mutual benefit of the bailor and bailee, the bailee is held to the exercise of ordinary care in relation to the property and is liable for ordinary negligence. Where the bailment is for the sole benefit of the bailor, the bailee is only bound to slight care and is liable for gross negligence. Where the bailment is for the sole benefit of the bailee, however, the bailee is bound to great care and is liable for slight negligence.[48] An involuntary bailee has no duty to care for the property unless he has knowledge that the property has come into his possession and in the event that he exercises some dominion over the property. He must refrain from reckless and willful acts which would injure or destroy the property.

As noted above, in a bailment for mutual benefit, the bailee, in the absence of a special contract, is held to the exercise of ordinary care in relation to the property and is responsible only for ordinary negligence. The bailee must exercise reasonable care, which is that care which a man of ordinary prudence would use in reference to his own property. A bailee for hire of property delivered on request for the purpose of exhibition is liable for any injury to such property resulting from his failure to use ordinary care in keeping it, but he is not liable as an insurer, nor is he bound to exercise an extraordinary degree of care.[49]

Example 19. Assume that the art collection noted in Example 18 above is stolen. If the bailment is for the mutual benefit of the parties, Museum X would not be liable as long as it exercised ordinary care in preventing theft.

If it is a bailment for the sole benefit of Museum X the museum would undoubtedly be liable for the value of the collection, as it would, in that case, be liable for the slightest negligence.

Where a bailment for the sole benefit of the bailor occurs, the bailee has the duty to exercise some care, but he is held merely to the exercise of slight care. The bailee is liable only for gross negligence or bad faith. The responsibility of a gratuitous bailee may be diminished or increased by contract, however. A gratuitous bailee may not use the property for his purposes or derive any benefit from the property without the consent of the owner.[50]

In a bailment for the sole benefit of the bailee, the bailee is bound to great care or extraordinary diligence and is responsible for slight neglect in relation to the subject matter of the bailment.[51] The right of the bailee to use the property bailed is strictly confined to such use, expressed or implied, as was anticipated by the bailor at the time of the bailment, and the bailee is responsible for any loss arising from an unauthorized use.

The parties to a contract are free to contract as they choose, provided that their agreement does not contravene public policy; consequently, one of the parties can be exempt from liability for his own negligence, assuming that there is equality of bargaining strength between the parties. A provision waiving liability may be valid against all fault except gross negligence; however, there is support for a view that denies validity to any contractual provisions exempting a bailee from liability for his own negligence.[52]

Example 20. Recall that a bailment for the sole benefit of the bailee requires extraordinary diligence and great care on the part of the bailee. Assume that the art collection loaned to Museum X in Example 18 is stolen or destroyed. Though X has insurance coverage, the art collection is priceless and cannot be replaced. Museum X should have contracted with A that its liability for the art collection would be limited to its insurance coverage or to some other stated amount.

In *Gardini v. Museum of City of New York*,[53] the court held a museum liable for the loss of a diamond brooch which had been entrusted to it for exhibition purposes. The owner of the brooch had been given a written receipt for the brooch which stated that the museum was not responsible for the safekeeping of articles entrusted to it for exhibition. The court held that the owner of the brooch could infer that the museum would exercise reasonable care in safeguarding the brooch, and the receipt did not absolve the museum from liability for gross negligence.

If a loss is caused by a third person, the bailee is not excused unless it clearly appears that the act could not have been foreseen or prevented and that no fault or neglect of the bailee contributed in any degree to create the loss. In *Colburn v. Washington State Art Association*,[54] a court held that one who places an exhibit in a museum which refuses to permit him to put a lock on the case assumes the risk of theft by leaving the exhibit there with knowledge of the method by which it might be protected. The court held that the bailment was for the mutual benefit of the parties and the bailee museum was required to exercise only ordinary diligence to prevent theft of the articles.

A bailee may be guilty of conversion if he unauthorizedly appropriates the property to his own use, if he uses the property in a way unauthorized by the terms of the bailment, or if he sells or transfers the property. If a bailee places the bailed property beyond his power to return it to the bailor, the bailee has committed an act of conversion. The negligence of the bailee in the care of the property does not constitute a conversion, but it has been held that where a bailee fails to use that degree of care which the circumstances of the case demands, the bailee can be liable to the bailor in an action in conversion for the consequent loss of the property or for its full value if it is rendered worthless.[55]

A bailee who has by his labor or skill added something of value to the property bailed has a lien on the property for the value of his work unless there is a special contract to the contrary. If the bailee voluntarily parts with possession of the property before receiving compensation, however, his lien may be lost.

On termination of a bailment, the bailee is ordinarily under an absolute duty to redeliver to his bailor the property bailed, in its original or altered form, or to account for the property in accordance with the contract of bailment. Where the manner of redelivery is specified, the bailee must comply strictly with such terms or be liable in the event of loss. Where the contract is silent on this question, the bailee's obligation is generally regulated by the custom and usage of the business at the place where the bailment is made. Where a bailee wrongfully delivers the property of a bailor, the bailee is liable for conversion.

A museum director should be aware of his status as a bailee in accepting or soliciting exhibits. The terms of the agreement of bailment should be expressly stated in a written contract whereby the museum limits its liability for such exhibits. (See appendix G for a sample bailment contract.)

Licensing Agreements

A museum may be interested in reproducing and marketing works of art from its collection. Such a program provides revenue to the museum and, given a product of quality, can enhance the overall reputation of the museum as well as expand its cultural and educational influence. Reproductions can be made in miniature or in facsimile. If the museum chooses to market such products and cannot reproduce the objects through its own resources and personnel, it should consider entering into a contract with a reputable firm to do so. The museum should investigate the firm's ability to create a product of quality, its ability to market effectively, and its financial stability and reputation. The rights and responsibilities of the museum and the firm should be carefully defined in a licensing agreement.

A licensing agreement authorizes a person or firm to manufacture and market reproductions. It is a contract between the parties and is construed like any other contract. It may limit the sale of the product to a specified territory or industrial area, or it may limit the manufacturer to a specific design or specified product. From the museum's standpoint, royalties from the sale of reproductions of its objects should be based upon gross sales and not upon net profit. (A computation of "net profit" depends upon accounting methods and concepts employed. It is subject to varied interpretations.) The agreement should contain clauses regarding assignability, termination, option to renew, and right of the museum to reject any product both initially and throughout the terms of the agreement. The museum should be the sole judge of whether a product has met the standards of quality established by the parties, and the licensee should be required to furnish the museum with evidence of the quality of the licensed products at periodic intervals. The museum should determine the rights of any artists in the objects. The artist may have a copyright to the object; if so, permission must be secured from the artist before the reproduction is made or marketed. The artist would, in that event, require a share of the royalties. (See appendix F for a sample licensing agreement.)

Copyright Law

If a museum produces models of its art objects or publishes articles or books based upon its operations or research, a knowledge of the law of copyrights is imperative. Article 1, section 8, of the U.S. Constitution grants Congress the power to promote the progress of the useful arts by securing for a limited time to authors the exclusive right to their respective writings.[56] To be copyrightable, then, a work would ordinarily be in the form of a "writing"; however, section 102 of the Copyright Act of 1976[57] extends copyright coverage to works of art. It provides copyright protection for "original works of authorship" fixed in tangible form. Literary works; musical works; dramatic works; pantomimes and choreographic works; pictorial, graphic, and sculptural works; motion pictures and other audiovisual works; and sound recordings are the seven broad categories of copyrightable works. Section 101 of the act defines "pictorial, graphic, and sculptural works" to include "two-dimensional and three-dimensional works of fine, graphic, and applied art, photographs, prints and art reproductions, maps, globes, charts, technical drawings, diagrams, and models." The design of a useful article is considered a pictorial, graphic, or sculptural work "only if, and only to the extent that such design incorporates pictorial, graphic, or sculptural features that can be identified separately from, and are capable of existing independently of, the utilitarian aspects of the article." To be copyrightable, a work must also be a product of original creative authorship.

A copyright owner has the exclusive right to reproduce the copyrighted work, to prepare derivative works, and to distribute the work publicly. A copyright owner also possesses the exclusive right to public performance and public display.[58] Once a work is sold, the exclusive right to sell is terminated; a copyright owner cannot in that event control future disposition of sold copies of the work. There are also limitations on the owner's exclusive right to use a copyrighted work; some copying without permission is permitted under the doctrine of "fair use,"[59] and certain performances and displays are exempt from copyright liability.

When an artist sells his work, he loses the display right in the work; however, he does not lose the right to reproduce the work. Section 109 of the Copyright Act states that the display right acquired by a purchaser of a work does not extend to one who merely rents the work or has it on loan.

Example 21. Museum X purchases a painting from the artist. Museum X has the right to display the work but may not make reproductions of the work without permission from the artist.

Example 22. Museum X has a painting on loan from someone other than the artist. It must ascertain the rights of the lender. If the lender does not own the painting, the lender may not have display rights and, in that event, may not transfer display rights to the museum. If such is the case, the museum must secure permission from the artist to display the work.

The owner, or co-owners, of a work are the source of copyright ownership.[60] If a work is made for hire, however, the employer is considered to be the author and is regarded as the initial owner of the copyright unless there is an agreement to the contrary. A "work made for hire" is a "work prepared by an employee within the scope of his employment," and certain categories of commissioned works, which are produced as a result of a special order. Commissioned works are "works made for hire" only if there is an express agreement in writing signed by the parties stating that the work shall be considered a work made for hire. If works are prepared within the scope of one's employment, the copyright is owned by the employer unless the parties agree otherwise in a written agreement signed by the parties. Consequently, if an employee of a museum produces a product as part of his regular duties of employment, the museum is the source of copyright ownership. If the museum commissions someone to design a product, it will be the source of copyright ownership only if there is a written agreement to that effect.

A copyright in a contribution is separate and distinct from a copyright in the collective work as a whole, and in the absence of an express transfer, the owner of the collective work obtains only certain limited rights to each contribution.[61] In the absence of an express transfer, the author of the separate individual article which appears in a collection retains all rights in the article except the right to reproduce and distribute the contribution as part of the collective work.

Example 23. An author submits an article to a literary magazine for publication. Unless the author transfers his copyright in the article to the publisher, he, the author, retains the copyright. The publisher of the magazine will have a copyright only in the collective work.

A copyright is valid for the life of the author and 50 years after his or her death for works created after January 1, 1978.[62] In the case of joint ownership, the 50 years are measured from the date of death of the last surviving author. For works made for hire, the term is 75 years from the first publication or 100 years from creation, whichever is shorter. For unpublished works in existence on January 1, 1978, the duration of copyright will generally be computed in the same manner as for new works—life plus 50 years or the 75- or 100-year terms apply to these works also. All works in this category are guaranteed at least 25 years of statutory protection. Works that were copyrighted before 1978 and consequently had been published by January 1, 1978, are eligible for copyright renewal for a term of 47 years; however, copyright renewal must be timely if the 47-year period of added protection is to pertain.

Once a work goes into the public domain, there is no copyright protection. Under the old law, publication without the statutory notice caused the work to fall into the public domain; the work then became available to everyone for use without payment or permission. Under present law, a work becomes a part of the public domain if the copyright owner has authorized publication of the work without the notice of copyright and fails to register a claim for copyright in the U.S. Copyright Office within five years of publication without the notice. Distribution of only a relatively small number of copies without the notice will not cause copyright to be lost if efforts are made to add the notice later.

To secure copyright protection, the owner of the work should place a notice on all visually perceptible copies that are distributed to the public.[63] The required elements for notice are: (a) the symbol © (the letter c in a circle), or the word "Copyright," or the abbreviation "Copr.," (b) the year of first publication of the work, (c) the name of the owner of copyright in the work, or an abbreviation by which the name can be recognized, or a generally known alternative designation of the owner. Copyright Office Circular 38, which contains general information about international copyright protection for U.S. authors, advises using the symbol ©, which not only fulfills U.S. copyright requirements, but also provides some advantages in securing copyright protection for U.S. works in other countries that are members of the Universal Copyright Convention. Consequently, notice of a copyright should be placed to provide "reasonable notice" of the copyright claim as follows:

© 1980 John Doe

Many publishers use the © symbol in combination with the word "Copyright" or its abbreviation:

Copyright © 1980 John Doe

Circular 38 also explains the widespread use of the phrase "All Rights Reserved," often seen immediately after the copyright notice. The term affords possible advantages for copyright protection for U.S. authors in South American countries that are parties to the Buenos Aires Convention of 1910, though not members of the UCC. If the expression is used, it should follow the name of the copyright owner:

© 1980 John Doe. All Rights Reserved

The year may be omitted for pictorial, graphic, or sculptural works where the work is reproduced in greeting cards, stationery, dolls, jewelry, or other such articles. If the notice is omitted or there is a serious error, there is no effect on copyright ownership as long as the claim to copyright is registered with the Copyright Office within five years of publication without the notice and "reasonable effort" is made to add the notice to copies that are later distributed within the United States.

Notice of copyright must be affixed to copies of a work in such a manner and location as to give reasonable notice of the claim of copyright. The Register of Copyrights prescribes by regulation specific methods of affixation and positions of the notice on various types of work to satisfy this requirement.[64] Regulations provide that for two-dimensional pictorial, graphic, or sculptural works, a notice can be placed on either the front or the back of the work or on a permanent mounting or framing. For three-dimensional works, a label on any visible portion, including a permanent base, is sufficient.[65] Artists who feel that a notice of copyright on the front of the work distracts from the work can place the notice elsewhere and still retain the copyright.

The notice of copyright should be placed on all publicly distributed copies of a work.[66] Section 101 of the act defines publication as the distribution of copies to the public by sale or other transfer of ownership or by rental, lease, or lending. It further provides that public display does not itself constitute publication.

Example 24. An exhibition of a painting does not require a notice of copyright. Public distribution would only occur when a sale or lease of the painting is consummated. Nonetheless, it is preferable that a notice be placed on the painting. Notice can be affixed on the back of the painting so as not to detract from the painting.

As noted above, works not published before January 1, 1978, and not in the public domain can now be copyrighted under the same terms as newly created works.[67] Consequently, works of art created before 1978 but not sold or otherwise transferred have the same copyright protection as newly created works.

Within three months after the work has been published with a copyright notice in the United States, the copyright owner must deposit two copies with the Library of Congress. (The Register of Copyrights, may by regulation, exempt certain categories of material from this required deposit.) On the other hand, registration of published or unpublished works, which is separate from depositing the work with the Library of Congress, is permissive; it can be made at any time during the copyright term. A claim can be registered by depositing copies of the work with the Copyright Office with a completed application form and a fee. Application forms may be obtained free of charge by writing: Information and Publications Section, Copyright Office, Library of Congress, Washington, D.C. 20559. The number of the form should be identified. There are five application forms: Form TX (for nondramatic literary works); Form PA (for works of the performing arts); Form VA (for works of the visual arts); Form SR (for sound recordings); and Form RE (for renewal registrations). Form GR/CP (an adjunct application to be used for registration of a group of contributions to periodicals) is also available. Form VA for registration for a work of the visual arts is used to register pictorial, graphic, or sculptural works. (See appendix F).

Registration is not a condition to copyright; however, it is required if a suit for infringement is instituted.[68] A copyright owner must register his claim to enforce his rights in court. In addition, if infringement occurs after registration, the copyright owner is entitled to extraordinary remedies of attorney's fees and statutory damages. If an infringement suit occurs before registration, the owner is entitled only to an injunction and actual damages. Further, a certificate of registration is given prima facie weight in a judicial proceeding if the registration was made within five years after first publication of the work; thereafter, the court has discretion as to what weight the certificate will be given.

Any or all of the exclusive rights of the copyright owner may be transferred; however, a transfer of exclusive rights is not valid unless the transfer is in writing and is signed by the owner of the rights or his duly authorized agent. Transfer of a right on a nonexclusive basis does not require a writing. Transfers of copyright are normally made by contract. These contracts can be recorded in the Copyright Office.[69] Although recordation is not required to make transfer between the parties valid, it does provide certain legal advantages and may be required to validate the transfer against third parties. A transfer of a copyright can be terminated by the author or creator or by his heirs at any time during a period of five years beginning at the end of thirty-five years from the date of the transfer. The termination is effected by serving an advance notice in writing upon the holder of the copyright.[70]

4

Rights of Artists
in Their Works

If a museum chooses to market reproductions of art objects from its collection, it must consider the rights of the creators of its museum pieces. If artists have a copyright in their creations, permission to reproduce the items must be obtained. Inasmuch as the right of reproduction belongs to the creator, the artist could limit use of the work. To bargain effectively both regarding reproductions of its art objects and initially in acquiring those objects, the museum director should know the underlying theories regarding an artist's rights in his works.

The concept of literary and artistic rights involves two elements—one is called a property right in the artist or author, while the other is called a moral right. The moral right protects the personality of the artist or author and is a recognition that literary or artistic works are extensions of the personalities of their creators, giving them special protection, or an inherent right in their works. The French law recognizes both elements of literary and artistic rights, whereas the United States does not.

Property Rights

In the United States, the economic right of an artist or author is protected through the copyright law. Such a property right is a temporary monopoly granted to the artist to prevent exploitation of his or her creation by others. It assures the artist of the exclusive right to control both the reproduction of the creation and the performance and exhibition of the work. Recall that copyright law in the United States was modified by the Copyright Act of 1976, which became effective January 1, 1978. Under the old law, the right of an artist or author to his or her creation had common-law protection which continued indefinitely until the work was published. This protection was regulated by the states. Because the federal government has preempted the field under the new law, state laws regarding copyright are no longer effective. There is now a single system of statutory protection for all copyrightable works, whether published or unpublished. The old law also provided that unless an artist or author expressly retained his copyright, he was presumed to have transferred it when he sold the object or article. The new law is just the opposite. It provides that rights in copyright are retained unless they are expressly transferred. As noted in chapter 3, property rights are now protected for the author's life plus fifty years after death. Under the old law, copyright protection was granted for an ititial term of twenty-eight years from the first publication; however, with proper renewal, an extension of another twenty-eight years was allotted.

An artist or author should place a copyright notice on his work when it is to be published or publicly displayed. (The simple steps required to place such a notice are discussed in chapter 3.) Many artists do not attempt to secure copyright protection. A Picasso maquette, given by Picasso to the Public Building Commission of Chicago, was held to have become a part of the public domain when it was displayed without statutory notice. In *Letter Edged in Black Press, Inc.* v. *Public Building Commission*,[1] the court held that common-law copyright protection was lost when the Picasso maquette was displayed; it then fell into the public domain because it was displayed without copyright notice. Under the old law, the common law provided protection for the author or artist before publication; however, this protection ended upon publication or display. If an article was published or an art object was displayed without copyright notice, it became a part of the public domain. Once a work is part of the public domain, it can no longer be copyrighted. Hence, the Public Building Commission of Chicago lost statutory protection.[2] Under the new copyright act, the Picasso maquette would not have lost its statutory protection. As noted above, the new law provides for a single statutory system of copyright protection; there is no longer common-law protection. Further, publication without notice will not necessarily cause a work to become a part of the public domain so long as there is a registration of one's copyright within five years after publication. Recall that display of itself is not publication under the new law. Thus, a painting on display need not have a copyright notice. (See chapter 3.) Nonetheless, it is always best to display the copyright notice for all exhibitions or publications. Without notice, a person copying the work would be an innocent infringer. Because notice need not be on the front of the work, the copyright notice will not distract from the work.

The French law enlarges upon the property right of the artist or author which, for the most part, is protected in the United States only through the copyright law. Le droit de suite provides the artist or the artist's heirs the right to collect a percentage of the price of each work on subsequent resale. This right protects artists who must sell works of art for economic reasons when they are virtually unknown and cannot secure fair prices. The artists are entitled to a portion of the increase in value of the objects. The droit de suite was not recognized in the United States for some time; however, in 1976, California added section 986 to its code to provide that when a work of art sells within the state of California for more than $1,000 and the seller resides in California, the seller must pay the artist 5 percent of the sales price. One author commented that this statute, rather than helping the artist, will tend to render less marketable the works of artists that are subject to the California statute.[3] He reasoned that if two works shared the same price and the same potential for appreciation in value, the art investor would be less willing to purchase that of the artist protected by legislation setting forth the droit de suite. A statute attributing a droit de suite to every art sale would make such artists involuntary investors in their own future reputations.

An artist can employ the concept of droit de suite by contract. Artists have used "reserved rights" contracts to effect sales of their works, in which the artist retained a percentage share of appreciation realized upon resale of the work. Such contracts are difficult to enforce, however, and a purchaser with any degree of bargaining power will generally not accept such a sales contract.

The recently recognized tort, the right of publicity, may provide artists with a property right in their creations. As noted in chapter 3, the right of publicity protects a person from the appropriation of personal name and likeness. It is a transferable interest, similar to a property interest.

The Supreme Court recognized the right of publicity in Zacchini v. Scripps Howard Broadcasting.[4] In that case a performer in a "human cannonball" act brought an action against a television broadcasting company to recover damages allegedly suffered when, against his wishes, the broadcasting company videotaped the entire performance and played the videotape on a television news program. The Supreme Court stated that the broadcast of a film of the performer's entire act posed a substantial threat to the economic value of that performance. According to the Court, the performer's act was the product of his own talents and energy, the end result of much time, effort, and expense, and much of its economic value lay in the right of exclusive control over the publicity given the performance. As the Court stated, if the public can see the act free on television, it will be less willing to pay to see it. The right of publicity may provide economic protection to an artist, should his name or product be used in any unauthorized manner.

Moral Rights

Le droit moral was developed principally by French and German jurists. It is the right of the artist or the author to safeguard his artistic reputation, as distinguished from the property aspects of his copyright.[5] Under the Berne Convention, the moral right has two components—the paternity right and the right to the integrity of the work.[6] Other writers have claimed other components of the moral right, such as the right to create a work, the right to publish the work, the right to withdraw a published work from sale, and the right to prevent excessive criticism of the work.[7]

Paternity Right

The paternity right is held to consist of the author's right to be made known to the public as the creator of a work, the right to prevent others from usurping the work by naming another person as the author, and the right to prevent others from wrongfully attributing to the artist a work he or she has not written.[8] French courts have extended the right by holding that an author's name must appear in the work without change even after sale of the work, unless the author has consented to the change, and, in the case of several authors, requiring that all names appear. A work may not be published anonymously unless the author so stipulates in the contract, and false attribution of authorship is prohibited under the general rules of law.[9] According to one author,[10] American law has a callous disregard for the paternity right of creative persons. He cited the provision in the Copyright Act which gives the employer the right to copyright a work made for hire. The work-made-for-hire arrangement presumably "severs completely the relation between the creator and ownership of the work."[11]

Though copyright law in the United States does not provide for the right of paternity, there is nonetheless a limited recognition of this concept in the United States. For example, the use of an author's name in a distortion of his work would possibly constitute the tort of libel. False attribution of authorship or the unauthorized disclosure of an author's name could constitute the tort of unfair competition or might be a violation of one's right of privacy or one's right of publicity. A court would probably uphold an author's right to have his or her name appear in connection with a publication of the work under a contract theory. Contributions to encyclopedic works are presumed to be anonymous; however, other contributions carry a presumption that the author's name will appear. The right of publicity, if recognized in a particular state, retains the artist's right to economic benefit from use of his or her name.

In an early case in New York, *Clemens v. Press Publishing Co.*,[12] a state court upheld an artist's right to payment for his manuscript even though the artist refused to allow publication of the article without his name. In a concurring opinion in that case, Justice Seabury stated that a purchaser of rights to literary property cannot "garble" the property "or put it out under another name than the author's." He further stated that a publisher could not omit the author's name altogether unless the contract with the author permitted anonymous authorship. In a later case, *Vargas v. Esquire, Inc.*,[13] a federal court of appeals held that the author, Vargas, waived his right to have his name appear in a magazine containing reproductions of his paintings because the contract between him and the publisher did not provide for attribution of authorship. Whether the court recognized the author's right to authorship and was of the opinion that the right had been waived by contract or whether it would permit such a right only if the contract specifically provided for it is not clear.

In 1979, the California legislature added section 987 to its code, formally recognizing a right of paternity in an artist. Section 987 provides that an artist has the right to claim authorship or, for just and valid reason, to disclaim authorship of a work of fine art. Section 987 creates a right in the artist similar to the right of publicity in the way that it provides for damages for the author.

Right to Integrity of a Work.

The right to the integrity of a work of art is the right of an artist or author to prevent all deformations of his work. By virtue of this right, the artist is entitled to make changes in the work or to authorize others to do so.[14] In the past, courts in the United States have provided little recognition of such a right. Protection for the author or artist, to the extent that it has been granted, has been through the torts of unfair competition or libel.

In an early case, *Crimi v. Rutgers Presbyterian Church in the City of New York*,[15] a state court in New York held that an artist could not prevent the owner of his artwork from destroying the work. In that case a church had commissioned an artist to paint a mural on the church wall. A later congregation decided that it did not like the mural and had it painted over when the church was redecorated. The artist sued the church to compel it to remove the obliterating paint from the mural. The court stated that the artist retained no rights in the work after he made an unconditional sale. In a later case, *Granz v. Harris*,[16] a federal court of appeals did hold that attributing authorship of abbreviated versions of an artist's musical performances to the artist would constitute the tort of unfair competition. The court also held that the contract between the artist and the purchaser of the master discs carried by implication, without the necessity of an express prohibition, the duty not to sell records which made the required legend a false representation. Hence, the court found that the sale of the abbreviated records also constituted a breach of contract. The court in *Granz* somewhat recognized an artists's right of integrity in their work. Justice Frank, in a concurring opinion, declared that an artist is entitled to prevent the publication of a garbled version as his product. Without rejecting the doctrine of moral right, however, he concurred that a court should not rest its decision on that doctrine if it is possible to rule for the artist under either a tort or contract theory.

The recent case of *Gilliam v. American Broadcasting Companies*[17] was the first direct attempt by a court to enlarge the copyright law and the tort of unfair competition to include a droit moral. In that case a group of British writers and performers known as Monty Python sought an injunction to restrain American Broadcasting Companies from broadcasting edited versions of three separate programs originally written and performed by Monty Python. The court held that the excising impaired the integrity of the original work. The court stated that one who obtains permission to use a copyrighted script in the production of a derivative work may not exceed the specific purpose for which permission was granted. The editing performed by American Broadcasting exceeded the scope of its license and was an infringement of the artists' copyright. The court asserted that copyright law should be used to recognize the important role of the artist in our society and to encourage production and dissemination of artistic works by providing adequate legal protection for one who submits his work to the public. The court further opined that while American copyright law seeks to vindicate the economic rather than the personal rights of authors and does not recognize moral rights of artists, the economic incentive for artistic and intellectual creation, which serves as the foundation for American copyright law, cannot be reconciled with the inability of artists to obtain relief for mutilation or misrepresentation of their work by the public on which the artists are financially dependent. The court recognized that relief has been granted for misrepresentation of an artist's work by relying on theories outside the statutory law of copyright, such as contract law or the law of unfair competition. As the court stated, though these decisions were clothed in terms of proprietary rights in one's creation, they also properly vindicated the author's personal right to prevent presentation of his work to the public in a distorted form.

The court in the *Gilliam* case found a violation of the Lanham Act,[18] the federal counterpart to state laws regarding unfair competition. The court stated that this act may be considered to have been violated if a representation of a product, although technically true, creates a false impression of the product's origin. Thus, an obligation to mention the name of the author carries the implied duty, as a matter of contract, not to make such changes in the work as would render the credit line a false attribution of authorship. Further, according to the court, an allegation that a defendant has presented to the public a garbled, or distorted, version of the artist's work seeks to redress the very rights that the Lanham Act sought to protect and should be a cause of action under that statute.

Section 987 of the California Code[19] recognizes that there is a public interest in preserving the integrity of cultural and artistic creations. That statute provides, effective January 1, 1980, that no person, except an artist who owns a work that he or she has created, may intentionally commit or authorize the commission of any physical defacement, mutilation, alteration, or destruction of a work of fine art. Hence California has also formally provided a right to integrity of a work of art.

Right to Create a Work

When an author or artist agrees to create a work and is later unwilling to do so, the right to create a work becomes a part of the artist's moral right. In the United States, this right is protected in that a court normally will not decree specific performance, though it will award damages.[20]

Right to Publish a Work

The right to publish or withhold a work from publication is a recognized right under the copyright law. It is also a part of the right of privacy. In *Chamberlain v. Feldman,*[21] a New York court held that Mark Twain's heirs could prevent the publication of one of Mark Twain's short stories by a person who had purchased the manuscript at an auction after the author's death. The court ruled that a purchase of the manuscript did not include a purchase of publication rights.

As a result of the *Chamberlain* case, the common law of copyrights came to be called the "right of first publication."[22] A New York court stated in *Estate of Hemingway v. Random House, Inc.*[23] that the common-law copyright enabled an author to control the first publication or to prevent publication entirely. Courts have been reluctant to find that an author had published a work because there was the possibility that the work had become a part of the public domain. Still, in *Pushman v. New York Graphic Society,*[24] an early court in New York held that an artist who had made an absolute sale of his painting without any condition, reservation, or qualification of any kind had abandoned his copyright, and the painting could be reproduced by anyone. The artist had contended that his sale of the painting did not transfer the right to reproduce the painting. Further, in *Giesel v. Poynter Products, Inc.,*[25] a federal district court held that, absent a reservation of the common-law copyright or other rights, the copyright and all rights pass with an absolute and unconditional sale. In that case, the court permitted a magazine which had acquired the rights to the "Dr. Seuss" cartoon to make and sell dolls based upon the cartoon. It held that a copyright in one medium empowers the copyright owner to copy the work in a different form. In an earlier case, *Warner Brothers v. Columbia Broadcasting System, Inc.,*[26] a federal court of appeals had held that a transfer of a right of copyright does not necessarily provide the transferee with complete ownership of the work. The court in the *Warner Brothers* case permitted the author Dashiell Hammett to use the characters of his work *Maltese Falcon* in subsequent works even though the author had given Warner Brothers the exclusive right to use the "Sam Spade" characters from *Maltese Falcon* in motion pictures, television, and radio media.

The new copyright law clarifies this area of copyright protection. It specifically provides that rights in a copyrighted work are divisible. Under present copyright law, an artist or author is granted five exclusive rights in copyrighted material: the right to reproduce the work, the right to prepare derivative works, the right to sell copies of the work, the right of performance, and the right to display the work publicly.[27] These rights may be owned and/or transferred singly or in their entirety.[28] Further, unless there is a specific transfer of any or all of the exclusive rights, the rights are retained by the author or artist.[29]

Right to Withdraw a Work and Right to Prevent Excessive Criticism

The right to withdraw a work from the market after it has been published is not recognized in the United States. The right to prevent excessive criticism is also not recognized; however, an injured party has an action for libel for damage to his reputation.

Freedom of Expression

The right of an artist or author to express his ideas freely is guaranteed by the First Amendment. This right is not without bounds, however. Some artists' expressions may be offensive to others; some may even violate community standards regarding obscenity and thus be subject to criminal sanctions. In *Close v. Lederle*,[30] an art instructor who displayed paintings offensive to others in a corridor of the university sued the university when he was ordered to remove the paintings. The court ruled that the university was warranted in finding that the exhibit was inappropriate, given the primary use to which the corridor was put. It held that the university could order removal of the paintings to afford protection to a captive audience, some of whom were children, in that the paintings could violate an unwilling bystander's right to privacy. Though paintings might not be regarded as obscene in a constitutional sense, the court held that their display need not be permitted in every context. The interest of others should be considered. According to the

court, freedom of speech must recognize, at least within limits, freedom
not to listen.

The museum director should be aware of the local statutes regarding display of obscene materials. Paintings or other art objects displayed in a museum would probably not violate a state's criminal
statutes; however, an awareness of local provisions regarding obscenity
is warranted in that current law affords no protection to explicitly sexual
scenes which might be offensive to the average person in the community. While the line dividing art from pornography may be ill defined,
some generalizations can be made.

The Supreme Court stated in 1957, in *Roth v. United States,* that
obscenity is not protected by the First Amendment. It declared:

> . . . all ideas having even the slightest redeeming social importance—
> unorthodox ideas, controversial ideas, even ideas hateful to the prevailing
> climate of opinion—have the full protection of the guarantees (of the First
> Amendment), unless excludable because they encroach upon the limited
> area of more important interest. But implicit in the history of the First
> Amendment is the rejection of obscenity as utterly without redeeming so-
> cial importance.[31]

The Court stated that obscene material is material which deals with sex
in a manner appealing to prurient interest; the mere portrayal of sex in
art, literature, and scientific works "is not itself sufficient reason to
deny material the constitutional protection of freedom of speech and
press." The Court adopted a standard to distinguish the two: whether to
the average person, applying contemporary community standards, the
dominant theme of the material taken as a whole appeals to the prurient interest. In 1966, however, the Supreme Court used a "social
value" test ("Is the material utterly without redeeming social value?")
to overturn a conviction under a state statute which had held the book
Fanny Hill to be obscene.[32] In *United States v. Ten Erotic Paintings,*[33] a
federal district court held that entry of allegedly obscene paintings into
the United States could not be barred in that the government presented
no factual basis to support a determination that any of the paintings
were "utterly without redeeming social value."

Following the decision concerning *Fanny Hill,* the Supreme Court
became somewhat divergent in its views on obscenity. Finally, in *Miller v. California,*[34] a majority of the justices agreed that the proper test
for obscenity should be: (a) whether "the average person, applying

contemporary community standards" would find that the work, taken as a whole, appeals to the prurient interest, (b) whether the work depicts or describes, in a patently offensive way, sexual conduct as specifically defined by the applicable state law, and (c) whether the work, taken as a whole, lacks serious literary, artistic, political, or scientific value. The Court in the *Miller* case offered examples of definitions that might appear in a state statute for purposes of regulation: patently offensive representations or descriptions of ultimate sexual acts, normal or perverted, actual or simulated, and patently offensive representations or descriptions of masturbation, excretory functions, and lewd exhibition of the genitals. The Court did acknowledge that no one would be subject to prosecution for the sale or exposure of obscene materials unless those materials "depict or describe patently offensive 'hard core' sexual conduct specifically defined by the regulating state law, as written or construed."[35] Books alone, containing only words and no pictures, may be obscene.[36]

In the *Miller* case, the Court held that obscenity is to be determined by applying contemporary community standards and not national standards, a ruling that can present a real problem. A display in a museum would undoubtedly have artistic value; nonetheless, a museum director in a puritanical community must be cautious regarding his art exhibitions. In *Pinkus v. United States*,[37] the Supreme Court clarified some aspects of application of the community standard. The Court ruled that children are not to be included as part of the community, though it is permissible to include "particularly sensitive" persons. In applying the community standard, however, one should not focus on the most susceptible and sensitive members of that community.

While an individual has a protected right to possess obscene material in the privacy of his home,[38] this zone of privacy does not extend beyond his home.[39] Further, the intended private use of materials is not relevant in determining whether the material is obscene.[40] The right to possess obscene materials in one's home does not imply nor establish the right of others to distribute those materials nor the right to bring them into the United States from abroad.[41] Obscene material can be confiscated at a port of entry.[42]

5

Museum Acquisitions

Museums generally acquire exhibitions and objects in one of three ways: by purchase, by gift, or on loan. It is imperative that the museum director be aware of the legal aspects of each.

Purchases

A museum which purchases museum objects wants assurance that it has legal title to the objects, that the objects conform to all representations regarding quality and origin, and that it has not violated any laws regulating acquisitions. In this regard, differing legal problems are involved in the acquisition of art objects, scientific specimens, and historical objects.

Application of Uniform Commercial Code

Museum objects are classified as personal property. Sales and purchases of personal property are governed in most states by the Uniform Commercial Code;[1] hence certain provisions of this code become relevant to the museum director. A sales contract is an ordinary contract subject to the common law relating to contracts; however, the Uniform Commercial Code contains a number of provisions which modify the common law of contracts. The Uniform Commercial Code adds to sales agreements much that is not expressed by the parties. It imposes obligations of good faith and permits the parties to prove "extrinsic" terms normally not permitted by the parol evidence rule. (See chapter 3 for a discussion of the parol evidence rule.) The principal modifications of the common law of contracts brought about by the Uniform Commercial Code are summarized below.

Terms of the Sales Agreement. The Uniform Commercial Code permits less certainty in a contract for the sale and purchase of goods than the common law of contracts. A valid contract of sale, for example, can exist even though the price is not settled. Section 2-204 (3) of the Uniform Commercial Code provides for the enforceability of contracts even though one or more terms is left open if the parties intended to make a contract and there is a reasonably certain basis for giving an appropriate remedy. Section 2-207 (3) provides that conduct by both parties which recognizes the existence of a contract is sufficient to establish a sales contract regardless of whether or not the terms are established. Section 2-204 (1) provides that a contract for the sale of goods may be made in any manner sufficient to show agreement, including conduct by both parties which recognizes the existence of a contract. An agreement is sufficient to constitute a contract for sale "even though the moment of its making is undetermined."[2] Under 2-207 (1) of the code, a definite and seasonable expression or acceptance or a written confirmation which is sent within a reasonable time operates as an acceptance even if it states terms additional to, or different from, those offered or agreed upon. Section 2-206 (1) provides that acceptance of an offer to make a contract can be made in any reasonable medium.

Statute of Frauds. The Statute of Frauds (see chapter 3) has been modified by the Uniform Commercial Code. Section 2-201 (3) provides that contracts for the sale of goods in excess of $500 will be enforceable even though they are not in writing if the goods are specially manufactured for the buyer and are not suitable for sale to others. If goods have been received and accepted, to the extent that they have been received and accepted, the contract need not be in writing. Further, if the person against whom enforcement is sought admits in his pleading, testimony, or otherwise in court that a contract or sale was made, the contract will be enforceable to the extent of the quantity of goods admitted, even though it was not in writing.[3]

Rejection of Goods. Under section 2-601 of the Uniform Commercial Code, the buyer of goods may reject an entire delivery of goods if the goods fail, in any respect, to conform to the contract. The buyer may reject the whole or may accept a part and reject the rest. This right in the buyer is subject, however, to the requirement that the buyer act in good faith and observe reasonable commercial standards of fair dealing in the trade.[4] As to goods to be delivered in separate lots, the buyer may reject any installment which is nonconforming if the nonconformity substantially impairs the value of that installment and cannot be cured.[5] If there is nonconformity which impairs the value of the whole contract, there is a breach of the whole; however, the buyer will reinstate the contract if he accepts a nonconforming installment without reasonable notification of cancellation.

Risk of Loss. Under section 2-509 (1), the risk of loss of shipped goods generally remains with the seller until the buyer receives the goods. In the absence of carrier shipment authorization, risk of loss passes to the buyer on his receipt of the goods if the seller is a merchant; otherwise, risk passes to the buyer on tender of delivery.

Warranties. Section 2-313 of the Uniform Commercial Code provides that a seller need not give the buyer an express warranty for a guarantee to attach to the goods. An affirmation of the value of the goods or a statement purporting to be merely the seller's opinion or commendation of the goods does not create a warranty; however, any description of the goods which is made a part of the basis of the bargain creates an express warranty that the goods will conform to the description. Any sample or model which is made a part of the basis of the bargain creates an express warranty that the whole of the goods will conform to the sample or model. In addition, any affirmation of fact or promise made by the seller to the buyer which relates to the goods and which becomes part of the basis of the bargain creates an express warranty that the goods will conform to the affirmation or promise. A warranty that the goods will be merchantable is implied in a contract of sale if the seller is a merchant as to the goods sold. Under section 2-316 of the Uniform Commercial Code, however, words in a contract negating or limiting warranty will be given effect. All implied warranties are excluded by expressions such as "with all faults" or "as is."

Art Objects

Because the Uniform Commercial Code is applicable to personal property in general, it does not provide discrete solutions to many problems unique to art objects. Fake works of art, for example, have presented major problems for museums and art collectors. The Uniform Commercial Code furnishes some remedies, should a museum purchase a forgery. As noted above, section 2-313 provides that goods sold shall conform to any affirmation of fact or promise made by the seller. On the other hand, section 2-316 provides that implied warranties are negated by expressions such as "with all faults" or "as is." Section 2-316 does state that negation or limitation of warranty is inoperative to the extent that such a construction is unreasonable. In addition, words or conduct relevant to the creation of an express warranty and words or conduct tending to negate or limit warranty are construed wherever reasonable to be consistent with each other.

Statutes in New York have gone beyond provisions of the Uniform Commercial Code to provide protection for art collectors. Article 12-D[6] states that language tending to negate or limit a warranty will not be operative unless the language is conspicuous and clearly and specifically apprises the buyer that the seller assumes no risk, liability, or responsibility for the authenticity of the authorship of a work of art. The New York statute also provides that a description furnished by a seller who is an art merchant, to a buyer, not an art merchant, which identifies the work with any author, becomes a part of the basis for the bargain and creates an express warranty of the authenticity of the authorship. Such a warranty cannot be negated or limited merely because formal words such as "warranty" or "guarantee" are not used.[7] Under the New York statute, any person who falsifies certificates of authenticity of works of fine art is subject to criminal prosecution.[8]

In *Weisz v. Parke-Bernet Galleries, Inc.*,[9] certain buyers of paintings listed in an auction catalogue as works of Raoul Dufy brought suit against the art gallery to recover the purchase price of such paintings when they discovered that the paintings were forgeries. The art gallery denied liability, stating that the catalogue described "conditions of sale" which included a disclaimer of warranty as to genuineness or authorship. The court found that because the dealer had superior knowledge and experience, the disclaimer was ineffective. The court stated that the fact that Parke-Bernet was offering a work of art for sale would inspire confidence that it was genuine and that the listed artist was, in fact, the creator of the work. A warning to the contrary had to be given special prominence or it would not be effective.

The fabrication of paintings has been accomplished by several methods.[10] A signature of a recognized painter may be added to an unsigned work, or an existing signature may be replaced with a more valuable one by painting over the original signature.[11] Some fabricators complete partially finished or discarded canvases which show the marks of age, while others reproduce and sell as genuine copies of specific originals.[12] Often imitators begin faked paintings and then pass them to specialists who add the finishing touches. Sometimes the paintings of students of a master are sold as the master's product.[13]

A museum should not only be careful regarding purchase of fake objects of art; it also should make certain the seller has legal title to the art object. In *Menzel v. List*,[14] the plaintiff purchased a Chagall painting for $4,000 from a New York art gallery. The New York gallery had purchased the painting from a Parisian art gallery. In 1932, however, the painting had been purchased by the Menzels at an auction in Belgium. When the Germans invaded Belgium, the Menzels fled, leaving their possessions, including the Chagall painting, in their apartment. When they returned six years later, the painting was gone. It had been removed by the German authorities; a receipt for it had been left. The Menzels learned that the painting was in List's possession from an art book which carried a reproduction of the painting plus a statement that it was in List's possession. The Menzels then sued List for a return of the painting, and List was ordered by the court to return it to the Menzels. He was awarded the value of the painting; the jury found the painting to be worth $22,500, and the New York gallery was ordered to pay List this amount. The court held that the painting could have been sold subject to any existing lawful claims unknown to the seller at the time of the sale. Because it was not, List was entitled to recover the value of the painting and was not limited to his purchase price.

Under Section 2-714 (2) of the Uniform Commercial Code, a purchaser who has received goods which were not as warranted may recover the difference between the value of the goods as accepted and the value the goods would have had if they had been as warranted. This provision provides the more expansive damages awarded List in the *Menzel* case rather than a remedy consisting simply of return of the purchase price. While this provision and the *Menzel* case provide protection for the innocent purchaser, there is a danger when the purchaser later sells the art object. The defective title will not have been cured, and should the rightful owner sue the purchaser, the latter may be compelled to respond in damages for the appreciated value of the object. Limitation on time during which suit may be brought does not begin until the rightful owner asserts a claim to the property. Should a museum sell an art object, the sales agreement should limit the purchaser to a refund of the purchase price for defective title.

Gifts

A gift is a voluntary transfer of property by one party, the donor, to another, the donee, without consideration. Unless the donor has less than absolute ownership or unless the language of the gift indicates a lesser interest, a gift normally passes absolute ownership in the property given. A gift taking effect during the lifetime of the donor is called an inter vivos gift, while a gift taking effect at death is called a testamentary gift. A testamentary gift can be effectuated only by a valid will; however, an attempted gift can be operative as a will if the testamentary formalities are complied with and if the instrument can be construed as a will. Partial interests in property may be the subject of a gift. Although a donor cannot retain the right to use and enjoy property during his lifetime and also direct its disposition after death (in any manner other than by the making of a will), he may reserve a life estate and give a present estate in the remainder of the property to the donee.

The requisites of a valid gift are: an intention to make a gift, a delivery of the property given, and an acceptance by the donee.[15] Freedom of will on the part of a donor is essential to the validity of a gift; if the donor has been induced to make a gift as a result of duress, fraud, or undue influence, the gift may be set aside.[16] Further, the donor must have sufficient mental capacity to make a gift; however, any person is deemed to have the capacity to accept a gift if the gift is for his benefit.[17] Intention to make a gift must be clear and unmistakable and must be a present intention; intention to make a gift in the future will not support a gift.[18]

Delivery of the subject of the gift must be complete and unconditional. The reason for this is that a gift is without consideration, and thus no action is available in court to enforce the gift if it has not been fully delivered. Delivery of the subject of the gift to the donee or his agent can be actual, constructive, or symbolic. It must transfer possession to the donee and must vest a present and irrevocable title in the donee. At the same time, the donor must be divested of control and dominion over the property. A gift of property evidenced by a written instrument executed by the donor can be consummated by a delivery of the instrument without a manual delivery of the property. The execution and delivery of a deed to land, for example, is a completed execution of a gift of the land.

An unmistakable and unconditional acceptance on the part of the donee is essential to the validity of a gift inter vivos; however, acceptance is presumed where the gift is beneficial to the donee. A gift inter vivos subject to a precedent condition to take effect in the future is invalid; however, a donor may limit his gift by a condition that is dependent on an expected state of facts, so that if the state of fact fails, the gift fails also. A reservation by the donor of certain proprietary rights in the subject of the gift, such as the use and enjoyment of the property, is not necessarily inconsistent with the absolute character of the gift, and gifts accompanied by such reservations have been repeatedly upheld.[19]

Where a gift inter vivos has been perfected by a sufficient delivery and acceptance, it cannot be revoked. Where some essential element necessary to make a perfected gift inter vivos is lacking, however, the donor may revoke the gift at any time before it is perfected.[20]

Cy Pres Doctrine

Property may be given to a charity in the form of a charitable trust wherein certain restrictions are placed upon use of the trust property. Such restrictions may become impossible to execute, however, an example being the gift of property to establish a university for white males only. The charitable trust is a fiduciary relationship arising as a result of an intention to donate property to a charity but also to subject the person by whom the trust property is held to equitable duties in dealing with the property for the charitable purpose. The so-called cy pres doctrine requires that administration of such a charitable trust be carried out with as close an approximation to the scheme (intent) of the donor as is reasonably practicable. In instances where a gift would fail because of the impossibility of administering it in light of its restrictions, however, a court may apply the cy pres doctrine to delete the restrictions. The basic premise for application of cy pres doctrine is to defeat the failure of the charitable bequest. The cy pres power is the power of the court alone. A charitable organization may not receive a gift for one purpose and use it for another unless the court, applying the cy pres doctrine, so commands.[21]

A charitable trust will generally not fail because of illegality, impossibility, or impracticality because of the court's power, by cy pres, to direct the application of the property to some other charitable purpose which can be attributed to the donor. In *Wooten v. Fitz-Gerald*,[22] property was left by will in trust for the use and benefit of the aged white men of a certain county in Texas. The state court deleted "white" from the trust provisions by applying the doctrine of cy pres. The court noted that the last reference in the will, as to the purpose of the trust, referred only to "aged men." The court stated that the decedent might have preferred the benefit of the property to be limited to white men but that this was not the dominant purpose of the bequest. In *Evans v. Abney*,[23] the Supreme Court of the United States held that the cy pres doctrine is *not* applicable in an instance where the donor manifested an intention that the gift lapse in the event that the particular purpose becomes impossible to accomplish. In the *Evans* case, the donor conveyed property in trust for the creation of a public park for the exclusive use of the white people of a city. The State Supreme Court ruled that the donor's intention had become impossible to fulfill and that the trust property would revert by law to the heirs of the donor. Black citizens challenged the termination of the trust, and the attorney general of the state argued that the court should apply the cy pres doctrine to amend the terms of the will by striking the racial restrictions and thus open the park to all residents of the city. The U.S. Supreme Court stated that the "whites only" provision was an essential and inseparable part of the donor's plan; because the sole purpose of the trust was in irreconcilable conflict with the constitutional mandate, the trust failed and the property reverted. The cy pres doctrine was not applicable.

When circumstances change after a gift is made, so that a literal compliance with the terms of the gift becomes impossible, a court may direct that the gift shall be so administered as to accomplish most effectively the donor's general purpose.[24] Further, where property is given in trust to be applied to a particular charitable use by a certain charitable institution which ceases to exist, courts have held that cy pres may be applied for the same purposes by another institution (unless the donor manifested an intent to restrict the gift to the institution which he named.[25]

Charitable Contributions Deduction for Gifts

Persons donating property to a museum are interested in the tax deductibility of such gifts. The Tax Reform Act of 1969 changed the rules regarding deductibility of charitable contributions considerably. Many former tax benefits no longer exist. As a general rule, contributions of money or property made to qualified organizations are deductible pursuant to section 170 of the Internal Revenue Code. If property is donated, the deduction is normally the fair market value of such property at the time of the contribution.

Limitations on Contribution Deductions. Charitable contributions are subject to several limitations. For example, contributions by individuals are limited to 50 percent of the taxpayer's adjusted gross income and 30 percent for contributions of capital gain property. Contributions to private foundations are subject to a 20 percent limitation. A corporation can only deduct 10 percent of its taxable income, computed without regard to the charitable contributions, in a taxable year. With the exception of contributions to private foundations, contributions in excess of these limitations may be carried forward five years and deducted in succeeding taxable years. Contributions to private foundations in excess of the 20 percent limitation may not be carried forward. In addition, gifts to public charities that qualify for the 50 percent limitation are considered first in determining the contribution deduction. Gifts to which the 20 percent limitation applies are considered afterward and only to the extent of the lesser of 20 percent of adjusted gross income or 50 percent of adjusted gross income less the amount of charitable contributions qualifying for the 50 percent limitation. The excess cannot be carried forward.

Example 1. *A*, an individual, has adjusted gross income of $20,000 for the taxable year. He gave $8,000 to his church and $5,000 cash to Museum *X*, a private foundation, during the year. The gift to Museum *X* is limited initially to 20 percent of adjusted gross income, or $4,000 ($20,000 × 20 percent). The gift to the church is applied first, however. *A* is entitled to the lesser of 20 percent of adjusted gross income ($4,000) or 50 percent of adjusted gross income less the amount of charitable contributions qualifying for the 50 percent limitation ($8,000 gift to the church in this example). Fifty percent of adjusted income is $10,000. This amount, less the $8,000 which qualifies for the 50 percent limitation, leaves only $2,000, which can be taken as a deduction for the contribution to Museum *X*. *A* can deduct $10,000 as charitable contributions for the taxable year; the remaining $3,000, which he donated to Museum *X*, cannot be carried forward. It is lost as a deduction.

If property when sold would produce ordinary income (as distinguished from capital gain), the charitable contribution deduction is equal to the fair market value of the property less the amount of ordinary income which would have been reported if the property were sold. This generally means that the deduction is limited to the cost (or cost less depreciation) of the property. Ordinary income property would include inventory in the contributor's business, works of art created by the donor, and capital assets owned less than a year. For a capital asset (an asset which if sold would produce a capital gain rather than ordinary income) which is held over a year, the charitable contribution deduction is equal to the fair market value of the property. If the capital asset is given to a private foundation, however, the contribution deduction must be reduced by 40 percent of the long-term capital gain that the donor would have realized if the property had been sold at its fair market value.

If tangible personal property is contributed to a public charity and is put to an "unrelated use," the charitable deduction is reduced by 40 percent of the potential long-term capital gain. A taxpayer-donor must establish that the property is not in fact being put to an unrelated use by the donee and that, at the time of the contribution, it was reasonable to anticipate that the property would not be put to an unrelated use. If an object is donated to or for the use of a museum and if the object is of a general type normally retained by a museum for museum purposes, Treasury Regulations[26] specify that it is reasonable for the donor to anticipate that the object will not be put to an unrelated use by the donee whether or not the object is later sold or exchanged by the donee museum, unless the donor has actual knowledge to the contrary. This regulation permits the donor a deduction for the fair market value of the object without the necessity of requiring the museum to hold the object until the time period for audit of the donor's income tax return has ended. The museum director should point out this regulation to the donor so that the museum will not be locked into an agreement prohibiting sale for an extended period of time.

Example 2. *A* contributes a Van Gogh painting to a museum. It has a value of $500,000; however, *A* paid only $100,000 for the painting. The painting was displayed by the museum for two years and was then sold. *A* has a charitable contribution deduction of $500,000. It is not reduced by 40 percent of the unrealized appreciation [40 percent × ($500,000 − $100,000)] because the painting was the kind of art normally retained by a museum.

Example 3. A is the creator of a painting which he, A, believes to be worth $100,000. The cost of the painting to A was $50 (the cost of the canvas, paints, and brushes). A donates the painting to Museum X. A has a charitable contribution deduction of $50. If the painting were sold by A, it would produce ordinary income; hence, A's deduction is limited to his cost in the painting.

Transfers of Less than a Donor's Entire Interest. A charitable contribution made by a transfer in trust of less than the donor's entire interest in the property is not generally deductible unless it consists of a "remainder" interest transferred to a pooled income fund, a charitable remainder annuity trust, a charitable remainder unitrust, or an "income" interest that is either a guaranteed annuity interest or a unitrust interest, with the donor being treated as the owner of the income interest.[27] A guaranteed annuity interest means an irrevocable right under the terms of the trust instrument to receive payment of a fixed amount periodically, at least annually. The amount cannot change from year to year. A unitrust interest is an irrevocable right under the terms of the trust instrument to receive payment, at least annually, of a fixed percentage of the net fair market value of the trust assets, determined annually.

A pooled income fund is a trust to which donors contribute an irrevocable remainder interest in property to or for the use of a qualified organization and retain an income interest for the life of one or more beneficiaries. The property transferred by each donor is commingled with property transferred by other donors. The trust fund cannot have investments in tax-exempt securities, and it must be maintained by the charity to which the remainder interest is contributed. Each beneficiary of an income interest receives income determined by the rate of return earned by the trust for the year. A charitable remainder annuity trust, on the other hand, is a trust from which at least 5 percent of the *initial* net fair market value of all property placed in the trust is paid at least annually, for twenty years or less, or for life, to one or more individuals who were living when the trust was created. No other amount can be paid to anyone, except the charity, and following the termination of the payments, the remainder interest is transferred to, or retained by, the charity. A charitable remainder unitrust is similar to a charitable remainder annuity trust except that the payments to the noncharity beneficiary must be a fixed percentage, not less than 5 percent for all beneficiaries taken together, of the net fair market value of the trust assets, *valued annually*.

A charitable contribution, *not* made by a transfer in trust, of less than the donor's entire interest in property may be deducted only as follows. (a) An undivided part of the donor's entire interest: If the donor owns a ten-acre tract of land, he can take a deduction for a gift of a 50 percent undivided interest in the land. (b) A remainder interest in a personal home or farm: A deduction is permitted for a remainder interest in a donor's home or farm which he retains for his lifetime. Nevertheless, the amount of the deduction is the fair market value of the partial interest at the time of the contribution, reduced by depreciation and discounted at the rate of 6 percent per year. (c) A remainder interest in real property granted to a public charity or a government unit to be used exclusively for conservation purposes: "Conservation purposes" is defined to include the preservation of land areas for public outdoor recreation or educational or scenic enjoyment; the preservation of historic land areas or structures; the preservation of open space; or the protection of natural environmental habitats for fish, wildlife, and plants.

If a contribution of a remainder interest in real property (which is a historically important land or a certified historic structure), or a restriction (granted in perpetuity) on the use which may be made of the real property, is made to a museum for historical preservation purposes, a charitable deduction for tax purposes of the value of the remainder interest or of the value of the restriction will be allowed.[28] A certified historic structure is one listed in the National Register or located in a restricted historic district and certified by the secretary of the interior as being of historic significance in the district.

An original work of art and a copyright interest in that work are treated as two interests in the same property; consequently, no charitable deduction is allowed for income tax purposes if an individual gives the original work of art to a charity and retains the copyright interest. (However, for transfers made after 1981, as to estate and gift taxes, these interests are treated as separate properties; a charitable deduction would be permitted for estate and gift taxes, even though the copyright interest was not transferred.)

A contribution of the right to use property, such as a rent-free building, is not deductible because it is considered a contribution of less than the donor's entire interest in the property. Payments to a charity for benefit performances can be deducted if the admission charge is more than the value of the benefits received. Dues, fees, or assessments are deductible if the amount paid exceeds the value of the benefits and privileges received by the donor.

Valuation. Often a donor will ask a museum director to value his gift. Whether or not a museum should render such a service to a donor depends upon the circumstances. It is not illegal to do so; however, a donee institution is considered an interested party by the Internal Revenue Service. Consequently, the IRS will give less weight to the museum director's appraisal. There are instances in which museum personnel will be the only qualified appraisers. Further, it may not be worthwhile to use outside appraisers for small gifts. For large gifts, it is usually preferable to obtain outside appraisers.

The Internal Revenue Code and the Treasury Regulations give very little guidance on the determination of the fair market value of property. Fair market value is defined by the IRS as "the price at which the property would change hands between a willing buyer and a willing seller, neither being under any compulsion to buy or sell and both having reasonable knowledge of relevant facts."[29] The IRS has published guidelines for making appraisals of donated properties such as art objects, literary manuscripts, and antiques.[30] Facts bearing on value are cost, selling price of the item, sales of comparable properties, cost of reproduction, opinion evidence, and appraisals. The weight to be given to opinion evidence depends on its origin and the thoroughness with which it is supported by experience and facts. Only where expert opinion is supported by facts having strong probative value will the opinion be given appropriate weight. The underlying facts must corroborate the opinion; otherwise the opinion will be discounted or disregarded.[31] The IRS gives an example of the kind of data which should be contained in a typical appraisal. According to the IRS, appraisals of art objects, and paintings in particular, should include (a) a complete description of the object, indicating the size, the subject matter, the medium, the name of the artist, the approximate date of creation, and the interest transferred; (b) the cost, date, and manner of acquisition; (c) a history of the item including proof of authenticity; (d) a photograph of a size and quality that permit full identification of the subject matter; (e) a statement of the factors upon which the appraisal was based, such as sales of other works by the same artist, quoted prices in dealer's catalogues of the artist's works, economic state of the art market at or around the time of valuation, a record of any exhibitions at which the particular art object had been displayed, and a statement as to the standing of the artist in his profession and in the particular school or time period.[32] The IRS does not accord recognition to any appraiser or group of appraisers to the extent of accepting their appraisals without question. The IRS uses distinguished art experts, members of an art advisory panel, to perform the public service of advising the Internal Revenue Service concerning the values that taxpayers give to particular works of art.

The IRS has issued two recent pronouncements regarding valuation of literary or art properties. In Revenue Ruling 79-491, a taxpayer attempted to deduct the fair market value of art books donated to various charities and purchased at a discount of as much as 75 percent off the listed retail price. A company located outside the United States had contacted individuals in high brackets, advising them of the availability of the "limited edition" art books at a quantity discount and apprising them of the advantages for federal income tax of purchasing the books at a discount and then contributing them to charitable organizations within the United States. A taxpayer purchased some of the books for $25 per book and attempted to deduct $100 per book as a charitable contribution. The IRS ruled that the taxpayer's activity was tantamount to that of a dealer selling books. Thus the books were considered ordinary income property under section 170 (e) of the Internal Revenue Code, and the taxpayer's deduction was limited to his cost of $25 per book. In Revenue Ruling 80-69, the IRS stated that the best evidence of fair market value depends on actual transactions and not on some artificially calculated estimate of value contrary to the prices at which items changed hands in the marketplace. In that ruling, the taxpayer purchased an assortment of gems for 500x dollars from a promotor who advised him that the price was wholesale and that the taxpayer would be entitled to a deduction of 1500x dollars should he donate the gems to a charity. Taxpayer donated the gems to a museum thirteen months after purchase and claimed a charitable contribution deduction of 1500x dollars; however, the IRS limited his deduction to 500x dollars.

Loans

As noted in chapter 3, a loan of an art object to a museum constitutes a bailment. Such a bailment can be for the sole benefit of the bailee museum, or it may be for the mutual benefit of both parties. Where a bailment is for the sole benefit of the bailee, the bailee is bound to great care and is responsible for slight neglect in relation to the subject matter of the bailment. If the bailment is for the mutual benefit of the bailor and the bailee, in the absence of a special contract, the bailee is held to the exercise of ordinary care and is responsible only for ordinary negligence. As noted in chapter 3, a museum director should be aware of his status as a bailee in accepting exhibits. The terms of the agreement of bailment should be expressly stated in a written contract, and the museum's liability should be limited to a stated amount for such exhibits. (Refer to chapter 3 for a discussion of the law of bailments.)

International loans of artistic treasures have been hindered in the past by the cost of insuring such exhibitions. Exhibitions of this sort provide increased knowledge and goodwill among nations, however. Consequently, to solve the problem of funds needed to acquire, on loan, international exhibitions, Congress passed the Arts and Artifacts Indemnity Act in 1975.[33] This act provides indemnification by the federal government for museum exhibitions of works of art, including tapestries, paintings, sculptures, folk art, graphics, and craft arts; manuscripts, rare documents, and books; photographs, motion pictures, audio and video tapes; and other objects or artifacts which are of educational, cultural, historical, or scientific value and which are certified by the secretary of state, or his designee, as being in the national interest. An indemnity agreement, if approved, will cover eligible items while on exhibition in the United States or elsewhere when the display is part of an exchange of exhibitions. The act is administered by the Federal Council on the Arts and the Humanities; applications for indemnity are submitted to this council. The applicant pledges the credit of the United States to pay any amount for which the council becomes liable under the agreement. Indemnification is limited to $50 million for a single exhibition, with the first $15,000 of loss being deductible ($25,000 is deductible for losses of more than $2 million and $50,000 for losses of more than $10 million). Private insurance must cover value above the $50 million. (The act provides for an aggregate limit of $400 million of indemnity outstanding at any given time.) The indemnification agreement, if approved, covers an exhibition from the date when the eligible items leave the premises of the lender or other place designated by the lender until the items are returned to the premises of the lender or other place designated by the lender. Several exhibitions have been insured pursuant to the act, including the Treasures of Tutankhamen.

Laws and Regulations

There are ethical and diplomatic problems, as well as legal problems, involved in acquiring museum objects and exhibits. Because large numbers of ancient artifacts have been stolen in the past, there has been widespread concern that the cultural heritage of the various nations might become obliterated. This concern led to legislation in various contries to protect historical, scientific, and art objects.

Historic Preservation

A small movement was started in the United States in the nineteenth century to save a few historic treasures such as the Casa Grande ruins in Arizona and Mount Vernon in Virginia. That movement has grown tremendously. Today a partnership, so to speak, exists between the federal government, the states, and the private sector to protect the nation's historic resources. Even today, however, historic preservation occurs principally at the state and local level, with the federal government providing, for the most part, only a leadership role. In this role, the federal government has adopted numerous statutes to protect both cultural and natural resources.

Vandalism at the Casa Grande ruins and at other archaeological sites led the Congress of the United States to respond to the problem for the first time in 1906 with its approval of the Antiquities Act. Significant acts since that date have included the Historic Sites Act of 1935, the Historic Preservation Act of 1966, the National Environmental Policy Act of 1969, and the Archaeological Resources Protection Act of 1979. In 1978, Congress passed the American Indian Religious Freedom Act to provide, in essence, that historic preservation laws not impinge upon the religious freedom of Native Americans.

Antiquities Act of 1906. The Antiquities Act of 1906[34] provided penalties for destroying or damaging any historic ruins on public lands. The act further provided that any person who appropriates, injures, or destroys any historic or prehistoric ruin or monument, or any object of antiquity on lands owned or controlled by the federal government without permission of the department of the federal government having jurisdiction over the lands shall be fined and may be subject to imprisonment. The act authorized the president to set aside historic places, landmarks, and structures, as well as other lands of scientific value, as national monuments. Pursuant to this act, permits are required (to be granted by the secretaries of the interior, agriculture, and army) to excavate upon federal property. Such permits are issued only to reputable institutions for scientific or historic preservation purposes.

In *U.S. v. Diaz*,[35] an individual was convicted under the Antiquities Act in a U.S. District Court in Arizona for appropriating objects of antiquity from government land. The Ninth Circuit Court of Appeals reversed the conviction stating that the act was too vague regarding the definition of "ruin," "monument," or "object of antiquity." The defendant in the *Diaz* case had appropriated face masks found in a cave on the San Carlos Indian Reservation. These masks were identified by a San Carlos medicine man as having been made in 1969 or 1970 by another medicine man and were used by the Apache Indians in religious ceremonies. After the religious ceremonies, the artifacts were traditionally deposited in remote places on the reservation for religious reasons and were never allowed to leave the reservation. According to a professor of anthropology who testified in the case, an "object of antiquity" could include something that was made just yesterday if it related to religious or social traditions of long standing. The Ninth Circuit Court of Appeals disagreed, stating that a person must be able to know, with reasonable certainty, what objects he may not take. It noted that the statute did not specify that the word "antiquity" can refer not only to the age of an object but also the use for which the object was made and to which it was put, subjects not likely to be of common knowledge. In *U.S. v. Smyer*,[36] the Tenth Circuit Court of Appeals upheld a conviction of a violation of the Antiquities Act, distinguishing the *Diaz* case. In the *Smyer* case, defendants excavated a prehistoric Mimbres ruin at an archaeological site which was inhabited about A.D. 1000–1250. The defendants alleged that the Antiquities Act was vague and thus unconstitutional, citing the *Diaz* case as authority. The Tenth Circuit Court of Appeals noted that the *Diaz* case involved newly created artifacts, however. According to the court in the *Smyer* case, a person of ordinary intelligence should know that it is prohibited to excavate a prehistoric Indian burial ground and to appropriate artifacts that were 800–900 years old. The court ruled that as the law had been applied in the prosecution of defendants for taking artifacts from ancient sites for commercial motives, the Antiquities Act is not unconstitutionally vague.

In 1971, the United States used the Antiquities Act to assert its title to a wrecked and abandoned vessel thought to be a Spanish vessel which had sunk in the sea off the Florida coast in 1622. The Fifth Circuit

Court of Appeals held, in *Treasure Salvors* v. *Unidentified Wrecked, Etc.*,[37] that the Antiquities Act applies by its terms only to lands owned or controlled by the United States government. Because the wreck of the vessel rested on the continental shelf, it was outside the territorial waters of the United States; hence, the United States did not have title to the vessel.

Historic Sites Act of 1935. The Antiquities Act became more effective when Congress passed the Historic Sites Act of 1935.[38] The Historic Sites Act declared it a national policy "to perserve for public use historic sites, buildings, and objects of national significance for the inspiration and benefit of the people of the United States." The secretary of the interior was authorized to restore, reconstruct, and maintain historic sites and properties and to establish and maintain museums for these purposes. The secretary may contract and enter into cooperative agreements with states, municipal subdivisions, and private organizations and individuals, to protect, preserve, maintain, or operate any historic or archaeologic building, site, object, or property connected with a public use.

Pursuant to the Historic Sites Act, the secretary of the interior determined in 1936 that certain lands in the city of St. Louis, Missouri, possessed exceptional value as an historic site, and, through the city of St. Louis, instituted condemnation proceedings to acquire the land. This action was challenged in *Barnidge* v. *United States*[39] based upon an allegation that the Historic Sites Act does not authorize the condemnation of property. The Eighth Circuit Court of Appeals stated that another act[40] grants the federal government condemnation power to acquire real estate for public use. Further, the Historic Sites Act authorizes the secretary of the interior to acquire property for the purposes of the act. As a result, the court ruled that the United States may acquire by eminent domain, or otherwise, sites of national historic significance for the purposes declared in the Historic Sites Act and preserve them to commemorate and illustrate the nation's history.

National Trust for Historic Preservation in the United States. In 1949, a National Trust for Historic Preservation in the United States, called the "National Trust," was chartered as a private, nonprofit organization.[41] The National Trust receives donations of sites, buildings, and objects significant in American history and culture, and preserves and administers them for the public benefit. The affairs of the

National Trust are under the director of a board of trustees composed of the attorney general of the United States, the secretary of the interior, the director of the National Gallery of Art, and six United States citizens.

Reservoir Act of 1960. In 1960, the Reservoir Act[42] was passed. It provided for the preservation of historical and archaeological data which might otherwise be lost or destroyed as a result of flooding or other alterations of the terrain caused by a federal construction project or a federally licensed activity or program. Whenever any federal agency finds, or is notified in writing by an appropriate historical or archaeological authority, that its activities in connection with any federal construction project or federally licensed project, activity, or program may cause irreparable loss or destruction of significant scientific or prehistorical properties, the agency is to provide such information to the secretary of the interior, who is to investigate the areas affected.

Historic Preservation Act of 1966. Congress added the Historic Preservation Act in 1966[43] to provide for the maintenance and expansion of a National Register of districts, sites, buildings, structures, and objects significant in American history, architecture, archaeology, and culture and to provide matching grants for the purpose of preserving historical properties for the public benefit. The act established a program of matching grants-in-aid to the National Trust for Historic Preservation in the United States. Under the act the head of any federal agency having direct or indirect jurisdiction over a proposed federal or federally assisted undertaking in any state must consider the effect of the undertaking on any district, site, building, structure, or object included in the National Register prior to approval of the expenditure of any federal funds on the undertaking or prior to the issuance of any license. An Advisory Council on Historic Preservation was established by the act.

National Environmental Policy Act of 1969. The National Environmental Policy Act of 1969[44] added the requirement that environmental and cultural values must be considered along with economic and technological values when proposed federal projects are assessed. The act states that the federal government is to use all practicable means to improve and coordinate federal plans, functions, programs, and resources to the end that the nation may preserve important historic, cultural, and natural aspects of the national heritage. If proposed major federal action "significantly affects the quality of the human environment," the appropriate government agency must prepare an "environmental impact statement."

Archaeological Resources Protection Act of 1979. The purpose of the Archaeological Resources Protection Act[45] was to secure, for the present and future benefit of the American people, the protection of archaeological resources and sites located on public and Indian lands and to foster increased cooperation and exchange of information between governmental authorities, the professional archaeological community, and private individuals having collections of archaeological resources and data obtained before 1979. An "archaeological resource" is defined as any material remains of past human life or activities which are of archaeological interest and which are at least 100 years of age. A permit to excavate or remove any archaeological resource located on public or Indian lands will not be issued if there may be harm to any religious or cultural site. In addition, permits to excavate on Indian lands will be granted only after obtaining the consent of the Indian tribe owning the land. Persons receiving permits pursuant to the 1979 act need not also obtain permits under the Antiquities Act of 1906.

Indian tribes or their members need not obtain a permit under this act or under the Antiquities Act for the excavation or removal of any archaeological resource located on their lands as long as tribal law regulates the excavation and removal of archaeological resources.

Pursuant to this act, the secretary of the interior may promulgate regulations providing for the exchange, between suitable universities, museums, and other scientific or educational institutions, of archaeological resources removed from public lands and Indian lands under this act, as well as the ultimate disposition of resources removed pursuant to the Antiquities Act. Any exchange of resources removed from Indian lands is subject to the consent of the Indian tribe which has jurisdiction over the land.

The purchase, transport, exchange, or receipt of any archaeological resource removed without permission after October 31, 1979, will subject the violator to a fine of $10,000 and/or imprisonment of not more than a year or, if the value of the object is more than $5,000, to a fine of $20,000 and/or imprisonment of not more than two years.[46] A second violation causes the penalty to be a fine of as much as $100,000 or imprisonment for as long as five years.

The act is not applicable to any person with respect to an archaeological resource which was in his lawful possession prior to October 31, 1979. Further, the act is not applicable to the removal of arrowheads located on the surface of the grounds. It does not cover archaeological resources on state or private lands.

1980 Amendments to the National Historic Preservation Act. The National Historic Preservation Act of 1966 was amended in 1980 to provide better definition and guidance for the national historic preservation program at the federal, state, and local levels.[47] The 1980 act provided for a loan insurance program, for the establishment of a national museum of the building arts, and for procedures for implementing the World Heritage Convention and contained provisions to ensure proper maintenance of archaeological resources. The act authorized programmatic grants to the states, in addition to direct project-by-project grants, to make it easier for private organizations and individuals to obtain grants. Pursuant to this act, studies were to be made to consider ways further to assist historic preservation, including studies to develop means of identifying and conserving America's folk heritage; to examine the effects of the tax laws on historic preservation, and to make recommendations concerning urban cultural parks and historic conservation districts.

The 1980 act provided for an insured loan program to stimulate private investments in the preservation of properties included in the National Register. Historic properties are often viewed as high-risk investments, and nonprofit organizations interested in saving historic structures would otherwise have difficulty qualifying for loans. Most of the loans which can be insured under this act would be for acquisition and development projects.

The 1980 act also provided legislative implementation for United States participation in the Convention Concerning the Protection of the World Cultural and Natural Heritage approved by the United Nations Education, Scientific, and Cultural Organization (UNESCO) on November 23, 1972, and approved by the United States Senate on October 26, 1973. The purpose of the convention was to establish an effective system of collective protection of the cultural and natural heritage "of outstanding universal value." Each participating nation was to identify and delineate the meritorious properties situated in its own territory and to integrate protection of that cultural and natural heritage into comprehensive planning programs. Each was directed to submit to the

World Heritage Committee (established within UNESCO) an inventory of such properties in its territory and suitable for inclusion on the world heritage list.

The Museum of the Building Arts established by the 1980 act will be the first institution in the United States founded solely to focus attention on the built environment through a national program of exhibitions and publications. It was established to serve as a central information bank for professional associations, unions, manufacturers, and professionals responsible for current building in our nation and as a collection and resource center for teachers, writers, and students concerned with past achievements and present efforts in the art of building.

American Indian Religious Freedom Act. Historic preservation laws have caused concern for native Americans. It has been their position that such laws were passed without consideration of their effect on traditional American Indian religions, that such laws often deny American Indians access to sacred sites required in their religions, including cemeteries, and often prohibit the use and possession of sacred objects necessary for the exercise of religious rites and ceremonies. As a result, the American Indian Religious Freedom Act was passed by Congress in 1978, [48] providing that the federal government would protect and preserve for American Indians their inherent right of freedom to believe and exercise their traditional religions. The president of the United States was to direct the various federal departments, agencies, and other instrumentalities responsible for administering relevant laws to evaluate their policies and procedures in consultation with native traditional religious leaders in order to determine appropriate changes necessary to protect and preserve native American religious cultural rights and practices. The purpose of the act was to insure that policies and procedures of various federal agencies are brought into compliance with the constitutional injunction that Congress shall make no laws abridging the free exercise of religion.

One concern of native Americans had been the removal of their offerings left at religious shrines. Because these articles were usually newly made, they were not subject to the Antiquities Act and thus, were often taken out of the country without interference by U.S. Customs officials. Recall the *U.S.* v. *Diaz* case,[49] in which a federal court determined that artifacts of recent origin were not antiquities subject to protection by the Antiquities Act. The Archaeological Resources Protection Act of 1979 will provide the Indian some protection, since it requires that a permit be obtained to excavate or remove any archaeological resource located on Indian lands and that the Indian tribe owning the land consent to the granting of such a permit. The taking of an archaeological resource without a permit will subject the violator to a substantial fine and/or imprisonment. The problem is that an archaeological resource must be at least 100 years of age. Inasmuch as permits can only be secured after the consent of the Indian tribe has been obtained, however, some pilfering of religious objects may be halted.

Another concern of native Americans is that their religious objects are often a part of museum collections. Efforts are being made by native Americans to regain these objects. Negotiations are currently under way between various Indian tribes and several museums regarding a return of such religious objects. Some museums have returned the objects; others have not. The American Indian Religious Freedom Act does not require that such religious objects be returned to native Americans. Further, the act is only directed to federal agencies. Unless state laws are implemented requiring such a return of these objects, most museums have no legal obligation to do so.[50] The Zuni have negotiated with the Smithsonian Institution to return certain of their artifacts which they allege were stolen from their reservation at the turn of the century.[51] Native Americans believe that the Smithsonian has an obligation to return such artifacts under the Religious Freedom Act because the Smithsonian is completely federally subsidized.[52] They further contend that those museums that are partially financed by the federal government and those that have tax-exempt status should also return such artifacts pursuant to the act.[53]

The Archaeological Resources Protection Act of 1979 will deter museums somewhat in the future regarding the acquisition of artifacts taken from Indian lands. Recall that the act provides criminal penalties for the purchase, transport, exchange, or receipt of any archaeological resource without permission after October 31, 1979. Museums must be especially careful regarding ownership of artifacts more than 100 years old.

Tax Incentives for Historic Preservation. Rehabilitation of historic structures has been aided somewhat by provisions of the Internal Revenue Code granting tax benefits for preserving historic structures. Recall that a charitable contribution deduction is allowed for grants of remainder interests in real property or for restrictions in perpetuity on the use to be made of real property, if such interests are donated to charities for historic preservation of such land or structures. Prior to 1982, a 10 percent investment tax credit was available for expenditures to rehabilitate buildings at least twenty years old.[54] An investment credit provides a direct credit against income tax liability; hence, it is more beneficial to a taxpayer than a tax deduction. Effective in 1982, the investment credit was increased to 15 percent for buildings thirty to thirty-nine years old, to 20 percent for buildings more than thirty-nine years old, and to 25 percent for certified historic structures.[55] Costs of restoring or renovating the interior or exterior of a building to extend its useful life, upgrade its usefulness, or to preserve it, will normally qualify for the credit, as will expenditures for replacement of plumbing, wiring, interior walls, flooring, and heating systems. The costs of acquiring a building or an interest in a building do not qualify for the investment credit, however. Neither do expenses for enlarging an existing building or for adding facilities to it.

For these purposes, a "certified historic structure" is a depreciable building or other edifice listed in the National Register of Historic Places or located in a registered historic district and certified by the secretary of the interior as being of historic significance to the district.[56] A registered historic district is a district listed in the National Register of Historic Places or a district designated under a statute of a state (or local government), but only if the secretary of the interior certifies that the statute contains criteria that achieve the purpose of preserving historically significant buildings and if the district meets substantially all the requirements for districts to be listed in the National Register.

Example 4. *A* owns a building that was constructed more than fifty years ago and is a certified historic structure. It had never been rehabilitated until *A* renovated the interior and exterior of the building in 1982, pursuant to a certified rehabilitation, at a cost of $360,000. *A* intends to use the building in his business. Because the building is a certified historic structure, the 25 percent investment credit is available. *A* may take an investment credit, as a direct reduction in his 1982 income tax liability, in the amount of $90,000 ($360,000 × 25 percent). *A* would also use the regular depreciation method (straight-line) to charge the cost of $360,000 against his taxable income in the form of depreciation. As a substantial improvement, a fifteen-year recovery period would be used. Hence, *A* would deduct $24,000 per year as depreciation expense.

Should a taxpayer tear down a certified historic structure (in the period after June 30, 1976, and before January 1, 1984), he will not be permitted to deduct, for tax purposes, the cost of demolition or any loss sustained because of the demolition. Pursuant to section 280B of the Internal Revenue Code, the cost of demolition must be added to the cost of the land.

State Preservation Laws. The past decade has been one of extreme growth in the area of historic preservation. Numerous state preservation programs have commenced, with most states now having established some form of state preservation agency. Activities by the state or by local governments to preserve historic properties at the possible expense of private enterprise were sanctioned by the Supreme Court in *Penn Central Transportation v. City of New York.*[57] In that case the Supreme Court likened the Landmarks Preservation Law of the city of New York to zoning laws that substantially relate to the promotion of the general welfare and require no payment to the property owner because of a diminution in property value brought about by the application of the law to one's property. Penn Central Transportation Company owned a building called the Terminal; it had been designated as one of New York City's most famous buildings. Penn Central wanted to construct an office building atop the Terminal and to tear down a portion of the old building. The city of New York refused to grant permission, and Penn Central brought suit, alleging that restrictions placed upon its property by the city of New York constituted a "taking" of its property without due process of law. The Supreme Court stated that the law does not interfere in any way with present uses of the Terminal. According to the Court, its designation as a landmark not only permitted the owner to continue to use the property but assumed that the owner would do so precisely as it had for the past sixty-five years—the building would remain a railroad terminal containing office space and concessions; consequently, Penn Central was not entitled to compensation for the law's restriction on its use of the Terminal. The Supreme Court noted that, over the past fity years, all fifty states and more than 500 municipalities have enacted laws to encourage or require the preservation of buildings and areas with historic or aesthetic importance. According to the Court, these nationwide legislative efforts were precipitated by two concerns. The first was recognition that, in recent years, large numbers of historic structures, landmarks, and areas had been destroyed without adequate consideration of either the values represented therein or the possibility of preserving the destroyed properties for use in economically productive ways. The second was a widely shared belief that structures with special historic, cultural, or architectural significance enhance the quality of life for all. The Court expressed the opinion that these buildings and their workmanship represent the lessons of the past, embody precious features of our heritage, and serve as examples of quality for today. According to the Court, historic conservation is but one aspect of a much larger problem, basically an environmental one, of enhancing—or perhaps developing for the first time—the quality of life for people. Three justices of the Supreme Court dissented in the *Penn Central* case. They stated, in a dissenting opinion, that an owner of a building might initially be pleased that his property has been chosen by a distinguished committee of architects, historians, and city planners for such a singular distinction, only to find that his property, once designated an historic structure, must be maintained forever in its present state. A landmark designation may well impose upon him a substantial cost, with little or no offsetting benefit except for the honor of the designation. The dissenting justices raised the question of whether the cost associated with the city of New York's desire to preserve a limited number of landmarks must be borne by all its taxpayers or whether it could instead be imposed entirely on the owners of the individual properties.

Some persons have expressed concern that the proliferation of historic preservation laws may cause an increased assertion of power by state and local authorities and that the decision of the Supreme Court in the *Penn Central* case will cause more growth in the public sector in preservation law. An alternative to the police power in the allocation of property rights would be private agreements among individuals.[58]

Smithsonian Institution. The federal government has provided protection of certain cultural property of national interest through its establishment of the Smithsonian Institution. All objects of art and of foreign and curious research, and all objects of natural history, plants, and geological and mineralogical specimens belonging to the United States, which may be in the city of Washington, are to be delivered to the board of regents of the Smithsonian Institution for examination and study.[59] The secretary of the Smithsonian Institution is authorized to cooperate with any state, educational institution, or scientific organization in the United States for continuing paleontological investigations, and the excavation and preservation of fossil remains, in areas which will be flooded by the construction of government dams. The Smithsonian Institution controls and directs the National Museum, the National Gallery of Art, the National Portrait Gallery, the Smithsonian Gallery of Art, the Joseph H. Hirshhorn Museum and Sculpture Garden, the National Air and Space Museum, the Woodrow Wilson International Center for Scholars, the John F. Kennedy Center for the Performing Arts, the Museum of African Art, and the National Zoological Park.

A 1980 federal court of appeals decision gave the secretary of the interior broad discretionary power to locate in the Smithsonian Institution specimens found on federal property. In 1976, a 6,070-pound meteorite was found on federal land in the Old Woman Mountain Range in Southern California. The Department of Interior and the Bureau of Land Management consulted with the Smithsonian to determine the procedures to be followed to transfer the Old Woman Meteorite to the Smithsonian. The meteorite was removed from its site in 1977 and was placed on public exhibition in the San Bernardino County Museum for one week and in the Los Angeles County Museum of Natural History for six weeks. The museum applied for a permit under the Antiquities Act to retain the meteorite and brought suit to enjoin the removal of the meteorite from California and to void the permit issued to the Smithsonian. The Ninth Circuit Court of Appeals[60] stated that officials of the Department of the Interior had not violated the Antiquities Act when they contacted the Smithsonian and not other institutions concerning the meteorite. The court stated that permits "may" be granted to institutions which officials of the Department of Interior deem properly qualified. The Smithsonian had not filed an application in compliance with the regulations, and the state of California contended that the secretary could not act until a formal application had been received. The court disagreed, stating that the regulations establish a uniform method of applying for antiquities permits, but do not limit the secretary's ability to act in absence of applications, nor do they require that the secretary solicit applications. According to the court, the status of the Smithsonian Institution as a national museum created by an act of Congress provides a rational basis for the secretary's decision to choose to contact the Smithsonian about the meteorite as opposed to another institution.

Importation of artifacts. In addition to drafting statutes to protect historical properties within the United States, Congress became concerned about the importation into the United States of unlawfully obtained artifacts. In 1972, an act was adopted which provided that no pre-Columbian monumental or architectural sculpture or mural may be imported in the United States unless the government of the country of origin of the sculpture or mural issues a certificate that the exportation of the object from that country does not violate any of its laws.[61] A pre-Columbian monumental or architectural sculpture or mural is defined as any stone carving or wall art, or any fragment or part thereof, which is the product of a pre-Columbian Indian culture of Mexico, Central America, South America, or the Caribbean Islands, is an immobile monument or architectural structure or part of such monument or structure, and is subject to export control by the country of origin. Under the act, any pre-Columbian monumental or architectural sculpture or mural imported into the United States in violation of the act is to be seized and is subject to forfeiture under the customs laws.

Control of the importation of art objects from other countries became the concern of several nations. At a meeting in Paris in 1970, the General Conference of the United Nations Educational, Scientific, and Cultural Organization (UNESCO) recognized that the illicit import, export, and transfer of ownership of cultural property had become one of the main causes of the impoverishment of the cultural heritage of the originating countries and that international cooperation constituted one of the most efficient means of protecting each country's cultural property against the dangers resulting from the illicit transfer of such properties. To accomplish this end, the parties to the convention agreed to oppose all such practices with the means at their disposal. While not made a part of United States law, the document drafted by UNESCO was adopted by some museums in the United States. The International Council of Museums adopted a resolution that any object acquired must have a full, clear, and satisfactory documentation as to its origin. Under the Joint Professional Policy on Museum Acquisitions, museums have agreed to refuse to acquire, through purchase, gift, or bequest, cultural property exported in violation of the laws obtaining in the countries of origin. Some museums have adopted policies that require the director to ascertain that any objects acquired were not stolen or wrongfully converted. No objects can be acquired by some museums unless the responsible museum official or committee is satisfied as to the legality of the exportation and the circumstances of the recovery of the object.

In the past, art institutions in the United States have been able to exhibit ancient, oriental, and primitive art because it was lawful under

United States law to collect such material, whether or not it was exported from another country in compliance with that country's export restrictions. The United States had refused to accede to pressure from other nations to make it illegal to bring into the United States art objects exported in violation of the laws of other countries. While it has taken steps in isolated instances to discourage the importation of ancient art, such as the statute regarding the importation of pre-Columbian artifacts, it had not imposed harsh sanctions. In an innovative decision in *U.S.* v. *McClain*,[62] however, the Fifth Circuit Court of Appeals ruled that the National Stolen Property Act[63] could be applied to the illegal exportation of artifacts declared by Mexican law to be the property of that nation. The National Stolen Property Act makes it a felony knowingly to sell or to receive stolen goods in interstate or foreign commerce. The court stated that illegal exportation constitutes a sufficient act of conversion to be deemed a theft. The court was of the opinion that the 1972 statute regarding importation of pre-Columbian artifacts, UNESCO negotiations, and the historical policy of the United States of encouraging the importation of art more than 100 years old did not have the effect of narrowing the National Stolen Property Act so as to make it inapplicable to artifacts declared to be the property of another country and illegally imported into this country. In a second hearing on the issue,[64] the court commented that procedures available under the 1972 act can be extremely expensive and time consuming and do not provide a meaningful deterrent to the pillage of pre-Columbian sites now taking place. It stated:

> Moreover, the Act covers objects imported from all the countries of Latin America. These countries may have acted quite differently to protect their cultural heritage, some by declaring national ownership and others merely by enacting stringent export restrictions. Because it covers artifacts from such a large number of countries, the Act is better seen not as an indication that other available penalties were thereby precluded, but rather as a recognition that additional deterrents were needed.

It then affirmed its earlier decision that it is proper to punish through the National Stolen Property Act encroachments upon legitimate and clear Mexican ownership even though the goods may never have been physically possessed by agents of that nation.

While the 1972 statute on pre-Columbian artifacts provides only for the civil penalty of forfeiture of the artifacts, the National Stolen Property Act provides for a fine of as much as $10,000 and imprisonment for as long as ten years. The Council of the American Association of Museums has expressed concern that the *McClain* decision, rather than helping, might actually discourage the growing cooperative efforts in international circles to find ways of regulating illegal traffic in cultural property.

Imported works of art for the use of charitable, nonprofit organizations or governmental institutions and those not imported for sale or commercial use are free of duty.[65] Importation of these items may require that forms be filed with custom officers. An institutional form (Customs Forms 3321 and 3325) and/or a bond (Customs Form 7565) may be required. These articles may be transferred from one institution to another upon an application in writing describing the articles and stating the name of the institution to which transfer is to be made. If any of the duty-free articles are sold within five years after the date of entry, the amount of duties which would have otherwise been collected will be collected immediately. After five years these duty-free articles may be freely exchanged. Destruction of items terminates liability.[66]

Systematic Collections

Scientific museums must be aware of the many statutes and regulations designed to curb misuse of natural resources. Specimens cannot be obtained or possessed without proper permits.[67] The problem in this area is that each state has varying laws and regulations. It is imperative that a museum seeking scientific specimens consult both local laws and federal laws regarding the particular specimens sought.[68] Here I will summarize only the requirements of federal law. The pertinent federal statutes are the Migratory Bird Treaty Act of 1918,[69] the Marine Mammal Protection Act of 1972,[70] and the Endangered Species Act of 1973.[71]

Migratory Bird Treaty Act. The Migratory Bird Treaty Act made it unlawful to pursue, capture, kill, purchase, transport, import, or carry any migratory bird (or any part of such a bird or a nest or egg of such a bird) that is included in the terms of the conventions between the United States and Great Britain, between the United States and the United Mexican States, between the United States and Japan, and between the United States and the Union of Soviet Socialist Republics. The law further made it unlawful to ship or transport from one state to another any bird (or any part of the bird or a nest or egg of the bird) which was captured or killed contrary to the laws of any state or contrary to the laws of Canada. An employee of the Department of the Interior authorized to enforce the provisions of the act has authority to arrest any person commiting a violation of the act. It is a felony offense to violate the act.

Marine Mammal Protection Act. The Marine Mammal Protection Act of 1972 provided for a moratorium on the taking and importation of marine mammals and marine mammal products because it was determined that certain species and population stocks of marine mammals were in danger of extinction as a result of man's activities. A marine mammal is any mammal which is morphologically adapted to the marine environment or which primarily inhabits the marine environment (such as the polar bear). No part of such a mammal, including its raw, dressed, or dyed fur or skin, may be taken or imported without a permit. Permits may be issued for taking and importation for purposes of scientific research and for public display if the taking or importation is first reviewed by the Marine Mammal Commission which was established pursuant to the act.

Without a permit, it is unlawful for any person or vessel to take any marine mammal in waters or lands under the jurisdiction of the United States or to use any port or harbor for any purpose in any way connected with the taking or importation of marine mammals or marine mammal products. It is also unlawful to possess, transport, or sell any such mammal. This act further prohibits the commercial taking of whales. Penalties for violation of the act include civil penalties of as much as $10,000 for each violation, as well as criminal penalties for any person who knowingly violates the act.

Endangered Species Act. Congress determined that certain species of fish, wildlife, and plants in the United States have been rendered extinct as a consequence of economic growth and development untempered by adequate concern and conservation and that other species of fish, wildlife, and plants have been so depleted in numbers that they are in danger of, or threatened with, extinction. As a result, it passed the Endangered Species Act in 1973 to provide a means to conservation of the ecosystems upon which endangered and threatened species depend and a program for protection of the affected species. Pursuant to the act, the secretary of the interior is to determine which species are endangered or threatened and is to set forth that determination in the course of regulation. Such species may not be possessed, sold, carried, transported, imported, or taken without a permit. Permits may be issued to acquire such species for scientific purposes or to enhance the propagation or survival of the affected species. Each application for a permit is published in the Federal Register, thereby inviting views or arguments regarding the application. The act does not apply to any Indian, Aleut, or Eskimo who is an Alaskan native or to any nonnative permanent resident of an Alaskan native village if the animal is taken primarily for subsistence. Nonedible by-products of species taken by these individuals may be sold in interstate commerce if they have been made into authentic native articles of handicrafts and clothing. A violation of the act subjects the violator to a civil penalty of as much as $10,000 for each violation and criminal penalties for a willful violation.

Other Acts Relating to Protection of Wildlife. It is a criminal offense to remove, or to convert to private use, a wild, free-roaming horse or burro on public lands without authority from the secretary of interior or secretary of agriculture.[72]

The American Eagle Protection Act[73] provides that the bald eagle, commonly known as the American eagle, or any golden eagle, may not be taken, possessed, sold, purchased, transported, exported, or imported at any time or in any manner. These prohibitions extend to any part of an eagle, including its nest or eggs, and apply whether the eagle is dead or alive. There are civil and criminal penalties for violation of the act. The bald or golden eagle may be taken or possessed for scientific or exhibition purposes of public museums, scientific societies, and zoological parks, but a permit must be secured from the secretary of the interior. An employee of the Department of the Interior authorized to enforce the act may arrest any person in possession of any part of the bald or golden eagle without a permit.

The Lacey Act[74] provides penalties (a fine of as much as $500 or imprisonment for as long as six months) for hunting, trapping, capturing, or willfully disturbing or killing any bird, fish, or wild animal of any kind (or destroying any eggs or a nest of birds or fish) on any lands or waters set apart or reserved as sanctuaries, refuges, or breeding grounds, unless authorized by a law. It also prohibits the importation of injurious mammals, birds, fish, amphibia, and reptiles without a permit and prohibits the transportation of wildlife (whether dead or alive and any parts thereof) captured, killed, purchased, or sold in violation of the law of any state or any federal or foreign law. (This prohibition extends to products made from wildlife.) There is a civil penalty of $5,000 for unlawful transportation of injurious mammals. Willful violation of the act subjects the violator to criminal penalties of a $10,000 maximum fine and/or imprisonment for as much as one year. The Lacey Act also provides penalties (maximum fine of $500 and/or imprisonment for at most six months) for shipping, transporting, carrying, or conveying in interstate or foreign commerce any package containing wild animals or birds, or the dead bodies or parts of them, without plainly marking such package with the names and addresses of the shipper and consignee and with an accurate statement showing the contents by number and kind. This prohibition extends to furs, hides, or skins of wild animals. The act further provides a fine of as much as $100 and/or imprisonment for trapping, capturing, possessing, or killing an Antwerp or homing pigeon (commonly called a carrier pigeon) owned by the United States or bearing a band owned and issued by the United States.

The Black Bass Act[75] provides penalties (a $200 maximum fine and/or imprisonment for three months or less) for transporting, purchasing, or receiving any black bass unlawfully obtained. It further provides that any package containing black bass must be clearly marked. An employee of the Department of Interior or Commerce authorized to enforce the act may arrest anyone in violation of the act.

Importation into the United States. For specimens to be imported into the United States, a completed Declaration for Importation of Fish or Wildlife (Form 3-177) must be filed by the importer with the district director of customs at the port of entry. The common and scientific name of the specimens must be listed as well as the name and address of the importer and the name of the carrier. If the laws or regulations of the country of origin restrict the possession or transportation of wildlife, the importer may be required to produce foreign documentation showing that those laws have not been violated. Such documentation must be in the form of original permits from the foreign country or copies of any importing contracts or agreements. If the specimens are imported for scientific use, they are duty free. Specimens of archaeology, mineralogy, or natural history (including specimens of botany or zoology other than live zoological specimens) imported for any public or private scientific collection for exhibition or other education or scientific use, and not for sale or other commercial use, are duty free.[76] An import-export permit (Form 3-200) must be obtained from the U.S. Department of the Interior, Director of Fish and Wildlife.[77]

Packages containing wild animals or birds cannot be shipped in interstate commerce unless they are plainly marked with the names and addresses of the shipper and consignee and with an accurate statement indicating the contents of the package.[78] "Marking permits" can be obtained from the U.S Fish and Wildlife Service[79] to permit shipping across the United States by merely marking each package with the label. For animals imported into the United States (except for those imported from Canada or Mexico), an import permit must also be secured from the U.S. Department of Agriculture. This department regulates care of live animals under the Animal Welfare Act.[80]

For those specimens capable of carrying human diseases, a permit must be obtained from the surgeon general through the U.S. Department of Health and Human Services.[81] Plants require additional registration through the U.S. Department of Agriculture.[82] Marine animals must have additional registration with the Department of Commerce (National Marine Fisheries Service).

Certain specimens can only be imported into the United States at certain designated port of entries. Upon receipt of an application, however, the director of the Bureau of Sport Fisheries and Wildlife can issue a permit authorizing a scientist to import wildlife, other than endangered wildlife, for scientific purposes at any Customs port of entry. There are also permits to import wildlife, including endangered species, at any Customs port of entry in order to minimize deterioration or loss.

A customs officer may refuse clearance of imported wildlife for the following reasons: a federal law or regulation has been violated; the correct identity of the wildlife has not been established; required foreign documentation is not authentic; or the importer has filed an incomplete declaration of importation.

Collection of Specimens. Before scientific specimens can be collected, permit applications must be submitted to the director of the Fish and Wildlife Service on official Form 3-200, indicating the common and scientific names of the species to be covered by the permit, the number, age, and sex of such species, and the activity to be authorized. The form must also describe the institution where the wildlife will be used or displayed and the facilities where the wildlife will be housed. The resume of the person who will care for the wildlife must be included. Copies of all contracts and agreements pursuant to the activities to be authorized must be attached, as well as a full statement of the reasons why the applicant should obtain the permit. For endangered species, the permittee must submit a written report to the director of the Fish and Wildlife Service of his activities pursuant to the permit not later than ten days after completion of the activity. The death or escape of all living wildlife covered by the permit must be immediately reported to the office of the Fish and Wildlife Service. The carcass of any dead wildlife covered by the permit must be stored in a manner which will preserve its use as a scientific specimen.

For marine animals, one must also contact the Department of Commerce (National Marine Fisheries Service). For live animals, a permit must be secured from the U.S. Department of Agriculture; for animals capable of carrying human disease, a permit is required from the Department of Health and Human Services. For collection of scientific specimens on National Wildlife Refuges, application for a research proposal should be submitted to the refuge manager detailing the scientific work. For collection of scientific specimens in a national park, a written permit must be obtained from the superintendent, and the research proposal must be described. Permits are only issued to persons officially representing reputable scientific or educational institutions. For interstate transportation of specimens, clearly mark all packages on the outside by using a marking label or by giving the name and address of the consignor and consignee and the contents of the package.

State permits are required in all the states. As a general rule, one may write the game and fish division at the state capitol. Either a permit or a hunting license is usually required. As noted above, there are criminal sanctions, as well as civil penalties, for possessing or transporting specimens without proper permits. The harshness of the criminal penalty can be an issue, however. For example, the Lacey Act[83] makes it a misdemeanor to engage in interstate commerce in wildlife taken in violation of state law; on the other hand, a violation of the National Stolen Property Act is a felony offense punishable with as much as ten years' imprisonment, as noted above. In *United States v. Long Cove Seafood, Inc.*,[84] the federal government attempted to file charges under the National Stolen Property Act against persons who held wildlife in violation of state conservation laws. Still, the Second Circuit Court of Appeals refused to accept the government's broad definition of "stolen" property. The court stated that wildfish, birds, and animals are, as a general rule, owned by no one. Property rights to them are obtained by reducing them to possessions. It decided that the state of New York had not asserted a true ownership interest in wildlife such as that indicated by Mexico with respect to pre-Columbian artifacts, and it held that the National Stolen Property Act was not applicable. While the defendants were held to have violated the Environmental Conservation Law and the Lacey Act, they had not transported "stolen" property. Another court might not be as lenient, however. It becomes imperative to comply with state and federal laws, as well as the laws of any foreign country involved.

Deaccessioning of Museum Objects

Before a museum disposes of its acquisitions, the museum director should exercise caution. He must weigh the museum's responsibility to the public to assure that prominent works of art remain accessible to the public. Possible restrictions placed upon donated objects must be considered. (In this regard, some restrictions on sale may be removed by a court by application of the cy pres doctrine.) The manner of sale should be carefully studied. Some museums sell valuable items only at public auction to assure the best price; others fear that the advance notice required for a public auction prohibits the confidentiality necessary to obtain the best price. An object which a public museum wishes to sell might be a desirable acquisition for another public institution. If so, a lower price may be warranted. The museum director must also consider the use of funds obtained through a sale of objects. Should the funds be used only for future acquisitions, or may they be used for operating expenses? Most museums have internal regulations to assure safeguard of the public's interest in its acquisitions. Museum pieces currently out of date should not be sold for that reason alone; future tastes might produce much higher future values. Many museums require a unanimous vote of an acquisitions committee as well as the board of directors to deaccession a work. (See appendix G for the guidelines of the New York State Association of Museums regarding disposition of collection materials.)

6

Employee Relations

Museums not under governmental control with an operating budget of at least a million dollars a year are subject to the National Labor Relations Act (NLRA);[1] consequently, directors of these museums may find that museum employees are union members, so that directors may be required to engage in collective bargaining. Even if a museum's budget does not meet federal guidelines,[2] the museum may still face unionization under state law.

Museums are also subject to federal laws and regulations prohibiting discrimination in programs or activities which are in any way federally assisted. The National Labor Relations Board (NLRB) will treat racial or sexual discrimination as an unfair labor practice.[3] Further, civil rights statutes passed during the Reconstruction Era,[4] as well as the Civil Rights Act of 1964,[5] the Equal Pay Act,[6] the Age Discrimination in Employment Act,[7] and the Vocational Rehabilitation Act of 1973,[8] provide redress for employees treated in a discriminatory manner. The museum director should be familiar with these provisions.

Labor Laws

Pursuant to the commerce clause of the federal Constitution, Congress may make laws regulating the relationship between employers and employees, may prescribe rules designed to settle labor disputes, and may regulate wages and working conditions. The National Labor Relations Act provides for the regulation of practices occurring in relations between employer and employees which provoke, or tend to provoke, strikes or labor disturbances affecting interstate commerce and establishes a single tribunal, the National Labor Relations Board, to administer the provisions of the statute, with adequate and exclusive opportunity for judicial review in a designated court.[9] Those labor-management relations not covered by the NLRA nonetheless affect the public interest and thus may be regulated by the states.

Labor relations statutes in general apply to private industry and not to public employment. The NLRA does not recognize the existence of the right of collective bargaining in public employment and expressly excepts from the definition of the term "employer" the United States or any wholly owned government corporation and any state or political subdivision thereof. A museum controlled by a state or the federal government would not, then, be subject to regulation by the National Labor Relations Board.[10] The NLRB has defined a state-controlled museum as one which is either responsible to the public or to the general electorate or is created directly by the state so as to constitute a department or an administrative arm of the government. In *Minneapolis Society of Fine Arts,*[11] the board ruled that the Minneapolis Society was subject to the NLRA because the society was not administered by individuals responsible to the public. It stated that occupancy by the society of city-owned property or the receipt of revenue from a state-established tax fund would not be enough to make the society a creature of the state.

There has been a question as to whether charitable, educational, and other nonprofit enterprises which are not agencies or political subdivisions of the state are subject to the NLRA. In 1951, the National Labor Relations Board indicated that it would not exercise jurisdiction over nonprofit educational institutions because to do so would not effect the purpose of the act.[12] In 1970, however, the board pointed to what it viewed as an increased involvement in commerce by educational institutions and concluded that this fact required a different position regarding its jurisdiction; consequently, it overruled its earlier decision.[13] The board then asserted jurisdiction over nonprofit private secondary schools and museums.[14] At present, the board asserts jurisdiction over all private nonprofit educational institutions with gross annual revenues that meet its jurisdictional requirements (at least $1 million a year) whether they are secular or religious;[15] consequently, a knowledge of the labor laws becomes important to the museum director.

History of the National Labor Relations Act

Congress enacted the National Labor Relations Act in 1935 to protect the right of American workers to bargain collectively. This legislation, known as the Wagner Act, assured workers of the right to organize to counterbalance the collective activities of employers. The Wagner Act provided that a representative chosen by a majority of the workers exclusively represented the workers in a voting district or unit, and the employer was obligated to bargain with the representative of the employees in that unit. The National Labor Relations Board was established by the Wagner Act as a uniform, national body to interpret the right of workers. The board was authorized to prevent and remedy unfair labor practices and to conduct elections to determine representation of employees.

The Wagner Act was weighted heavily in favor of labor. Management was given some relief in 1947 with the passage of the Taft-Hartley Act. This act contained provisions relating to union violence and prohibited unions from interfering with the right of management to select its own representatives for purposes of collective bargaining. The closed shop was made illegal.[16] In addition, employees were given the right to refrain from self-organization and collective bargaining. The Taft-Hartley Act provided that unions must also bargain in good faith, that union dues and fees could not be excessive, and that there could be no strikes or lockouts for sixty days before the termination of a contract, with a provision that mediation agencies be given an opportunity to intervene. The Taft-Hartley Act excluded supervisors from the bargaining units. Three other classes of employees—professional employees, craftsmen, and plant guards—were given special treatment. This provision was especially beneficial in preventing all employees, a group with few common interests, from being treated alike as one bargaining unit. Professionals were not to be included with nonprofessionals in a bargaining unit unless the majority of the professionals voted for inclusion. Further, plant guards, those individuals employed as guards to enforce rules against employees and other persons to protect the property of the employer or to protect the safety of persons on the employer's premises, could be included only in a unit composed exclusively of guards.

The Taft-Hartley Act amended the definition of "employer" to exclude nonprofit hospitals.[17] There was some discussion of the scope of the National Labor Relations Board, but the consensus was that nonprofit institutions in general did not fall within the board's jurisdiction because they did not affect commerce.[18] That act expanded the board to five members and provided for an independent board counsel appointed by the president. This change was effected to cause the board to function as a court and to be divorced from a prosecutory function. (Charges had been made that the board functioned as both a prosecutor and a judge.)

In 1959, the Landum-Griffin Act was passed to close loopholes regarding secondary boycotts. It prevented so-called hot cargo agreements by which employers bind themselves in advance to boycott any other employer with whom the union has a dispute. The most recent significant amendment to the National Labor Relations Act was passed in 1974, removing the previous exemption of nonprofit hospitals.[19]

The Supreme Court has clouded the scope of the National Labor Relations Act as it relates to nonprofit educational institutions in two of its recent decisions. In *N.L.R.B.* v. *Catholic Bishop of Chicago,*[20] the National Labor Relations Board had relied on the 1974 amendment to the National Labor Relations Act to assert jurisdiction over a church-operated school. The Supreme Court stated, however, that in the absence of a clear expression of congressional intent to bring teachers in church-operated schools within the jurisdiction of the board, the Court would not construe the act in such a way as to call for the resolution of difficult and sensitive First Amendment questions. The Court ruled that there would be a significant risk of infringement of the religion clause of the First Amendment if the NLRA gave the board jurisdiction over church-operated schools. (Actually, the Taft-Hartley Act was to have provided an exception for enterprises operated exclusively for religious, charitable, scientific, literary, or educational purposes where no part of the net earnings inured to the benefit of any private shareholder or individual, but the proposed exception was not enacted. The Senate proposed an exception limited to nonprofit hospitals and passed the bill in that form.)

The National Labor Relations Board approved the formation of bargaining units composed of faculty members of a university within a year after it had asserted jurisdiction over a university.[21] In *N.L.R.B.* v. *Yeshiva University,*[22] however, the U.S. Supreme Court ruled that faculty members are managerial employees and thus are excluded from the act's coverage. According to the Court, respect for the board's expertise exists when the board's conclusions are rationally based on articulated facts and are consistent with the act. In reference to the board's determination that faculty members are professional employees entitled to the act's protection, the Supreme Court determined that the board's decision satisfied neither criterion. While the Court disagreed with the board's determination that faculty members are not managerial, it did not specifically address the issue of whether a university should be covered by the NLRA. The Court did find no evidence that Congress had considered whether a university faculty may organize for collective bargaining under the NLRA and that the authority structure of a university does not fit neatly within the statutory scheme of the act. The Court further stated, however, that the absence of explicit congressional direction does not preclude the board from reaching any particular type of employment.

Procedure under the National Labor Relations Act

If a majority of the workers in an appropriate bargaining unit wish to be represented before management by a labor union, management must then engage in collective bargaining with the designated union regarding mandatory subjects of bargaining. The first step in this procedure is the official recognition of labor's representative.

Recognition of the Labor Representative. The National Labor Relations Act provides that representatives designated or selected for the purposes of collective bargaining by a majority of the employees in a unit appropriate for these purposes shall be the exclusive representative of all the employees in the unit for collective bargaining in respect to rates of pay, wages, hours of employment, or other conditions of employment.[23] It is unlawful for an employer to recognize a union that does not represent a majority of the employees in a bargaining unit. Hence, in this way, the act imposes the will of the majority upon the minority.

A labor organization wishing to be certified as the exclusive bargaining unit must acquire authorization from 30 percent of the workers of a particular unit. Recall that professional and nonprofessional employees may not be in the same unit unless a majority of the professional employees vote to be included, and plant guards must be in a unit composed exclusively of plant guards. If an employer is presented with a demand for recognition by a union, the employer may voluntarily recognize the union (assuming that it represents a majority of the employees), or it may insist that the question of representation be settled by an NLRB election.

Generally, employees select a union as their representative in a secret ballot election in which a majority of the employees voting cast their ballots in favor of a particular union to represent them for the purpose of collective bargaining. Before an employer agrees to meet with a union, he should determine that the union does, in fact, represent a majority of the employees in an appropriate bargaining unit. If there is reasonable doubt concerning a union's majority status, an election by secret ballot should be requested. This is true even though the union presents cards indicating that it represents a majority of the employees. An employer is required to recognize a majority union, but the employer can refuse to recognize a union with only authorization cards. Further, the employer is under no duty to ask for an election; the union has the burden of taking the next step in invoking the board's election procedure if management does not do so.

In *Linden Lumber Division v. N.L.R.B.*,[24] a union obtained authorization cards from a majority of employees and demanded that it be recognized as the collective bargaining representative of those employees. Management doubted the union's claim to majority status, alleging that the union's claimed membership had been improperly influenced by supervisors. The union struck for recognition, charging management with an unfair labor practice based on its refusal to bargain. The Supreme Court held that management may have rational, good-faith grounds for distrusting authorization cards in a given situation. It stated that in instances where an employer has not engaged in an unfair labor practice impairing the electoral process, the employer does not violate a duty to bargain simply because of a refusal to accept evidence of the union's majority status other than the results of a board election. Further, in the absence of any agreement to permit majority status to be determined by means other than a board election, the union has the burden of taking the next step in invoking the board's election procedure.

A petition for investigation by the National Labor Relations Board of the question as to whether a union represents a majority of an appropriate grouping of employees can be initiated by the employer, by any person, or by a labor organization acting on behalf of a substantial number of employees. In addition, if there is a certified or currently recognized representative, any employee, or group of employees, may also file decertification proceedings to test the question of whether the certified union still represents the employees.[25] A union must have been designated by at least 30 percent of the employees before the board will cause an election. A person seeking decertification must have the signatures of at least 30 percent of the employees covered by an expiring collective bargaining agreement in his petition. If the employer is the petitioner, however, the 30 percent proof of representation is not needed.

Union organizers often seek to enlist a majority of the workers of a particular business through solicitation on the employer's premises. In *Republic Aviation Corp. v. N.L.R.B.*,[26] the Supreme Court upheld the rights of employees to solicit for a union during nonworking time where efficiency was not compromised. The Court also held, however, that the private property rights of an owner prevailed over the intrusion of nonemployee organizers, even in nonworking areas of the business and during nonworking hours.[27] The Court stated that an employer may not affirmatively interfere with organization; however, the union may not always insist that the employer aid organization. The Court was of the opinion that the distinction between employees and nonemployees is one of substance. While no restriction may be placed on the employees' right to discuss self-organization among themselves (unless the employer can demonstrate that a restriction is necessary to maintain production or discipline), no such obligation is owed nonemployee organizers. Their access to company property is governed by a different consideration. If the locations of the place of business and the living quarters of the employees place the employees beyond the reach of reasonable union efforts to communicate with the workers, then the employer must allow the union to approach his employees on his property. Where these conditions do not exist, the employer may validly post his property against nonemployee distribution of union literature. According to the Court, the act requires only that the employer refrain from interference, discrimination, resraint, or coercion in the employees' exercise of their own rights. It does not require that the employer permit the use of its facilities for organization when other means are readily available.

The National Labor Relations Board, upon receipt of a petition regarding the question of union representation, will conduct an investigation to determine (a) whether the board has jurisdiction, (b) whether there is an appropriate unit of employees for the purposes of collective bargaining, (c) whether the election would reflect the free choice of employees in the appropriate unit, and (d) whether, if the petitioner is a labor organization seeking recognition, there is a sufficient probability that the employees have selected it to represent them. (It must have been designated by at least 30 percent of the employees, as noted above.) The board makes available to the parties two types of informal consent procedures through which representation issues can be resolved without recourse to formal procedures.[28] These informal arrangements are referred to as consent election agreements. A board agent will arrange the details incident to the mechanics and conduct of the election. The actual polling is conducted and supervised by board agents.

Duty to Bargain in Good Faith. Once a union is established as the representative of a majority of the employees in a specific bargaining unit, the National Labor Relations Act requires that the employer and the union meet at reasonable times to confer in good faith and to reduce to writing the agreement reached, if either party requests a written agreement.[29] This obligation does not require that either party agree to a proposal, however, nor does it require the making of a concession. The National Labor Relations Board is empowered to determine appropriate collective bargaining units, its decision being subject to judicial review.

Supervisors or managerial employees are not entitled to protection of the act, nor are they employees with whom an employer is under a duty to bargain. This is generally the rule under both federal and state statutes, the reason being that supervisors and managerial employees formulate and effect policies by expressing and making operative the decisions of their employer. The employer is entitled to the undivided loyalty of its representatives; thus these employees must be aligned with management. For a museum, supervisors or managerial employees would include curators, the editor of the museum publication, its publicity director, its librarian, and its coordinators. Employees who have supervision over other employees, the authority to hire and fire and to approve wage increases, and the right to formulate policies, would be classified as supervisors or managerial employees.[30]

The duty to bargain in good faith assumes that the parties will meet at mutually convenient places and will be willing to devote a reasonable amount of time to the bargaining process. The parties must be represented in the bargaining process by someone who has authority to speak for the principals and who is not merely a messenger. The parties must reply to each other's proposals within a reasonable period of time, and they must not impose unfair conditions upon bargaining, such as settlement of outstanding grievances or unfair labor practice charges.

The parties must not bypass each other's designated representatives and must supply each other with any reasonable information required to bargain effectively.

Subject Matter of Bargaining. Management and labor are required to bargain on some subjects; others are permissive. Each party, on the request of the other, must bargain with respect to mandatory subjects. Mandatory subjects of bargaining include terms and conditions of employment, such as rates of pay, wages, and hours of employment. Other matters which have been held to be mandatory subjects of bargaining include duration of a collective bargaining contract, health and welfare programs, a group insurance program, health insurance coverage, holidays, job security, grievance procedures, payments of bonuses, pension plans, compulsory retirement, stock purchase plan which involves the employer's contributions, a nonstrike provision, paid vacations, promotions, and seniority rights. Various subjects held to be permissive include: a check-off of union dues, whether a union is the representative and appropriate unit for bargaining purposes, an employer's decision to liquidate a part of its business, and benefits for retired workers.[31] Neither party may be required to bargain on permissive subjects. Further, if the parties do bargain on permissive subjects, neither party may insist on bargaining to the point of an impasse. Illegal subjects, such as hot cargoes, are not subjects of bargaining, and any agreement about them is unenforceable.

Unfair Labor Practices. The National Labor Relations Act defines certain practices on the part of labor and management as constituting unfair labor practices. Employers are prohibited from (a) interfering with, restraining, or coercing employees in the exercise of their right to self-organization and to bargain collectively, or their right to refrain from so doing, (b) discriminating against employees to discourage or encourage union membership (except that a lawful union security clause may be signed), (c) discriminating against employees because they have given testimony or filed charges with the board, and (d) refusing to bargain in good faith with the representative union. Labor organizations are prohibited from (a) restraining or coercing employees or interfering with management's selection of its bargaining representative, (b) causing an employer to discriminate against employees in violation of the act, (c) refusing to bargain in good faith with the employer, (d) engaging in secondary boycotts or jurisdictional strikes, (e) charging excessive or discriminatory initiation fees, (f) engaging in featherbedding, and (g) engaging in organization or recognition picketing.

If either management or labor commits an unfair labor practice, the aggrieved party may file a formal complaint with the National Labor Relations Board. More than forty regional offices handle such complaints. A field examiner reviews the complaint and recommends to the regional director that a complaint be issued or that the charge be dismissed. If a charge is dismissed, the charging party may appeal to the board's general counsel in Washington. If a complaint is issued, the respondent must answer the charge. If differences are not settled, a hearing will be held in the community where the unfair practice occurred. Following the hearing, a formal decision and recommendation are filed by the hearing judge. Either party may file exceptions to the judge's finding with the board at its Washington office. The board will then review the record and will issue its decision. The final decision of the board may be appealed to a federal court of appeals. If there is no appeal, the respondent can wait for the board to seek enforcement of its order in the courts. Courts are empowered to enforce, modify, or set aside the board's orders, subject to the limitation that the findings of the board regarding facts are conclusive if they are supported by evidence. There may be contempt proceedings for failure to comply with the court's order.[32]

Strikes. Economic strikes often occur when employees cease work to achieve a labor objective classed as a mandatory subject of bargaining. Such strikes most often occur after negotiations for an initial or renewal labor agreement have deadlocked. On-the-job slowdowns designed to place economic pressure on the employer are partial economic strikes. Such strikers may be terminated in instances where their activities breach the employer's work rules. Strikes also occur to protest alleged employer unfair labor practices. A strike to secure an initial labor agreement generally does not require notice to the employer or to governmental agencies. Should the employer refuse to continue the bargaining process over mandatory subjects during such a strike, the strike will be transformed from an economic to an unfair labor practice strike in which management's prerogatives will be limited. If a union insists that management bargain over a permissive subject to the point of a bargaining impasse, the union has committed an unfair labor practice. A strike under these circumstances constitutes an unfair labor practice on the part of the union. The employer may file an unfair labor practice charge with the NLRB and seek an injunction to prohibit the strike.

A union violates its contract with management if it strikes during the term of a labor contract which has a no-strike clause. In these circumstances, management may seek damages against the union and request an injunction against the strike.

Rights of Strikers. An "economic" worker on strike, one who is trying to force a concession which the employer is not required to make, is entitled to reemployment after the termination of a lawful action if a vacancy exists for which the striker is qualified. Still, the employer is permitted to replace economic strikers permanently by employing new workers. On the other hand, employees who strike because management has committed an unfair labor practice are protected with respect to their reemployment even if the employer has hired replacements. If a striker has violated an employee unfair labor practice, he may be discharged from employment lawfully on a nondiscriminatory basis. Also, an employer does not commit an unfair labor practice by denying reinstatement to an employee who engaged in an illegal strike—a strike for an unlawful purpose or objective, for example.

Striking employees have the right to establish a picket line, to use arguments in support of their position, and to attempt by proper means to induce other persons not to work at jobs which they have vacated by striking or not to patronize the establishment. On the other hand, the employer and other employees have a right to be free from the harassment of illegal picketing. Picketing is permissible where the object sought reasonably relates to a legitimate and lawful interest of organized labor and where such concerted action is carried out peaceably and honestly. If the purpose is unlawful or is carried out forcibly or untruthfully, the picketing is unlawful.[33] An employer who is subjected to an unlawful strike may sue for damages.

Public employees are not covered by the National Labor Relations Act, as noted above. These employees would only be regulated by state statutes; state statutes which prohibit public employees from striking have been held to be valid.

Right-to-Work Laws. Section 14 (b) of the Taft-Hartley Act[34] states that the act does not require membership in a labor organization as a condition of employment in any state or territory in which membership or application for membership is prohibited by state or territorial law. This provision prevents the federal government from preempting the field of labor law so as to deprive the states of their powers to prevent compulsory unionism. Section 14 (b) removes all federal restrictions upon existing and future state legislation prohibiting compulsory unionism even where such legislation may affect employees engaged in interstate commerce. The effect of the provision is to allow the states to ban a union shop. The closed shop is prohibited under the federal act; however, a union shop is permitted. A union shop requires that all new and present employees must become union members within a certain period of time and must remain in good standing with the union. This compulsory unionism clause of the NLRA cannot be enforced in a right-to-work state.

With or without right-to-work laws, most employers are free to hire whomever they choose. The concern, then, is principally over workers' rights—whether or not a majority of workers should have the right to force an unwilling minority to join a union after the workers have been hired.

How Labor Laws Affect a Museum. A museum which is covered by the National Labor Relations Act must recognize the right of its workers to organize. Under nonunion conditions, the museum directors unilaterally establish the rules on wages and other labor matters (with the exception of certain antidiscrimination requirements imposed by other federal statutes, as noted below). These rules may be largely implicit. Under union conditions, the rules are typically written down in explicit terms and result from negotiation with the union through collective bargaining. An organization which has established rules providing for grievance procedures for workers and which prohibits arbitrary dismissal often provides the worker satisfaction that prevents employees from desiring union representation. Dissatisfied workers generally cause un-ionization.

What does management of a museum do when a union is just beginning to organize the workers? A policy of trying to keep the union out is not unrealistic, but it does require that the manager handle himself with great care. Management interference with employees in the exercise of their right to self-organization is an unfair labor practice, as noted above. Management may not counter the union drive with threats or discrimination or promises of benefits. At the early stages of a union drive, union organization is generally conducted secretly, with the union contacting employees who might join the union. Only after a number of employees have shown an active interest will the organization normally conduct its campaign for members in the open. The law restricts the use of picketing by unions as a means of persuading employers to grant recognition in those instances where federal or state labor relations statutes are applicable. In addition, recall that nonemployee union members can be prevented from soliciting employees to join the union on company property so long as the employees are reasonably accessible to union organizers at their homes after work.

Assuming that the majority of the workers want a union to represent them in collective bargaining and assuming that the union can satisfy the museum director that it does represent a majority of the workers within a bargaining unit, the museum director may voluntarily recognize the union. If the director is not satisfied that the union represents a majority of the workers within the bargaining unit, he may require an election conducted by secret ballot or he may insist that the question of representation be settled by an NLRB election. Once management is required to "recognize" the union as the bargaining agent for the employees (this occurring voluntarily if the museum director is satisfied that the union represents a majority of workers within the bargaining unit, otherwise by election), museum management is required to negotiate in good faith with the union regarding those mandatory subjects of bargaining.

Those museums which are subject to the National Labor Relations Act should carefully articulate job descriptions. Recall that supervisors and managerial employees are not covered by the act; the museum director may forbid them to join a union. (As noted above, supervisors or managerial employees would include curators, the editor of a museum publication, its publicity director, its librarian, and its coordinators.) Further, bargaining is only required for mandatory subjects. A museum director should generally exercise his discretion to refrain from bargaining on permissive subjects so as not to lose management prerogatives regarding these subjects.

Those museums which are controlled by a state, or a political subdivision thereof, are not subject to the act and, unless there is a state labor relations act that covers public employees, will not be required to bargain with labor representatives. Employees of federal museums are covered by federal collective bargaining provisions.

Discrimination in Employment

A museum which receives federal funds is subject to certain federal statutes relating to discriminatory practices in employment. Even though a museum receives no federal funds, however, it may still be subject to some of these provisions. The pertinent statutes regarding discrimination in employment are the Civil Rights Act of 1871,[35] the Civil Rights Act of 1964[36] (commonly called Title VII), the Equal Pay Act.[37] the Age Discrimination in Employment Act,[38] the Vocational Rehabilitation Act,[39] and the Vietnam Era Veterans Readjustment Act.[40] The Fourteenth Amendment and the Fifth Amendment to the U.S. Constitution provide further restrictions upon those museums that are state or federally controlled. The extent of coverage of a particular museum, then, depends in part at least on its legal status.

Employment Policies

A museum should have a sound personnel program, which includes an adequate program of wages and benefits, provisions for upward mobility, positive internal communication, and a grievance procedure for employees. Job descriptions can provide more certainty for employees and can be beneficial for the employer as well. As noted above, adequate job descriptions will identify those employees who are managerial and thus not subject to collective bargaining. It will also establish qualifications for certain positions so as to provide guidelines to answer possible discrimination charges. In this context, the museum director must be aware of the pertinent provisions of discrimination statutes so as to structure museum employment policies correctly. Provisions of these statutes are summarized.

Civil Rights Act of 1871. If the museum is an agency or arm of the state, its officials are subject to the Civil Rights Act of 1871. Section 1983 of the act provides that a "person" who, under color of any statute, ordinance, regulation, custom, or usage of any state, deprives another of any rights, privileges, or immunities secured by the Constitution and any federal laws is liable to the injured party. Pursuant to this statute, if an official of a state-controlled museum deprives a person of any rights under a federal statute or under the U.S. Constitution, he or she is acting under color of the state and may be subject to liability. Section 1981 of the act prohibits racial discrimination in the making and enforcement of private contracts. It has been held that private institutions are subject to section 1981 but not to 1983.

Civil Rights Act of 1964. Public museums, as well as private museums which affect commerce and which have fifteen or more employees for each working day in each of twenty or more calendar weeks in the current or preceding calendar year, are subject to the Civil Rights Act of 1964, which is referred to as Title VII. Title VII forbids discrimination on the basis of race, color, creed, national origin, and sex by employment agencies, labor organizations, and private and public employers. Title VII is enforced by the Equal Employment Opportunity Commission.[41] This commission has the authority to prevent any person from engaging in any unlawful employment practice as defined by the act and investigates each charge of discrimination filed with it.

Claims of employment discrimination under Title VII generally arise in one of two ways—disparate treatment or disparate impact. "Disparate treatment" means that an employer treats a person differently because of race, color, creed, national origin, or sex. Discriminatory intent is critical in such cases. "Disparate impact" involves employer practices which may be neutral on their face but which more harshly affect a protected group and are not related to job performance. Discriminatory intent is not required to establish a case of disparate impact.

The appropriate starting point for evaluation of a personal claim of disparate treatment is *McDonnell Douglas Corp. v. Green.*[42] In that case the Supreme Court stated that a complainant in a Title VII trial must carry the initial burden of establishing a prima facie case of racial or sex discrimination. The complainant may do this by showing that he or she is a member of a minority, that he or she applied and was qualified for a position for which the institution was seeking applicants, that despite proper qualifications the applicant was rejected, and that, after the rejection, the position remained open and the institution continued to seek applicants from persons with the complainant's qualifications. The burden then shifts to the institution to articulate some legitimate, nondiscriminatory reason for the applicant's rejection. If the institution is able to sustain this burden, the burden shifts back to the complainant to demonstrate that the institution's stated reason for the complainant's rejection was in fact pretext. In *Furnco Construction Corp. v. Waters,*[43] the Supreme Court held that to dispel an adverse inference from a prima facie showing of employment discrimination, the employer need only articulate some legitimate, nondiscriminatory reason for the applicant's rejection. Statistical proof that the work force was racially imbalanced or contained a disproportionately higher percentage of minority employees could be considered in determining motivation; however, courts cannot require different business practices for an employer until a violation of the Civil Rights Act has been proven. If there is such a showing, the burden which shifts to the employer is merely proving that its employment decision was based on a legitimate consideration and not an illegitimate one such as race. (According to the Supreme Court, Title VII forbids an employer from having as a goal a work force selected by any proscribed discriminatory practice, but it does not impose a duty to adopt a hiring procedure that maximizes the hiring of minority employees.) If some such reason is advanced by the employer, the focus returns to the employee to show that the employer's stated reason for the employee's rejection was in fact pretext.[44]

Practices, procedures, or tests neutral on their face, and even neutral in terms of intent, cannot be maintained if they have a disparate impact on certain persons. *Griggs v. Duke Power Company*[45] established the rule that employment practices which operate to exclude certain persons from employment must be related to job performance, or the practice is in violation of Title VII. Discriminatory intent need not be shown. In the *Griggs* case a high school education or the passing of a standardized general intelligence test was a condition of employment. The Supreme Court held that neither requirement was related to successful job performance and that both requirements did operate to disqualify black applicants at a substantially higher rate than white applicants; consequently, the practice was held to be prohibited by Title VII regardless of discriminatory purpose. While disproportionate impact might cause further inquiry, an inference of discrimination may nonetheless be negated by an employer's affirmative efforts to recruit minorities.[46]

The objective of Congress in the enactment of Title VII is obvious from the language of the statute. It is to achieve equality of employment opportunities and to remove barriers that have operated in the past to favor an identifiable group of white employees over other employees. Discriminatory preference for any group, minority or majority, however, is precisely and only what Congress has proscribed. In this regard, it is a violation of Title VII for a job advertisement to indicate preference, limitation, specification, or discrimination based on sex or race, though specification based on sex is permitted if sex is a bona fide occupational qualification for a particular job. A bona fide occupational qualification exception as to sex is interpreted narrowly. Refusal to hire a woman cannot be based on assumptions of the comparative employment characteristics of women in general. Further, it may not be based on stereotyped characterizations of the sexes, nor may the preferences of coworkers, the employer, clients, or customers be considered. Benefits provided employees must be the same for male and female.[47]

A museum covered by Title VII should have an affirmative action plan which would establish procedures to increase the minority applicant pool and the number of minorities interviewed and employed and would attempt to steer persons who are not qualified for one position so that they find another within the museum. A museum should not use any selection procedure which has an adverse impact on the hiring, promotion, or other employment of members of any race, sex, or ethnic group.

Equal Pay Act. Pursuant to the Equal Pay Act, an employer may not pay different wages to employees of opposite sexes for equal work on jobs the performance of which requires equal skill, effort, and responsibility and which are performed under similar working conditions, except where such payment is made pursuant to a seniority system, a merit system, a system which measures earnings by quantity or quality of production, or a differential based on any other factor other than sex.[48] The Equal Pay Act is administered by the Equal Employment Opportunity Commission.[49] (It was formerly administered by the Department of Labor.)

Age Discrimination Act. Any employment decision relative to a person between forty and seventy years of age must be based on the individual's ability or capacity to perform the work in question. Title VII standards have been applied to charges of age discrimination.[50] In *Schwager v. Sun Oil Company*,[51] the court noted that the Age Discrimination Act is a remedial act, its purposes being to promote employment of older persons based on their ability rather than on age, to prohibit arbitrary age discrimination in employment, and to help employers and workers find ways of meeting problems arising from the impact of age on employment. According to the court, with the enactment of the legislation age became a proscribed basis for employment decisions in much the same manner as under Title VII. The purposes and structure of the acts are similar. Mandatory retirement for persons under age seventy is prohibited. Still, persons over sixty-five who for two years prior to retirement are employed in executive or high policy-making positions are exempted from the act if such persons are entitled to an immediate nonforfeitable retirement benefit equivalent to a straight-line annuity of $27,000 or more, excluding social security benefits.

An employer may not differentiate as to age unless age is shown to be a bona fide occupational qualification necessary to the normal operation of the particular business. A business necessity test, not a business convenience test, is used. *Hodgson v. Greyhound, Inc.*[52] is a case in which the employer demonstrated that its maximum-hiring-age policy was founded upon good-faith judgment concerning safety needs of its passengers and others and that its hiring policy was not the result of an arbitrary belief lacking in objective reason or rationale. The Age Discrimination Act is administered by the Equal Employment Opportunity Commission. (It was also formerly administered by the Department of Labor.)

Vocational Rehabilitation Act. Section 503 of the Vocational Rehabilitation Act of 1973[53] provides that persons or firms who have contracts with the federal government in excess of $2,500 must take affirmative action to employ and advance qualified handicapped individuals. Such a contractor must also make reasonable allowances for a person's handicap unless doing so would impose an undue hardship.[54] An individual who believes that a contractor has not complied with this act may file a complaint with the Department of Labor.

Under section 504 of the Rehabilitation Act, an organization receiving federal financial assistance, or under any program or activity conducted by an agency of the executive branch of the federal government, may not discriminate against "otherwise qualified" handicapped individuals.[55] Section 504 applies to universities and to states and municipalities which receive federal grant funds.

In *Southeastern Community College v. Davis*,[56] the Supreme Court stated that an educational institution need not lower or substantially modify its standards to accommodate a handicapped person. In that case, a person suffering from serious hearing disabilities sought to be trained as a registered nurse. The Supreme Court ruled that admission to the program could be denied because the applicant was not "otherwise qualified." According to the Court, ability to understand speech without reliance on lipreading is necessary for the safety of patients; hence the applicant was not qualified. The Court stated that an "otherwise qualified person" is one who is able to meet all the program's requirements in spite of his handicap.

The language and history of section 504 of the Rehabilitation Act of 1973 indicate that Congress intended that those institutions subject to the act should make positive efforts to eliminate discrimination against the handicapped; however, section 504 does not impose a general requirement with respect to affirmative action. Unlike the requirements of affirmative action, regulations of the act do not compel the use of different selection criteria for handicapped students, nor does the act require achievement of any particular rate of participation by handicapped individuals in any programs.[57]

Modifications to accommodate the handicapped may include making facilities accessible to disabled persons, restructuring jobs, modifying work schedules and equipment, and providing interpreters or readers. A museum director must make such changes unless they constitute undue hardship as indicated by the size and type of museum operations and the nature and cost of the adjustment.[58]

Vietnam Era Veterans Readjustment Act. Any person or organization having a contract in the amount of $10,000 or more with the federal government for the procurement of personal property and nonpersonal services (including construction) must take affirmative action to employ and advance in employment qualified disabled veterans and veterans of the Vietnam era.[59] An aggrieved person who believes a federal contractor is not complying with this act may file a complaint with the Department of Labor.

Termination of Employment

According to the Second Circuit Court of Appeals in *Powell v. Syracuse University*,[60] the law requires not that employment be rational, wise, or well considered but only that it be nondiscriminatory. The general rule is that, in the absence of a contract to the contrary, an employer has the authority to discharge an employee with or without reason. Because affirmative action requirements regarding hiring and terms and conditions of employment apply also to termination of employees, however, this general rule has been limited by affirmative action requirements of state and federal statutes. Further, tenure rules and regulations, present for the most part in colleges and universities, provide restrictions on termination policies.

The Fourteenth Amendment provides that no person shall be deprived by a state government of "life, liberty or property, without due process of law." It further prohibits a state from denying anyone "equal protection of the law." The Fifth Amendment, applicable to the federal government, also provides that no person shall be deprived of life, liberty, or property without due process of law. If the museum is state or federally controlled and the employee can demonstrate a "property" or a "liberty" interest in reemployment, notice and a "for cause" hearing must be given the employee before termination. (In the absence of such an interest, no due process protections attach.)

Property Interest. The Supreme Court in *Board of Regents* v. *Roth*[61] and *Perry* v. *Sindermann*[62] defined a "property" interest in employment as a legitimate claim of entitlement. A person must have more than a unilateral expectation of reemployment to have such an interest, but if one is found to exist by reason of some independent source, the Fourteenth Amendment protects it.[63] The Supreme Court stated that property interests are not created by the Constitution; rather, they are created, and their dimensions are defined, by existing rules or understandings. A tenured faculty member has a property right; thus he cannot be terminated without a hearing based on cause. A nontenured faculty member, on the other hand, has no right of reemployment; a hearing is not required prior to termination. In the *Perry* v. *Sindermann* case, the Court did state that an institution which has no explicit tenure system may have created a de facto system by its practices. Existing rules and understandings, promulgated and fostered by state officials, may justify a legitimate claim of entitlement to continued employment. If this is the case, the employee does have a property interest in reemployment and must be afforded a hearing before termination.

Liberty Interest. In the *Roth* case, the Supreme Court stated that a "liberty" interest would be violated if an institution brought charges against an employee that imposed a stigma or other disability, foreclosing the employee's freedom to take advantage of other employment opportunities. This suggests that liberty interests are implicated when a charge regarding an individual's honesty or morality has been made. A charge must be made publicly before a termination will infringe a liberty interest, however. In *Ortwein* v. *Mackey*,[64] the Fifth Circuit Court of

Appeals stated that a "liberty" interest of an employee is not infringed by the mere presence of derogatory information in confidential files; a "liberty" interest has not been infringed unless untrue charges are perpetuated by the institution. Because the institution, in Ortwein, did not make public the reasons underlying its decision not to renew the employment, the employee could show no violation of his liberty interests. In Bishop v. Wood,[65] a policeman was terminated for reasons privately communicated to him. The Supreme Court stated that even if reasons for termination were not well founded, the fact that the communication was not made public offered no basis for a claim that the policeman's interest in his "good name," reputation, honor, or integrity was thereby impaired.

The mere fact of nonretention is not sufficiently stigmatizing to implicate a liberty interest.[66] In Davis v. Oregon State University,[67] the Ninth Circuit Court of Appeals stated that the embarrassment and reflection on professional competence that usually accompany a denial of academic tenure and subsequent termination are not sufficient to implicate a liberty interest; the fact that the professor is unsuccessful in seeking other employment is immaterial.

Procedural Due Process. The Fourteenth Amendment provides that a person may not be deprived by a state of "property" or "liberty" without "due process of law." The question arises as to what constitutes "due process." In Prebble v. Brodrick,[68] the Tenth Circuit Court of Appeals stated that a consideration of the "due process" procedures that may be required under any given set of circumstances must begin with a determination of the precise nature of the government function involved as well as of the private interest that has been affected by governmental action. The court recognized that there is no controlling decision by the Supreme Court establishing a procedural route which must be followed in a termination case. In the Prebble case, a faculty member was permitted to have counsel present at the termination hearing; he was given the right to testify and to present witnesses in his behalf; and he was furnished a written decision stating the reasons for the committee's conclusion. The court found that the procedures followed afforded procedural due process.

The faculty member was permitted to have counsel in the Prebble case; whether this is a requirement of due process has not been addressed by the courts. In Ferguson v. Thomas,[69] the Fifth Circuit Court of Appeals stated that the following minimum requirements must be followed in a for cause hearing: (a) the employee must be advised of the cause of his termination in sufficient detail to enable him to show any error that may exist; (b) he must be advised of the names and nature of testimony of the witnesses against him; (c) within a reasonable time thereafter, he must be accorded a meaningful opportunity to be heard in his own defense; and (d) a hearing should be held before a tribunal that both possesses some expertise in the area and has an apparent impartiality toward the charges. Right to counsel was not listed as a requirement for due process.

Museums controlled by the federal or state governments will be subject to the requirements of the Fifth or Fourteenth Amendments, respectively. Directors of government-controlled museums should be careful that they not establish an expectancy of continued reemployment on the part of their employees so as to cause the museum to be saddled with a de facto tenure system. Directors of all museums should make certain that hiring and termination practices are not based upon discriminatory motives that run afoul of Title VII.

Safety Requirements

In 1970, Congress determined that those employers whose businesses affect commerce must provide each employee employment and a place of employment free from recognized hazards that are causing, or are likely to cause, death or serious physical harm to the employees. With the passage of the Occupational Safety and Health Act of 1970,[70] broad authority was delegated to the secretary of labor to promulgate standards to ensure safe and healthful working conditions for the nations' workers. The Occupational Safety and Health Administration (OSHA) is the agency responsible for carrying out this authority. For those businesses affecting interstate commerce, the standards for safety and health at their places of employment, as set by the secretary of labor, are mandatory.[71]

Under regulations adopted by the secretary of labor, nonprofit and charitable organizations are covered by the act.[72] The United States and any state or political subdivision of a state are not included, however. Any entity created directly by the state so as to constitute an arm of the government or one administered by individuals who are controlled by public officials or the general electorate would be excluded from the act. Except for government-controlled museums, then, museums would be covered by the act.

The act's purpose is to provide for the general welfare and to assure as far as possible to every working man and woman safe and healthful working conditions and thus to preserve human resources. The act authorizes the secretary of labor to set health and safety standards, to conduct inspections, and to issue citations and proposed penalties. Any employer who has received a citation for a serious violation of the requirements of the act or of any standard, rule, or order of the regulations, will be assessed a civil penalty of as much as $1,000 for each such violation.[73]

Employers were to be stimulated to institute new safety programs and to improve existing programs. The act envisioned cooperative efforts between the employer, the employees, researchers, and federal and state safety officials. Voluminous regulations have been adopted since the act was passed.[74] An employer's task in attempting to comply with these regulations is formidable. The intent of the act was to compel employers to scrutinize their places of employment in an effort to locate and remedy hazardous conditions. Given the myriad standards which have been promulgated, a conscientious employer, even one with a small or medium-sized facility, will likely expend significant time and effort in bringing his facility into compliance with existing health and safety standards. In *Donlop v. Rockwell International*,[75] the court stated that the employer's task is difficult enough without adding the responsibility for potentially hazardous circumstances of which the employer is unaware and which he could not discover with the exercise of reasonable diligence. That court stated that the employer is to make a reasonable and a diligent effort to comply with the safety standards and that he would not be liable for penalties under the act if he has done so. The court stated that the employer will not be subjected to a higher standard and that the act does not make the employer an insurer of the safety of his employees.

The Supreme Court limited the otherwise extensive powers of the secretary of labor to promulgate voluminous standards in *Industrial Union v. American Petroleum*.[76] The Court stated that the secretary must first make a finding that the workplaces in question are not safe. "Safe" is not the equivalent of "risk-free," however. Consequently, the Court ruled that the secretary must make a threshold finding that the place of employment is unsafe in the sense that significant risks are present and can be eliminated or lessened by a change in practices before it may make public any permanent health or safety standard.

To enforce provisions of the act, the Secretary of Labor is empowered to inspect any place of employment covered by the act during regular working hours as well as at other reasonable times. Inspections follow a schedule established by OSHA or pursuant to complaints filed by employees. The act authorizes inspection of a business premise without a search warrant.[77] In *Marshall v. Barlow's, Inc.*,[78] however, the Supreme Court ruled that inspection without a warrant of a commercial premise violates the Fourth Amendment of the Constitution. The Court stated that the Fourth Amendment protects commercial buildings as well as private homes from unwarranted searches by government officials. The Court commented that the owner of a business has not, by the necessary utilization of employees in his operation, thrown open areas where employees alone are permitted to the warrantless scrutiny of government agents. According to the Court, the fact that an employee is free to report, and the government is free to use, any evidence of noncompliance with OSHA that an employee observes furnishes no justification for federal agents to enter a place of business from which the public is restricted to conduct their own warrantless search.

7

Duties of Museum Directors and Trustees

Directors of a museum board or trustees of a museum have the duty to manage the affairs of the museum so that its property will not be diverted from the public purposes for which it was entrusted. In recent years, the public has demanded increased accountability from trustees of all charitable organizations. The duties of trustees of charitable organizations are owed to the public at large and are enforced by the attorney general of the particular state. There have been problems in defining their roles and responsibilities, however. There is no clear-cut body of law establishing the legal standards to be applied. Courts in the various states may differ in the principles used to determine the extent of the duties and liabilities of such trustees. Standards must be borrowed from laws pertaining to corporations and trusts. Duties of a similar nature are required of both corporate directors and trustees of trust property; however, the trustee is held to a higher duty than that of a corporate director. Which body of law should apply to the museum director or trustee?[1] This chapter summarizes the laws applicable to corporate directors and to trustees in an effort to provide guidance to the museum director or trustee as to the duties to which he should be subjected, whether legally or ethically.

General Duties of Trustees

A trustee occupies a fiduciary relationship with respect to beneficiaries of the trust. As such, he has certain responsibilities regarding trust property. Once he accepts an appointment as trustee, he is under a duty to administer the trust so long as he remains trustee. The scope of a trustee's power depends upon the scope of his duties. Should he violate a duty, he will be subject to liability to the beneficiaries. He is not relieved of liability merely because he received no compensation for his services.

The most fundamental duty owed by a trustee to beneficiaries of the trust is the duty of loyalty. The fiduciary relationship between the trustee and the beneficiaries of a trust is an especially intense one. The trustee has the duty to administer the trust solely in the interest of the beneficiaries; consequently, he is not permitted to place himself in a position where it would be for his own benefit to violate this duty. When a trustee's personal interest comes into conflict with his duty to beneficiaries of the trust, courts have fixed a high and strict standard for the trustee's conduct. His interest must yield to that of the beneficiaries. In this regard, a transaction involving the trustee personally which was in all respects fair and reasonable might stand if the trustee dealt directly with the beneficiaries, made full disclosure, and did not take advantage of his position. Should he act without consent of the beneficiaries, however, the transaction will be set aside even though it was otherwise fair and reasonable. A purchase of trust property by a trustee individually, or a sale to the trust of the trustee's individual property, can be set aside no matter how fair the sale may have been. A trustee violates his duty to the beneficiaries not only where he purchases trust property for himself individually but also where he has a personal interest in the purchase of such a substantial nature that it might affect his judgment in making the sale.[2] The Uniform Trust Act[3] forbids a trustee from directly or indirectly buying or selling any property from the trust, from or to himself, or from or to any relative, employee, partner, or other business associate.

A trustee is also subject to a duty of care. This requires that the trustee, in administering the trust, exercise the care and skill that a man of ordinary prudence would exercise in dealing with his own property. The trustee is held to the standards of a man of ordinary prudence whether he receives compensation or whether he acts gratuitously. (In the case of bailments and in the case of agency, the courts have ordinarily fixed a higher standard of care for bailees and agents who are compensated than they have fixed for those who act gratuitously. There is no similar distinction as to trustees, however.) If the trustee has greater skill or more facilities than others have, he is under a duty to employ the greater skill and facilities. Moreover, if a trustee has represented himself as having a higher degree of skill or greater facilities than others have, he may incur a liability by failing to measure up to the standard he has set for himself. A person who induces another to employ him as a trustee by representing that he has special knowledge or special skill is held to the standard of skill which he represents himself to have.[4]

Another fundamental duty owed by the trustee to beneficiaries of the trust is the duty not to delegate to others the administration of the trust or the performance of acts in the administration of the trust. While this does not mean that the trustee must personally perform every act that may be necessary or proper in the execution of the trust, the trustee must remain the executive manager of the trust. As a general rule, discretionary acts must be exercised by the trustee himself; ministerial powers may be delegated.[5]

A trustee is under a duty to beneficiaries of the trust to keep clear and accurate accounts. If the trustee fails to keep proper accounts, all doubts are resolved against him. He must maintain separate accounts for trust property and must properly invest such funds. He must make certain that funds committed to his trust are used for their intended purposes. He must not engage in acts which might cause the trust to lose its exempt status.

General Duties of Corporate Directors

The board of directors of a corporation represents the corporate body; the directors are the executive representatives of the corporation. A board of directors is likened to an agent (a fiduciary who acts for another called the principal), but it also resembles the principal, for a corporation must act through its directors. Management and control of a corporation is under the board of directors, not the shareholders. Hence a board of directors becomes both a principal and an agent. (See chapter 3 for a discussion of the agency theory.)

As an agent owes certain fiduciary duties to his principal, so the directors of a corporation owe duties to the corporation. The duties of a director resemble those of a trustee. A director is subject to a duty of loyalty and a duty of care. The duty of loyalty requires that board members not exploit corporate opportunities or misuse inside information. Only reasonable salaries may be paid board members, and often board members serve without compensation. A board member must account to the corporation for any profits he receives as a result of his directorship. The duty of care requires that a board member exercise the same care and skill which an ordinarily prudent man would exercise under similar circumstances in his own personal affairs.

Corporate law evolved from trust law; hence contracts between directors and their corporations were originally prohibited. As corporate law divorced itself from trust law, however, duties of directors became less stringent than those required of trustees. At present, interested transactions are not prohibited as long as they are fair. While a trustee may not properly delegate the exercise of his powers, this rule is not applicable to a corporate director. The element of reliance upon personal judgment and discretion is wanting in the case of a corporation because it can only act through its directors and officers, and these may change from time to time. Nevertheless, a director is liable for an improper delegation of his powers and duties, should he permit others to perform acts which should be performed by the corporate officers or employees.[6] Board power can be delegated to an executive committee if the articles or bylaws permit. Because board members may live in different areas, it is sometimes necessary that power be delegated.

The duty of care requires that directors exercise reasonable skills in the exercise of their responsibilities. In *Litwin v. Allen*,[7] a New York court stated that while directors are liable for negligence in the performance of their duties, they are not insurers and thus are not liable for errors of judgment or for mistakes so long as they act with reasonable skill and prudence. A director is required to conduct the business of the corporation with the same degree of fidelity and care as an ordinarily prudent man would exercise in the management of his own affairs of like magnitude and importance. According to the court in the *Litwin* case, however, whether or not a director has discharged his duty depends upon the facts and circumstances of a particular case, the kind of corporation involved, its size and financial resources, the magnitude of the transaction, and the immediacy of the problem presented. A director is called upon "to bestow the care and skill" which the situation demands. In this context, a director of a bank is held to a stricter accountability than the director of an ordinary business corporation.

The liability of corporate directors for damages caused by negligent or unauthorized acts rests upon the common-law rule which renders every agent liable who violates his authority or neglects his duty to the damage of his principal. By accepting the office, directors implicitly undertake to give their best judgment to the enterprise. The acceptance of the office of director implies a competent knowledge of the duties assumed. Directors cannot be excused because of their lack of experience or ability. Still, directors are not responsible for mere errors of judgment or want of prudence short of clear and gross negligence. If the power of a director in dealing with corporate funds is doubtful, the directors are entitled to some protection for their negligent acts when they act under advice of counsel. Where the terms of their power are explicit, however, advice of counsel is of no avail.[8]

The duty of loyalty prohibits a director from obtaining a private or secret profit as a result of his official position; he must give the corporation the benefit of any advantage he has acquired. With respect to a director's duty regarding use of inside information, the law is not well defined. Under some state law and under federal law, it is a higher duty, resembling the duty of a fiduciary. Pursuant to section 16(b) of the Securities Exchange Act of 1934, insiders of a corporation (directors and stockholders with at least a 10 percent ownership) must return to the corporation all profits derived from sales or purchases of corporate stock within a six-month period, and liability attaches regardless of the intention of the insider. This federal rule generally was not a part of state corporate law. In *Diamond* v. *Oreamuno*,[9] however, in a derivative suit brought by the corporation's shareholders, a New York court held that the inside information of a corporate officer or director is an asset of the corporation, acquired by the insider as a fiduciary of the company; a misappropriation of such information is a violation of that trust. The New York court quoted the well-established rule that a person who acquires special knowledge or information by virtue of his fiduciary relationship with another is not free to exploit that knowledge or information for his own personal benefit but must account to his principal for any profits derived therefrom. It then likened a corporate director to a trustee in this regard and stated that "just as a trustee has no right to retain for himself the profits yielded by property placed in his possession but must account to his beneficiaries, a corporate fiduciary, who is entrusted with potentially valuable information, may not appropriate that asset for his use even though, in so doing, he causes no injury to the corporation." The New York court was of the opinion that when officers and directors abuse their position in order to gain personal profits, the effect is to cast a cloud on the corporation's name, thereby injuring stockholder relations and undermining public regard for the corporation's securities.

The Court's decision in the *Diamond* case has not been accepted in every state. In *Freeman* v. *Decio*,[10] an Indiana court refused to permit a suit by stockholders against corporate officers and directors for alleged illegal trading of corporate stock on the basis of material inside information. The Indiana court stated that it is not at all clear that current corporate law contemplates such an extensive notion of fiduciary duty as that enunciated in the *Diamond* case. The court in the *Freeman* case was of the opinion that it would be better to determine whether there is any potential loss to the corporation from the use of inside information before deciding to characterize inside information as an asset with respect to which the insider owes the corporation a duty of loyalty. It stated that this approach would be in keeping with the modern view of the corporate opportunity doctrine, discussed below. Before a court requires a director or officer to account automatically to the corporation for diversion of a corporate opportunity to personal use, it first inquires as to whether there was a possibility of a loss to the corporation (whether in fact the corporation was in a position to avail itself of the opportunity) before deciding that a corporate opportunity existed. According to the Indiana court, courts should scrutinize transactions between a director or officer and the corporation, under the duty of loyalty, in the same fashion. Courts should inquire as to whether there was any injury to the corporation and whether the transaction was fair and in good faith. In *Schein v. Chasen,*[11] a Florida court refused to extend what it termed the "innovative ruling" of the New York court in *Diamond* to someone who gave a tip of inside information. The federal court of appeals in the *Schein* case noted that derivative actions by shareholders of a corporation are permitted so that individual shareholders can be private attorney generals to enforce proper behavior on the part of corporate officials. The court stated, however, that this action should not be extended to cover outside individuals, corporations, or institutions subject to other private and governmental restraints on their behavior. It noted that the *Diamond* doctrine applies only to corporate fiduciaries who actually profit by inside information and does not cover inside aiders, abettors, or conspirators. The court commented that the *Diamond* rule is a significant alteration of the common-law principles applicable to officers and directors.

A corporate director is under a fiduciary obligation not to divert a corporate business opportunity for his own personal gain. This so-called doctrine of corporate opportunity is a species of the duty of a fiduciary to act with undivided loyalty. The doctrine charges any interest acquired by the director with a trust for the benefit of the corporation. The theory is that an insider should not use his inside position to benefit himself by seizing an investment opportunity available to and suitable for the corporation. It operates because the corporation was not given the opportunity to engage in a transaction. If a business opportunity comes to a corporate director in his individual capacity rather than his official capacity, however, and the opportunity is one which is not essential to the corporation and in which it has no interest or expectancy, the director is entitled to treat the opportunity as his own. The test in determining whether a corporate officer or director has appropriated a corporate opportunity is whether there was a specific duty on the part of the director to act or contract in regard to the particular matter as the representative of the corporation.

Transactions between a corporation and its officers or directors are not void and are only voidable at the option of the corporation. Such transactions are subject to the closest scrutiny, however, and must be characterized by absolute good faith. Where the corporation is represented in a transaction by interested directors or officers who deal with themselves, the contract is voidable at the option of the corporation merely because of the relationship; proof of actual fraud or of injury to the corporation is not required. In addition, while corporate directors are not absolutely precluded by their official position from purchasing property constituting a corporate asset, the corporation may have a purchase of its property by a director set aside if the contract is unfair. Here the courts will apply a more stringent test to determine fairness. Occasionally, statutes or a provision of the corporate charter or articles of incorporation may provide that corporate directors may not be interested directly or indirectly in dealings with the corporation.

A corporate director may not cast a vote upon a matter in which he has an adverse interest. Still, there has been some support for the possibility that a vote of an interested director, while not necessarily valid, may be counted in favor of a transaction between the director and the corporation if the transaction appears to be fair and characterized by good faith.

Duties of Museum Officers and Employees

Museum Trustees

A museum may be a nonprofit corporation, a charitable trust, or an agency of the government. The duties imposed upon the trustees or directors of the museum may vary according to the type of entity. In addition, standards used to determine proper conduct of trustees or directors may not be uniform in the different states. Those museums which are agencies of the state or the federal government may be subjected to state or federal statutes regarding conflicts of interest. The attorney general of the state is the enforcer of the trust position of the museum director or trustee.

In *Stern v. Lucy Webb Hayes National Training School*,[12] a federal district court noted that the charitable corporation does not fit neatly into the established common-law categories of a corporation or a trust. That court was of the opinion, however, that corporate rather than trust principles should be applied in determining the liability of the directors of a charitable organization, for as the court reasoned, their functions are virtually indistinguishable from those of their "pure" corporate counterparts.

Plaintiffs in the *Stern* case alleged that directors of the Sibley Hospital failed to supervise investments and failed to attend meetings of committees charged with such supervision. The court considered charges of mismanagement and self-dealing on the part of the hospital trustees. It noted that while both trustees and corporate directors are liable for losses occasioned by their negligent mismanagement of investments, the degree of care required differs. A trustee is uniformly held to a high standard of care and will be held liable for simple negligence, while a director must have committed gross negligence or must otherwise be guilty of more than mere mistakes of judgment. According to the court, this distinction is a recognition of the fact that corporate directors have many areas of responsibility, while the traditional trustee is often charged only with the management of the trust funds and can therefore be expected to devote more time and expertise to that task. The court was of the opinion that board members of most large charitable corporations fall within the corporate rather than the trust model; therefore, they should be held to the less stringent corporate standard of care. With respect to nonmanagement, the court stated that directors of charitable corporations, like corporate directors, should be permitted to delegate investment decisions to a committee of board members as long as all directors assume the responsibility for supervising the committee by scrutinizing their work periodically. As to the charge of self-dealing, the court again applied the less stringent corporate rule to the charitable organization.[13] It stated that while a trustee may be found guilty of a breach of trust even for mere negligence in the maintenance of accounts in banks with which they are associated, corporate directors are generally only required to show "entire fairness" to the corporation and "full disclosure" of the potential conflict of interest to the board. The court in the *Stern* case listed the following acts as those which would cause a trustee or director of a charitable organization to be in default of his fiduciary duty.

1. While assigned to a particular committee of the board having general financial or investment responsibility under bylaws, he failed to use due diligence in supervising the actions of those officers, employees, or outside experts to whom responsibility for making day-to-day decisions was delegated.

2. He knowingly permitted the organization to enter into a business transaction with himself or with any corporation, partnership, or association in which he then had a substantial interest or with which he held a position as trustee, director, general manager, or principal officer, without having previously informed the persons charged with approving the transaction of his interest or position or of any significant reasons why the transaction might not be in the best interests of the charity.

3. He actively participated in or voted in favor of a decision by the board to transact business with himself or with any corporation in which he then had a substantial interest, or with which he held a position as director or principal officer.

4. He otherwise failed to perform his duties honestly, in good faith, and with a reasonable amount of diligence and care.

The judge in the *Stern* case found the hospital trustees to have breached their fiduciary duty to supervise the management of Sibley's investments even though he imposed the less stringent corporate standards of conduct. He did not order the trustees removed but rather required that all dealings with board members or their affiliated organizations be disclosed. He also required that all new trustees read his opinion and signify in writing that they had done so.

It is imperative that a museum director familiarize himself with the laws within his jurisdiction regarding his duties and liabilities. Recall that in those states which follow the *Diamond* rule, the corporate duty of loyalty will be more stringent. For those museums which are governmentally controlled, there are conflict-of-interest statutes in some of the respective jurisdictions which specify further requirements for conduct. For federal agencies, such as the Smithsonian Institution, the federal law regarding conflicts of interest governs.

The question arises as to whether a director of a charitable organization, such as a museum, should meet a substantially higher ethical standard than individuals in the private sector. Consider the following transactions.

Example 1. *A*, a trustee of Museum *X*, is a collector and dealer in fine art. *A* obtains inside information about good buys in the art field. He purchases an art work as a result of information obtained as a trustee of Museum *X* and sells it to a third party at a substantial profit.

Example 2. *A*, a trustee of Museum *X*, has a proprietary interest in a firm which does business with the museum. The museum awards contracts to his firm at a substantial profit to *A*'s firm.

Example 3. A museum director sells objects from the museum's collections to a dealer at prices advantageous to the dealer in return for discounts on his private purchases from that same dealer.

Example 4. As director of a museum, *A* discovers an exceptionally good bargain on a valuable art collection. *A* buys the collection for himself.

Example 5. *A*, a director of Museum *X*, periodically takes valuable paintings from the museum collection and hangs them at his private residence or in his office.

Museums receive favorable tax treatment and are often supported for the most part through public funds. These considerations should require the highest moral principles of museum trustees. To provide for the highest standards of conduct on the part of museum officials, self-regulatory codes of behavior have been implemented within the museum profession. The code of ethics adopted by the Association of Art Museum Directors (see appendix H) provides that the position of a museum director is one of trust, involving great responsibilities. It declares it to be unprofessional for a museum director to use his influence or position in the art market for personal gain. In this regard, he should not traffic in works of art for monetary reasons nor be a party to the recommendation of works of art for purchase by a museum in which he has any undisclosed financial interest. If he himself is a collector, he should grant the museum's governing board the first option to acquire a work of art. Infractions of the canons of professional conduct will render a member of the association subject to discipline by reprimand, suspension, or expulsion.

Museum Employees

Conflict-of-interest principles should also be applicable to museum employees. The American Association of Museums adopted a code of ethics for museum workers in 1925 (see appendix H). It provides general guidelines for behavior of museum trustees, directors, and workers.

Employees of a museum should be subject to certain standards of conduct. An employee is subject to agency laws which provide that one cannot serve two masters. The employee must not violate the fundamental principle of primary loyalty to his museum employer. Before undertaking outside employment he should secure written permission from his employer. If the employee has outside employment, he should make it clear that he is not representing the museum, he should perform all work off museum premises, and he should make a full disclosure of all such outside employment. Curators often have separate standards of conduct. A curator should first offer any gifts obtained as a result of his employment to the museum and should give the museum first option to purchase before selling a private collection or art object. Any purchases made during official trips should be offered to the museum.

Methods to Remedy Conflict-of-Interest Problems

There are several methods which can be employed to remedy conflict-of-interest problems. A museum can exclude from its board anyone who has a potential conflict of interest. This may not be advisable, however, in that the best trustees will undoubtedly be those who have interests or prior experience in the museum or art field. One method is to eliminate the conflict—the so-called divestiture approach used in politics. A trustee should be disqualified from any decision making in which his conflict of interest comes into play. Full disclosure, requiring a statement in advance of all the trustee's holdings, interests, and activities, will reveal potential conflicts of interest so that the trustee's future actions can be evaluated by his associates, himself, and the public. For those museums which are private foundations for tax purposes, the penalties attached to acts of self-dealing and other prohibited acts (see chapter 2) should deter museum directors from participating in transactions with the museum. Further, the extensive reporting required for tax purposes from both private foundations and public charities, plus the threat of the loss of exempt status, should cause charities to be more responsible in their activities. Officers, directors, and employees of museums should be made aware of any conflict-of-interest statutes in their particular state, the code of ethics of the American Association of Museums, and the general law regarding duties and responsibilities of directors and trustees.

Appendices
Glossary of Legal Terms
Table of Selected Cases
Table of Statutes
Notes
Bibliography
Index

Appendix A
Sample Documents for Establishing a Museum

Trust Indenture for a Charitable Museum
Articles of Incorporation for a Museum of Art
Bylaws
Corporation Minutes

Trust Indenture for a Charitable Museum

The Department of the Treasury, Internal Revenue Service, has promulgated a sample declaration of trust to establish and govern a charitable trust which will qualify as being exempt from federal income taxes.[1] The following sample declaration of trust is modified from the IRS's sample. It would serve to establish a museum as a charitable trust.

THE HISTORICAL MUSEUM CHARITABLE TRUST

Declaration of Trust made as of the _____ day of _____ , 19_____ , by _____ of _____ and _____ _____ of _____ , who hereby declare and agree that they have received this day from _____ , as Donor, the sum of Ten Dollars ($10) and that they will hold and manage the same, and any additions to it, in trust, as follows:

First: This trust shall be called "The Historical Museum Charitable Trust."

Second: The trustees may receive and accept property, whether real, personal, or mixed, by way of gift, bequest, or devise, from any person, firm, trust, or corporation, to be held, administered, and disposed of in accordance with and pursuant to the provisions of this Declaration of Trust; but no gift, bequest, or devise of any such property shall be received and accepted if it is conditioned or limited in such manner as to require the disposition of the income or its principal to any organization other than "The Historical Museum," or as shall in the opinion of the trustees, jeopardize the Federal income tax exemption of this trust pursuant to section 501(c) (3) of the Internal Revenue Code of 1954, as now in force or afterward amended.[2]

169

Third: A. The principal and income of all property received and accepted by the trustees to be administered under this Declaration of Trust shall be held in trust by them, and the trustees may make payments or distributions from income or principal, or both, to or for the use of "The Historical Museum," in such amounts and for such charitable purposes of the trust as the trustees shall from time to time select and determine; and the trustees may make payments or distributions from income or principal, or both, directly for such museum purposes, within the meaning of charitable purposes as used in section 501(c)(3) of the Internal Revenue Code of 1954, but only such purposes as also constitute public charitable purposes under the law of trusts of the State of _____ . Income or principal derived from contributions by corporations shall be distributed by the trustees for use solely within the United States or its possessions. No part of the net earnings of this trust shall inure or be payable to or for the benefit of any private shareholder or individual, and no substantial part of the activities of this trust shall be the carrying on of propaganda, or otherwise attempting, to influence legislation. No part of the activities of this trust shall be the participation in, or intervention in (including the publishing or distributing of statements), any political campaign on behalf of any candidate for public office.

B. Any other provisions of this instrument notwithstanding, the trustees shall distribute its income for each taxable year at such time and in such manner as not to become subject to the tax on undistributed income imposed by section 4942 of the Internal Revenue Code of 1954, or corresponding provisions of any subsequent Federal tax laws. Any other provisions of this instrument notwithstanding, the trustees shall not engage in any act of self-dealing as defined in section 4941(d) of the Internal Revenue Code of 1954, or corresponding provisions of any subsequent Federal tax laws; nor make any investments in such manners as to incur tax liability under section 4944 of the Internal Revenue Code of 1954, or corresponding provisions of any subsequent Federal tax laws; nor make any taxable expenditures as defined in section 4945(d) of the Internal Revenue Code of 1954, or corresponding provisions of any subsequent Federal tax laws; nor retain any excess business holdings as defined in section 4943(c) of the Internal Revenue Code of 1954, or corresponding provisions of any subsequent Federal tax laws.[3]

C. The trust shall continue forever unless the trustees terminate it and distribute all of the principal and income, which action may be taken by the trustees in their discretion at any time. On such termination, the trust fund as then constituted shall be distributed to or for the use of charitable organizations, in such amounts and for such charitable purposes as the trustees shall then select and determine.

Fourth: This Declaration of Trust may be amended at any time or times by written instrument or instruments signed and sealed by the trustees, and acknowledged by any of the trustees, provided that no amendment shall authorize the trustees to conduct the affairs of this trust in any manner or for any purpose contrary to the provisions of section 501(c) (3) of the Internal Revenue Code of 1954 as now in force or afterward amended. An amendment of the provisions of this Article Fourth (or any amendment to it) shall be valid only if and to the extent that such amendment further restricts the trustees' amending power. All instruments amending this Declaration of Trust shall be noted upon or kept attached to the executed original of this Declaration of Trust held by the trustees.

Fifth: Any trustee under this Declaration of Trust may, by written instrument, signed and acknowledged, resign his office. The number of trustees shall be at all times not less than two, and whenever for any reason the number is reduced to one, there shall be, and at any other time there may be, appointed one or more additional trustees. Appointments shall be made by the trustee or trustees for the time in office by written instruments signed and acknowledged. Any succeeding or additional trustee shall, upon his acceptance of the office by written instrument signed and acknowledged, have the same powers, rights and duties, and the same title to the trust estate jointly with the surviving or remaining trustee or trustees as if originally appointed.

None of the trustees shall be required to furnish any bond or surety. None of them shall be responsible or liable for the acts of omissions of any other of the trustees or of any predecessor or of a custodian, agent, depositary, or counsel selected with reasonable care.

The one or more trustees, whether original or successor, for the time being in office, shall have full authority to act even though one or more vacancies may exist. A trustee may, by appropriate written instrument, delegate all or any part of his powers to another or others of the trustees for such periods and subject to such conditions as such delegating trustee may determine.

The trustees serving under this Declaration of Trust are authorized to pay to themselves amounts for reasonable expenses incurred and reasonable compensation for services rendered in the administration of this trust, but in no event shall any trustee who has made a contribution to this trust ever receive any compensation thereafter.

Sixth: The trustees' powers are exercisable solely in the fiduciary capacity consistent with and in furtherance of the purposes of this trust as specified in Article Third and not otherwise.

Seventh: Any person may rely on a copy, certified by a notary public, of the executed original of this Declaration of Trust held by the trustees, and of any of the notations on it and writings attached to it, as fully as he might rely on the original documents themselves. Any such person may rely fully on any statements of fact certified by anyone who appears from such original documents or from such certified copy to be a trustee under this Declaration of Trust. No one dealing with the trustees need inquire concerning the validity of anything the trustees purport to do. No one dealing with the trustees need see to the application of anything paid or transferred to or upon the order of the trustees of the trust.

Eighth: This Declaration of Trust is to be governed in all respects by the laws of the State of _____ .

Trustee—

Trustee—

Articles of Incorporation for a Museum of Art

ARTICLES OF INCORPORATION

The undersigned, acting as incorporators of The South Plains Museum of Art, under the Nonprofit Corporation Act of the State of _____ adopt the following Articles of Incorporation for such corporation.

First: The name of the corporation is The South Plains Museum of Art.

Second: The period of its duration is _____ .

Third: The purposes for which the corporation is organized are as follows:

(1) The corporation shall receive and maintain a fund or funds of real or personal property, or both, and, subject to the restrictions and limitations hereinafter set forth, shall use and apply the whole or any part of the income therefrom and the principal thereof, exclusively for the operation of a museum of art and shall stimulate and enhance public awareness of, interest in, and appreciation of art.

(2) The corporation shall distribute its income for each taxable year at such time and in such manner as not to become subject to tax on undistributed income imposed by section 4942 of the Internal Revenue Code of 1954 or corresponding provisions of any subsequent federal tax laws.

(3) The corporation shall not engage in any act of self-dealing as defined section 4941(d) of the Internal Revenue Code of 1954 or corresponding provisions any subsequent federal tax laws.

(4) The corporation shall not retain any excess business holdings as defined in section 4943(c) of the Internal Revenue Code of 1954 or corresponding provisions of any subsequent federal tax laws.

(5) The corporation shall not make any investment in such manner as to subject it to tax under section 4944 of the Internal Revenue Code of 1954 or corresponding provisions of any subsequent federal tax laws.

(6) The corporation shall not make any taxable expenditures as defined in section 4945(d) of the Internal Revenue Code of 1954 or corresponding provisions of any subsequent federal tax laws.[4]

Notwithstanding any of the above statements of purpose, the corporation shall not, except to an insubstantial degree, engage in any activities not in furtherance of the exempt purposes of the corporation.

The corporation is not organized for pecuniary profit, and no part of the net earnings shall inure to the benefit of any member or individual, including its members, trustees, or officers, except that the corporation shall be authorized and empowered to pay reasonable compensation for services rendered and to make payments and distributions in furtherance of the purposes set forth in Article Third hereof. No substantial part of the activities of the corporation shall be the carrying on of propaganda, or otherwise attempting to influence legislation, and the corporation shall not participate in, or intervene in (including the publishing or distribution of statements) any political campaign on behalf of any candidate for public office.

Fourth: Upon the dissolution of the corporation, the Board of Trustees shall, after paying or making provision for the payment of all of the liabilities of the corporation, dispose of all of the assets of the corporation exclusively for the purposes of the corporation in such manner, or to such organization or organizations organized and operated exclusively for charitable, educational, religious, or scientific purposes as shall at the time qualify as an exempt organization or organizations under section 501(c) (3) of the Internal Revenue Code of 1954 (or the corresponding provision of any future United States Internal Revenue Law), as the Board of Directors shall determine. Any such assets not so disposed of shall be disposed of by the Court of the county in which the principal office of the corporation is then located, exclusively for such purposes or to such organization or organizations, as said Court shall determine, which are organized and operated exclusively for such purposes.

Fifth: The address of the initial registered office of the corporation is _____ _____ , and the name of its initial registered agent at such address is _____ .

Sixth: The number of directors constituting the initial Board of Directors of the corporation is _____ , and the names and addresses of the persons who are to serve as the initial directors are:

           Name   *Address*

Seventh: The name and address of each incorporator is:

           Name   *Address*

In Witness Whereof, we have hereunto subscribed our names this _____ day of _____ , 19_____ .

_____

_____

_____

                          Incorporators

Bylaws

BYLAWS OF THE SOUTH PLAINS MUSEUM OF ART,
A NONPROFIT CORPORATION

ARTICLE 1
OFFICES

The principal office of the corporation in the State of _____
shall be located in the City of _____ . The corporation shall have and
continuously maintain in the State of _____ a registered
office, and a registered agent whose office is identical with such registered
office.

ARTICLE 2
MEMBERS

The South Plains Museum of Art shall have _____ (number)
members. The qualifications and rights of the members shall be as follows:

Each member shall be entitled to one vote on each matter submitted to a
vote of the members.

Any member may resign by filing a written resignation with the Secretary,
but such resignation shall not relieve the member so resigning of the obligation
to pay any dues, assessments, or other charges theretofore accrued and unpaid.

ARTICLE 3
MEETING OF MEMBERS

An annual meeting of the members shall be held on the _____ day of _____
_____ in each year for the purpose of electing Directors and for the
transaction of other business as may come before the meeting. If the day fixed
for the annual meeting shall be on a legal holiday, such meeting shall be held
on the next succeeding business day. If the election of Directors shall not be
held on the day designated herein for any annual meeting, or at any adjourn-
ment thereof, the Board of Directors shall cause the election to be held at a
special meeting of the members as soon thereafter as possible.

Special meetings of the members may be called by the President, the Board
of Directors, or not less than one-tenth of the members having voting rights.

The Board of Directors may designate any place, either within or without
the state, as the place of meeting for any annual meeting or for any special
meeting called by the Board of Directors. Written notice of any meeting of
members shall be delivered to each member entitled to vote at such meeting,
not less than ten nor more than sixty days prior to the date of such meeting. A

majority of the voting members constitutes a quorum. At any meeting, a member may vote by proxy.

ARTICLE 4
BOARD OF DIRECTORS

The affairs of the corporation shall be managed by its Board of Directors. The number of directors shall be _____ . Each Director shall hold office until the next annual meeting of members and until his successor shall have been elected and qualified.

A regular annual meeting of the Board of Directors shall be held immediately after the annual meeting of members. Special meetings of the Board of Directors may be called by the President or by any two Directors. Notice of any special meeting shall be given at least five days prior thereto by written notice to each Director. A majority of the Board of Directors shall constitute a quorum for the transaction of business.

Any vacancy occurring in the Board of Directors shall be filled by majority vote of the remaining Directors.

ARTICLE 5
OFFICERS

The officers of the corporation shall be a President, a Vice President, a Secretary, and a Treasurer. The officers shall be elected annually by the Board of Directors at the regular annual meeting of the Board of Directors. Any officer elected or appointed by the Board of Directors may be removed by the Board of Directors whenever, in its judgment, the best interests of the corporation would be served thereby. Any vacancy in any office shall be filled by the Board of Directors.

ARTICLE 6
AMENDMENTS TO BYLAWS

These bylaws may be amended by a majority of the Directors present at any regular meeting or at any special meeting, if at least ten days' written notice is given of an intention to amend the bylaws at such meeting.

Corporation Minutes

MINUTES OF THE FIRST MEETING OF THE BOARD OF DIRECTORS
OF THE SOUTH PLAINS MUSEUM OF ART,
A NONPROFIT CORPORATION

The following are the minutes of the first meeting of the Board of Directors of The South Plains Museum of Art, a corporation in the State of _____ _____ , held at _____ on _____ , 19_____ , said meeting having been held on the call of all the incorporators named in the Articles of Incorporation.

Present at the meeting were _____ , _____ , and _____ who are the persons named as the initial Directors of the corporation in its Articles of Incorporation.

These Directors have filed their written waivers of notice and consents to the holding of this meeting which waivers and consents have been filed with the corporate records and are made a part of the minutes of this meeting.

On motion duly made, _____ was elected Chairman of the meeting and _____ was elected to act as Secretary.

A document consisting of _____ pages entitled "Bylaws of the South Plains Museum of Art" was then presented to and considered by the Directors. After a review of such bylaws and a discussion of particular parts, on motion duly made and seconded, it was unanimously:

Resolved, that the bylaws presented to and considered at this meeting are adopted as the bylaws of this corporation.

A corporate seal was then presented to the meeting and on motion duly made and seconded, it was unanimously:

Resolved, that a corporate seal, consisting of _____ , containing the words "The South Plains Museum of Art," is adopted as the corporate seal of the corporation, and the Secretary is instructed to impress such seal on the minutes of this meeting.

The Chairman stated that nominations were in order for the election of officers of the corporation, which would be a President, a Vice President, a Secretary, and a Treasurer. Therefore, the following slate of officers was nominated:

There being no other nominations, on motion made, seconded, and unanimously carried, the slate of officers nominated was duly elected to hold office until their respective successors are duly elected. Each officer so elected, being present, accepted his office.

The following motions were adopted:

Resolved, that this corporation establish in its name a deposit account with the _____ Bank and that the following named officers of this corporation be, and they hereby are, authorized to establish such accounts; and

Resolved, that the following officers be, and they hereby are, authorized to withdraw funds of this corporation from said account signed as provided herein, and said bank is hereby authorized to honor and pay any and all checks so signed; and

Resolved, that the fiscal year of this corporation be from _____ to _____ of each year; and

Resolved, that the treasurer of this corporation be, and he is hereby authorized to pay the expenses of incorporation and organization of this corporation.

There being no further business to come before the meeting, on motion duly made, seconded, and unanimously carried, the meeting was adjourned.

_____

Secretary

Approved:

_____

Chairman

Appendix B

Income Tax Return of a Private Operating Foundation

Return of Private Foundation Exempt from Income Tax (Form 990-PF), with Schedule of Depreciation
Annual Report of Private Foundation (Form 990-AR)

The South Plains Museum Association was organized in 1977. The initial contribution was made by John Doe. The board of directors consists of the John Doe family. The association applied for and received 501(c) (3) status but as a private operating foundation. On January 1, 1980, the museum had the assets listed below.

Cash	$10,000
Savings accounts	20,000
Equipment	20,000
Building	40,000
Land	30,000

The fund had for 1980 the receipts shown below.

Interest on savings accounts		$1,200
Contributions		
	John Doe	12,000
	Mrs. John Doe	1,000
	General public	300
Admission fees		4,000
Total		$18,500

Disbursements are shown below.

Insurance	$200
Repairs	500
Supplies	500
Salaries	2,000
Taxes	200
Compensation to foundation manager (John Doe, Jr.)	3,000
Purchase of artifacts	2,000
Total	$8,400

The equipment has a useful life of ten years with no salvage value, while the building has a useful life of forty years. Straight-line depreciation is used.

Form 990-PF

Part I

Column A. Column A requires that all items of receipts and expenditures be listed according to the accounting method used by the foundation. If any contributions or gifts entered on line 1 exceed $5,000 from any one person, a schedule should be attached showing the name of that person, the date received, and the total amount received from each such person. If a contribution is in the form of property, the foundation must furnish a description and a fair market value of the property. Gross profits from all business activities are entered on line 11. (Any unrelated business income reported on Form 990-T is included here. If any business activity is not reported on Form 990-T, a statement must be attached indicating how such trade or business contributed to the exempt purpose of the foundation.) Total compensation of officers, directors, and trustees is entered on line 15. (Part VI must be completed with respect to this compensation.) With respect to depreciation on line 20, a schedule must be attached showing description of the property, date acquired, cost or other basis, depreciation allowable in previous years, method of computing depreciation, rate or life years, and depreciation claimed in the current tax year.

South Plains Museum's return would list $13,300 on line 1 (contributions from John Doe, Mrs. John Doe, and the general public total $13,300), $4,000 on line 3 (admission fees for the year), $1,200 on line 4 (interest), and total of $18,500 on line 13. It would enter $3,000 on line 14, $2,000 on line 15, and $3,200 on line 22 (insurance, $200; repairs, $500; supplies, $500, purchase of artifacts, $2,000). It would enter $3,000 on line 20 as depreciation. This is computed by dividing the cost of the equipment, $20,000, by ten years, and by dividing the cost of the building, $40,000, by forty years. Depreciation on the equipment would be $2,000, while depreciation on the building would be $1,000. Taxes of $200 are entered on line 19; however, total taxes would be $224. An additional tax of $24 must be paid as an excise tax on net investment income. This tax is computed on line 1 of Part II. The total on line 24 would be $11,424. Line 25(a) represents the excess of receipts over expenditures. This would be $7,076 ($18,500 receipts less $11,424 expenditures including depreciation).

Column B. All amounts that are included in the computation of net investment income are listed in Column B. Amounts from Column A that will not be used to compute net investment income are shaded; however, the amounts remaining may still be different from the amounts for Column B. For example, if amounts listed in Column A pertain to both investment activities and exempt activities, only the amount relating to investment activities will be listed in Column B. Further, if amounts listed in Column A include amounts reported on Form 990-T in computing unrelated business taxable income, those amounts will not be included in Column B. Tax-exempt income is not included in computing net investment income. All other investment income, even though derived from assets devoted to charitable purposes, is included in Column B. Gains from the sale or other disposition of property used for the production of income are included in Column B. If these gains are subject to the tax on unrelated business income, however, they are not also included here, though any excess not included in unrelated business taxable income would be. (Part VII of Form 990-PF is used to determine the total gains or losses, the net gain or loss then being entered on line 8, part 1.) Gains or losses from the sale or exchange of property used primarily for exempt purposes are excluded from the computation of net investment income. If the property is also used for investment purposes (other than incidentally), the gain or loss is apportioned; the part that pertains to the investment use is included in the computation of net investment income. If the sale or exchange of investment properties resulted in a net loss, the loss may not be subtracted from other investment income, nor may it be carried back or forward to other taxable years. Losses on exchange of property can only offset gains. Deductions on Column B are those expenses that are paid or incurred for the production or collection of investment income. Expenses that are allowable to tax-exempt income are not included. Only straight-line depreciation may be used. Taxes deductible in Column B include only those taxes that relate to investment income. Tax paid on net investment income is not included; however, operating foundations can deduct this tax. The difference between total receipts and total expenses from investment is entered on line 24. This amount is carried to Part II and multiplied by 2 percent to determine the excise tax on net investment income.

South Plains Museum would enter only its interest income of $1,200 in Column B; it has no other investment income. (Assume that it had no savings in 1979. It would therefore have paid no tax in tax year 1979 and would have no tax deduction in Column B.) The excise tax for South Plains Museum computed in Part II would be $24 ($1,200 × 2 percent).

Column C. Column C is used to compute adjusted net income, which figure is used in Part VIII for a nonoperating foundation to determine the amount of charitable distributions that the foundation is required to make to avoid paying a penalty tax for failure to distribute income. A private operating foundation, such as South Plains Museum, does not complete Part VIII. The amount determined in Column C is carried to Part XII to determine if the foundation qualifies as an operating foundation (substantially all of adjusted net income computed in Column C must be distributed in the form of qualifying distributions.) All income derived from, or in connection with, property held by the foundation is included. Deductible expenses include operating expenses paid or incurred for the production or collection of gross income. Deductions relating to property used for exempt purposes are excluded. If only a portion of property-produced income was included in Column C, the expenses relating to that property must be apportioned between exempt and nonexempt uses. Income in Column C includes all tax-exempt income; consequently, expenses relating to the production of tax-exempt income are deductions in Column C. Interest income, dividends, gross rents, and royalties entered in Column C should be the same amounts entered in Column A. Income modifications are amounts previously claimed as qualifying distributions that have been received in the taxable year or have been reclassified in the current taxable year. If the acquisition of property was previously claimed as a qualifying distribution and the property is sold in the taxable year, the amounts received on the sale are income modifications to the extent the acquisition was a qualifying distribution. Further, amounts set aside for a specific project and claimed as qualifying distributions are income modifications to the extent that the amount previously set aside was not necessary for the project. Only straight-line depreciation may be used. The deduction for taxes does not include income taxes paid on unrelated taxable business nor the tax on net investment income for nonoperating foundations. (These taxes are deductions on Part VIII for a nonoperating foundation, as amounts distributed.) For private operating foundations the tax on net investment can be deducted in Column C.

South Plains Museum will enter its interest income and its tax on net investment income in Column C. Its adjusted net income on line 25(c) will be $1,176. This amount will be entered on Part XII to determine whether the foundation qualifies as an operating foundation.

Column D. Expenditures for exempt purposes are listed in Column D. The amounts must be determined by using the cash method of accounting. Administrative expenses related to the organization's exempt purpose and contributions, gifts, and grants to charitable organizations not controlled by the grantor foundation qualify. The total of these amounts is entered on Part X as "qualifying distributions."

Parts III and IV

The beginning and ending net worths of the foundation are entered on the balance sheet in Part III. An organization's net worth is determined by subtracting its liabilities from its total assets. For South Plains Museum its assets at the beginning of the year include cash and savings accounts of $30,000; depreciable assets of $60,000 (equipment of $20,000 and building of $40,000) less depreciation from date of acquisition of $9,000 ($3,000 each year for three years); and land of $30,000. It had no outstanding liabilities; hence, its net worth totals its assets. Net worth is composed of initial contributions by the Doe family of $100,000 plus net earnings of the foundation since 1977 of $11,000. The ending balance sheet is composed of cash and savings accounts of

$40,010 (beginning balance of $30,000 plus receipts of $18,500 minus expenditures of $8,400); depreciable property of $60,000 less depreciation of $12,000 (depreciation for past years of $9,000 plus $3,000 depreciation for the current year); and land of $30,000. Assets total $118,100. This amount corresponds to liabilities of $24 (tax on net investment income which will not have been paid by the end of the tax year) plus net worth of $118,076. Ending net worth is computed by adding the excess of expenditures over receipts of $7,076 from line 25(a) to net worth at the beginning of the year. Changes in net worth are computed in Part IV. Any changes in net worth not caused by receipts or expenditures must be explained in Part IV.

Part V

Part V has a series of questions to determine whether a foundation or its manager have engaged in any acts that would cause the imposition of a penalty tax. Form 4720 (see appendix E) must be filed (with Form 990-PF) if acts of self-dealing between the foundation and disqualified persons took place or if the foundation failed to distribute income, had excess business holdings, made investments that jeopardized the foundation's exempt purposes, or made expenditures not in furtherance of the foundation's exempt purposes.

Part VI

Those persons who become substantial contributors during the year must be listed in Part VI. This category would include any person who made contributions to the foundation of more than $5,000, if the amount is more than 2 percent of the cumulative total contributions received by the foundation before the close of the taxable year. Once a person becomes a substantial contributor, he remains a substantial contributor for all subsequent years; consequently, even though John Doe contributed $12,000 during the year, he would have been listed as a substantial contributor in previous years and need not be listed on the current return.

Part VII

This part also requires a listing of compensation paid all officers, directors, and trustees during the year and a separate listing of compensation paid other employees that was more than $30,000. In addition, any professional fees paid persons in excess of $30,000 must be separately listed.

Part VIII

This need not be completed because most museums would choose to satisfy the operating test by meeting the assets test rather than the endowment test. This part is completed only if an operating foundation chooses the "endowment alternative test" to satisfy its operating status.

Part IX

This is not completed by operating foundations. It is completed, along with Part XI, for nonoperating foundations to determine if the foundation distributed sufficient "qualifying distributions" to avoid paying the 15 percent tax on undistributed income.

Part X

Total qualifying distributions for the year are computed in Part X. Qualifying distributions are amounts expended for exempt purposes. They include the amount computed in Column D, Part I; amounts spent for program-related investments (investments made to accomplish the exempt purposes of the foundation where no significant purpose is the production of income or the appreciation of property and no purpose is political in nature); amounts paid to acquire assets used directly in promoting charitable purposes; and amounts set aside for a specific project which will be paid for within sixty months from the date of the first set-aside and which is better accomplished by set-aside funds than by the immediate payment of funds. Total distributable amount computed in Part X is carried to Part XII for operating foundations. South Plains Museum would enter $8,400 computed in Column D, Part I. This amount is then carried to line 2(c) of Part XII.

Part XI

This is not completed for an operating foundation as it is not liable for a penalty tax for failure to distribute income.

Part XII

Part XII resembles the form that must be completed by private operating foundations when they are applying for exempt status. An operating foundation must furnish the same information each year to retain its status as an operating foundation. It must expend substantially all its adjusted net income directly for the active conduct of its exempt functions. In addition, it must meet either the assets test, the endowment test, or the support test. These tests can be satisfied in any three years of a four-year period.

South Plains Museum will enter its adjusted net income from line 25(c) of $1,176. It will compute 85 percent of $1,176, which is $1,000. It must have at least $1,000 of qualifying distributions to qualify as an operating foundation. Its qualifying distributions total $8,400; consequently, it meets this test. It would choose to satisfy the assets test which requires that 65 percent or more of its assets be devoted directly to the exempt functions of the foundation. The value of all its assets is entered on line 3(a) (i) with those assets used directly for exempt purposes listed on line 3(a) (ii). Assume the equipment ($20,000 and building $40,000 less depreciation of $12,000) plus the land and $20,100 cash are used directly for its exempt purposes. As this is more than 65 percent of the value of all the assets, South Plains Museum qualifies as an operating foundation.

Form 990-AR

Because South Plains Museum has at least $5,000 of assets, it must file Form 990-AR. Total gifts are entered on line 1 and gross income on line 2. Gross income would include interest income of $1,200 and admission fees of $4,000. Disbursements and expenses should be divided between those incurred to earn contributions and those attributable to gross income as listed on line 2. Assume half the salaries, compensation to the manager and depreciation of $2,000 is attributable to collection contributions. This, plus the $2,000 for purchase of artifacts, would total $6,500. The remaining expenditures, as listed on Form 990-PF, Part I, Column A of $4,924, would be entered on line 5 of Form 990-AR. The beginning balance sheet from Part III of Form 990-PF is entered on page 3 of Form 990-AR. The building and land are listed together under real estate.

Form 990-AR must be made available for public inspection. South Plains Museum must publish a notice in the local newspaper that the form is available for inspection.

Form 990-PF

Department of the Treasury
Internal Revenue Service

Return of Private Foundation
Exempt from Income Tax
Under Section 501(c)(3) of the Internal Revenue Code

For the calendar year 1980, or tax year beginning _____, 1980 and ending _____, 19___

Please type, print, or attach label. See Specific Instructions	Name of organization South Plains Museum Association	Employer identification number 75 : 1000000
	Address (number and street) 1000 - 10th Street	If the foundation is in a 60-month termination under section 507(b)(1)(B) check here . ▶ ☐
	City or town, State, and ZIP code Anytown, Texas 79000	Fair market value of assets at end of year

If address changed, check here ▶ ☐   Foreign organizations, check here ▶ ☐   120,000

The books are in care of ▶ John Doe, Jr.

Located at ▶ Anytown, Texas   Telephone no. ▶ 806-742-2000

If exemption application is pending, check here . . . . . ▶ ☐

Part I — Analysis of Revenue and Expenses (See instructions for Part I)

		(A) Revenue and expenses per books	(B) Computation of net investment income	(C) Computation of adjusted net income	(D) Disbursements for exempt purpose
1	Gross contributions, gifts, grants, etc. (see instructions) .	13,300			
2	Contributions from split-interest trusts (see instructions) .				
3	Gross dues and assessments	4,000			
4	Interest	1,200	1,200	1,200	
5	Dividends				
6	Gross rents and royalties				
7	Net gain or (loss) from sale of assets not on line 11 . . .				
8	Capital gain net income (see instructions) . . .				
9	Net short-term capital gain (see instructions) . .				
10	Income modifications (see instructions) . . .				
11	Gross profit from any business activities: (Gross receipts ▶ $ .... minus cost of sales ▶ $ ....) (see instructions)				
12	Other income (attach schedule)				
13	Total—add lines 1 through 12	18,500	1,200	1,200	
14	Compensation of officers, etc. (see instructions)	3,000			3,000
15	Other salaries and wages	2,000			2,000
16	(a) Pension plan contributions (enter number of plans ▶ ....)				
	(b) Other employee benefits				
17	Investment, legal, and other professional services				
18	Interest				
19	Taxes (see instructions)	224		24	200
20	Depreciation, amortization, and depletion (see instructions)	3,000			
21	Rent				
22	Other expenses (attach schedule)	3,200			3,200
23	Contributions, gifts, grants (see instructions) .				
24	Total—add lines 14 through 23	11,424	-0-	24	8,400
25 (a)	Excess of revenue over expenses: Line 13 minus line 24 . .	7,076			
(b)	Net investment income (if negative enter -0-) . .		1,200		
(c)	Adjusted net income (see instructions) (if negative enter -0-)			1,176	

Part II — Excise Tax On Investment Income

1 Domestic organizations enter 2% of line 25(b). Foreign organizations enter 4% of line 25(b)   24

2 Credits: (a) Foreign organizations—tax withheld at source . . | |

    (b) Tax paid with application for extension of time to file (Form 2758) . . . . . | |

3 Tax due—line 1 minus line 2. Pay in full with return. Make check or money order payable to Internal Revenue Service (write employer identification number on check or money order) . . . . ▶   24

4 Overpayment—line 2 minus line 1 . . . . ▶

Foreign organization—Enter book value ▶ $ _____ and fair market value ▶ $ _____ of investment assets held in U.S.

Under penalties of perjury, I declare that I have examined this return, including accompanying schedules and statements, and to the best of my knowledge and belief it is true, correct, and complete. Declaration of preparer (other than taxpayer) is based on all information of which the preparer has any knowledge.

▶ _____ Signature of officer or trustee   Date   ▶ _____ Preparer's signature

▶ _____ Title   ▶ _____ Preparer's address (or employer's name and address)

313-057   52-0237640

Page

Part III Balance Sheets

Assets	Beginning of tax year		End of tax year	
	(A) Amount	(B) Total	(C) Amount	(D) Total
1 Cash:				
(a) Savings and interest-bearing accounts	20,000		20,000	
(b) Other	10,000	30,000	20,100	40,100
2 Accounts receivable net				
3 Notes receivable net (attach schedule)				
4 Inventories				
5 Government obligations:				
(a) U.S. and instrumentalities				
(b) State, subdivisions of States				
6 Investments in corporate bonds, etc. (attach schedule) .				
7 Investments in corporate stocks (attach schedule) . .				
8 Mortgage loans (number of loans ▶.................) . .				
9 Other investments (attach schedule)				
10 Depreciable (depletable) assets (attach schedule):				
(a) Held for investment purposes				
(b) Minus accumulated depreciation				
(c) Held for charitable purposes	60,000		60,000	
(d) Minus accumulated depreciation	9,000	51,000	12,000	48,000
11 Land:				
(a) Held for investment purposes		30,000		30,000
(b) Held for charitable purposes				
12 Other assets (attach schedule)				
13 Total assets		111,000		118,100
Liabilities				
14 Accounts payable				24
15 Contributions, gifts, grants, payable				
16 Mortgages and notes payable (attach schedule) . . .				
17 Other liabilities (attach schedule)				
18 Total liabilities				
Net Worth (Fund Balances)				
19 Principal fund ▶		100,000		100,000
20 Income fund ▶		11,000		18,076
21 Total net worth (fund balances)		111,000		118,076
22 Total liabilities and net worth (line 18 plus line 21) . .		111,000		118,100

Part IV Analysis of Changes in Net Worth

1 Total net worth at beginning of year—Part III, Column B, line 21	111,000
2 Enter amount from Part I, line 25(a)	7,076
3 Other increases not included in line 2 (itemize) ▶	
4 Total of lines 1, 2, and 3	118,076
5 Decreases not included in line 2 (itemize) ▶	
6 Total net worth at end of year (line 4 minus line 5)—Part III, Column D, line 21	118,076

Form **4562**
Department of the Treasury
Internal Revenue Service

Depreciation

► See instructions on back.
► Attach this form to your return.

Name(s) as shown on return	Identifying number
South Plains Museum Association	75-1000000

For grouping assets, see instructions for line 3.

a. Description of property	b. Date acquired	c. Cost or other basis	d. Depreciation allowed or allowable in earlier years	e. Method of figuring depreciation	f. Life or rate	g. Depreciation for this year
Total additional first-year depreciation. See instructions for limitation. ──────────►						
Class Life Asset Depreciation Range (CLADR) System depreciation from Form 4832 . .						
Other depreciation: Buildings	1977	40,000	6,000	SL	2.5%	1,000
Furniture and fixtures . . .						
Transportation equipment . .						
Machinery and other equipment .	1977	20,000	3,000	SL	10%	2,000
Other (Specify)						
4 a Totals (add amounts in columns c and g) .		60,000				3,000
b Total current year acquisitions (included in line 4a, column c)		-0-				

Individual and partnership filers enter the totals from line 4a on the corresponding lines of their regular depreciation schedule. Other filers should attach Form 4562 to their return and enter line 4a, column g, on the depreciation expense line in the "Deductions" section of their return.

Form **4562** (1980)

Form 990–PF (1980)   Pag

Part V Statements Regarding Activities

File Form 4720 if you answer "No" to question 10(b), 11(b), or 14(b); or if you answer "Yes," to question 10(c), 12(b), 13(a), or 13(b).   **Yes** |

1 (a) During the tax year, did you attempt to influence any national, State, or local legislation? . . . .

(b) During the year did you participate or intervene in any political campaign? . . . .

(c) Did you spend more than $100 during the year (either directly or indirectly) for political purposes (see instructions for definition)? . .

If you answered "Yes" to 1(a), (b), or (c), attach a detailed description of the activities and copies of any materials published or distributed by the organization in connection with the activities.

(d) Did you file Form 1120–POL? . . . .

2 Have you engaged in any activities which have not previously been reported to the Internal Revenue Service? . . .

If "Yes," attach a detailed description of the activities.

3 Have you made any changes, not previously reported to the IRS, in your governing instrument, articles of incorporation, or bylaws, or other similar instruments? . . . .

If "Yes," attach a conformed copy of the changes.

4 (a) Did you have unrelated business gross income of $1,000 or more during the year? . . . .

(b) If "Yes," have you filed a tax return on Form 990–T for this year? . . . .

5 Was there a liquidation, termination, dissolution, or substantial contraction during the year? . . . .

If "Yes," attach a schedule for each asset disposed of showing: the type of asset, the date of disposition, its cost or other basis, its fair market value on date of disposition, and the name and address of each recipient to whom assets were distributed.

6 (a) Did you have at least $5,000 in assets at any time during the year?   X

(b) If "Yes," did you file the annual report required by section 6056 (see Form 990–AR for instructions)?   X

7 Are the requirements of section 508(e) (relating to governing instruments) satisfied? (See instructions) . . . .   —X—

If "Yes," are the requirements satisfied by:

(a) Language in the governing instrument (original or as amended), or   X

(b) Enactment of State legislation that effectively amends the governing instrument with no mandatory directions in the governing instrument that conflict with the State law? . . . .

8 (a) Enter States to which the foundation reports or with which it is registered (see instructions) ▶
   Texas, Oklahoma, New Mexico

(b) If you answered 6(a) "Yes," have you furnished a copy of Form 990–AR (or equivalent report) to the Attorney General (or his/her designate) of each State as required by General Instruction K.1?   X
If "No," attach explanation.

9 Are you claiming status as an operating foundation within the meaning of sections 4942(j)(3) or 4942(j)(6) for calendar year 1980 or fiscal year beginning in 1980 (see instructions for Part XII)?   X
If "Yes," complete Part XII.

10 Self-dealing (section 4941):

(a) During the year did you (either directly or indirectly):

(1) Engage in the sale or exchange or leasing of property with a disqualified person?   X

(2) Borrow money from, lend money to, or otherwise extend credit to (or accept it from) a disqualified person? .   X

(3) Furnish goods, services, or facilities to (or accept them from) a disqualified person?   X

(4) Pay compensation to or pay or reimburse the expenses of a disqualified person?   X

(5) Transfer any of your income or assets to a disqualified person (or make any of either available for the benefit or use of a disqualified person)?   X

(6) Agree to pay money or property to a government official? (Exception: check "No" if you agreed to make a grant to or to employ the official for a period after he or she terminates government service if he or she is terminating within 90 days.)   X

(b) If you answered "Yes" to any of the questions 10(a)(1) through (6), were the acts you engaged in excepted acts as described in the instructions for this line? . . . .

(c) Did you engage in a prior year in any of the acts described in 10(a), other than excepted acts, that were acts of self-dealing that were not corrected by the first day of your tax year beginning in 1980?   X

11 Taxes on failure to distribute income (section 4942) (does not apply for years you were an operating foundation as defined in section 4942(j)(3) or 4942(j)(6)):

(a) Did you at the end of tax year 1980 have any undistributed income (lines 6(b) and (c), Part XI) for tax year(s) beginning before 1980?   X
If "Yes," list the years ▶................, ..., ..., ...

(b) If "Yes," to (a) above, are you applying the provisions of section 4942(a)(2) (relating to incorrect valuation of assets) to the undistributed income for ALL such years? . . . .

(c) If the provisions of section 4942(a)(2) are being applied to ANY of the years listed in (a) above, list the years here and see the instructions ▶................, ..., ...

12 Taxes on excess business holdings (section 4943):

(a) Did you hold more than 2% direct or indirect interest in any business enterprise at any time during the year? . .

(b) If "Yes," did you have excess business holdings in 1980 as a result of any purchase by you or disqualified persons after May 26, 1969; after the lapse of the 5-year period to dispose of holdings acquired by gift or bequest; or after the lapse of the 10-year first phase holding period?   X
Note: You may use Schedule C, Form 4720 to determine if you had excess business holdings in 1980.

art V Statements Regarding Activities (continued)

	Yes	No
Taxes on investments which jeopardize charitable purpose (section 4944):		
(a) Did you invest during the year any amount in a manner that would jeopardize the carrying out of any of your exempt purposes?		X
(b) Did you make any investment in a prior year (but after December 31, 1969) that could jeopardize your charitable purpose that you had not removed from jeopardy on the first day of your tax year beginning in 1980?		X
Taxes on taxable expenditures (section 4945):		
(a) During the year did you pay, or incur any amount to:		
(1) Carry on propaganda, or otherwise attempt to influence legislation by attempting to affect the opinion of the general public or any segment thereof, or by communicating with any member or employee of a legislative body, or by communicating with any other government official or employee who may participate in the formulation of legislation?		X
(2) Influence the outcome of any specific public election, or to carry on, directly or indirectly, any voter registration drive?		X
(3) Provide a grant to an individual for travel, study, or other similar purposes?		X
(4) Provide a grant to an organization, other than a charitable, etc., organization described in paragraph (1), (2), or (3) of section 509(a)?		X
(5) Provide for any purpose other than religious, charitable, scientific, literary, or educational purposes, or for the prevention of cruelty to children or animals?		X
(b) If you answered "Yes" to any of questions (a)(1) through (a)(5), were all such transactions excepted transactions as described in the instructions?		
(c) If you answered "Yes" to question 14(a)(4), do you claim exemption from the tax because you maintained expenditure responsibility for the grant (as explained in item (12) of the instructions for line 14)? . . . . . . If "Yes," attach the statement required.		

art VI Statement Regarding Contributors, Compensation, etc.

ersons who became substantial contributors in 1980 (if more space is needed, attach schedule):

Name	Address

fficers, directors, trustees, foundation managers and their compensation, if any, for 1980:

Name and address	Title, and time devoted to position	Contributions to employee benefit plans	Expense account, other allowances	Compensation
John Doe, Jr.				3,000
al . . . . ▶				3,000

ompensation of five highest paid employees for 1980 (other than included in 2 above—see instructions):

Name and address of employees paid more than $30,000	Title, and time devoted to position	Contributions to employee benefit plans	Expense account, other allowances	Compensation

al number of other employees
l over $30,000 . . . . . ▶

Page

Part VIII Minimum Investment Return for 1980
(Operating Foundations—See instructions)

1 Fair market value of assets not used (or held for use) directly in carrying out exempt purposes:

   (a) Average monthly fair market value of securities . . . .

   (b) Average of monthly cash balances . . . .

   (c) Fair market value of all other assets (see instructions) . . . .

   (d) Total (add lines (a), (b), and (c)) . . . .

2 Acquisition indebtedness applicable to line 1 assets . . . .

3 Line 1(d) minus line 2 . . . .

4 Cash deemed held for charitable activities—enter 1½% of line 3 (for greater amount, see instructions) . . .

5 Line 3 minus line 4 . . . .

6 Enter 5% of line 5 . . . .

Part IX Computation of Distributable Amount for 1980
(See instructions—not applicable to operating foundations)

1 Adjusted net income from Part I, line 25(c) . . . .

2 Minimum investment return from Part VIII, line 6 . . . .

3 Enter the larger of line 1 or line 2 . . . .

4 Total of:

   (a) Tax on investment income for 1980 from Part II, line 1 . . . .

   (b) Income tax on unrelated business income for 1980 (Form 990–T) . . . . . .

5 Distributable amount (line 3 minus line 4) . . . .

6 Adjustments to distributable amount (see instructions) . . . .

7 Distributable amount as adjusted (line 5 plus or minus line 6)—also enter in Part XI, line 1 . . . .

Part X Qualifying Distributions in 1980
(See instructions)

1 Amounts paid (including administrative expenses) to accomplish charitable purposes:

   (a) Expenses, contributions, gifts, etc.—total from Part I, column (D), line 24 . . . . | 8,400

   (b) Program-related investments (see instructions) . . . .

2 Amounts paid to acquire assets used (or held for use) directly in carrying out charitable, etc., purposes . . .

3 Amounts set aside for specific projects which are for charitable purposes . . . .

4 Total qualifying distributions made in 1980 (add lines 1, 2, and 3)—also enter in Part XI, line 4 . . . . . . | 8,400

Part XII Private Operating Foundations
(See instructions and Part V, Question 9)

(a) If the foundation has received a ruling or determination letter that it is an operating foundation, and the ruling is effective for 1980, enter the date of the ruling . . . . . ▶
(b) Check box to indicate whether you are an operating foundation described in section ☐ 4942(j)(3) or ☐ 4942(j)(6) (see
instructions).

	Tax year	Prior Three Years			
	(a) 1980	(b) 1979	(c) 1978	(d) 1977	(e) Total
(a) Adjusted net income (from Part I, line 25(c) for 1980. Enter corresponding amount for prior years)	1,176				
(b) 85% of line (a)	1,000				
(c) Qualifying distributions from Part X, line 4 for 1980 (enter corresponding amount for prior years) .	8,400				
(d) Amounts included in (c) not used directly for active conduct of exempt activities	-0-				
(e) Qualifying distributions made directly for active conduct of exempt purposes (line (c) minus line (d)) .	8,400				
Complete the alternative test in (a), (b), or (c) on which the organization relies:					
(a) "Assets" alternative test—enter:					
(1) Value of all assets	118,100				
(2) Value of assets qualifying under section 4942(j)(3)(B)(i) .	98,100				
(b) "Endowment" alternative test— Enter ⅔ of minimum investment return shown in Part VIII, line 6 for 1980 (enter ⅔ of comparable amount for prior years)					
(c) "Support" alternative test—enter:					
(1) Total support other than gross investment income (interest, dividends, rents, payments on securities loans (section 512(a)(5)), or royalties)					
(2) Support from general public and 5 or more exempt organizations as provided in section 4942(j)(3)(B)(iii)					
(3) Largest amount of support from an exempt organization (see instructions)					
(4) Gross investment income . .					

☆ U.S. GOVERNMENT PRINTING OFFICE: 1980—313-057   52-0237640

Form 990–AR

Annual Report
of Private
Foundation

South Plains Museum Association
Name

Under Section 6056 of the Internal Revenue Code

This Annual Report and
the annual return of the foundation
filed on Form 990–PF are available for
public inspection. Consult an
Internal Revenue Service office for
further information.

Department
of the
Treasury
Internal
Revenue
Service

Annual report for calendar year 1980, or fiscal year beginning	, 1980, and ending , 19

Name of organization	Employer identification number
South Plains Museum Association	75 ⋮ 1000000

Address of principal office

1000 - 10th Street, Anytown, Texas   79300

If books and records are not at above address, specify where they are kept	Name of principal officer of foundation
	John Doe, Jr.

Public inspection (see instruction C):

(a) Enter date the notice of availability of annual report appeared in newspaper ▶ May 1, 1981.............

(b) Enter name of newspaper ▶ ....

(c) Check here ▶ ☒ if you have attached a copy of the newspaper notice as required by instruction C. (If the notice is not attached, the report will be considered incomplete.)

Check box for type of annual return ▶ ☒ Form 990–PF ☐ Form 5227	Check this box if your private foundation status terminated under section 507(b)(1)(A) ▶		☐

Revenues

Amount of gifts, grants, bequests, and contributions received for the year	13,300
2 Gross income for the year	5,200
3 Total	18,500

Disbursements and Expenses

4 Disbursements for the year for exempt (charitable) purposes (including administrative expenses)	6,500
Expenses attributable to gross income (item 2 above) for the year	4,924

Foundation Managers

5 List all managers of the foundation (see section 4946(b)):

Name and title	Address where manager may be contacted during normal business hours
John Doe, Jr.	1000 - 10th Street, Anytown, Texas 79300

5a List here any managers of the foundation who have contributed more than 2% of the total contributions received by the foundation before the close of any tax year (but only if they have contributed more than $5,000). (See section 507(d)(2).)

None

5b List here any managers of the foundation who own 10% or more of the stock of a corporation (or an equally large portion of the ownership of a partnership or other entity) of which the foundation has a 10% or greater interest.

None

Balance Sheet Per Books at the Beginning of the Year

Assets			Liabilities	
Cash		30,000	Accounts payable	
Accounts and notes receivable			Contributions, gifts, grants, etc., payable	
Inventories			Bonds and notes payable	
Securities:			Mortgages payable	
Government obligations			Other liabilities	
Corporate bonds			Total liabilities	
Corporate stocks			**Net Worth**	
Mortgage loans			Principal fund	100,000
Real estate . . .	70,000	67,000		11,000
Less: Depreciation .	3,000		Income fund	
Other assets . . .	20,000	14,000		
Less: Depreciation .	6,000		Total net worth	111,000
Total assets		111,000	Total liabilities and net worth	111,000

Itemized Statement of Securities and All Other Assets Held at the Close of the Tax Year

Asset	Book value	Market value

Total . . . . ▶

Appendix C

Income Tax Returns of Public Charities with and without Unrelated Business Taxable Income

Return of Organization Exempt from Income Tax (Form 990)

Organization Exempt under 501(c) (3) (Schedule A, Form 990)

Public Charity without Unrelated Business Taxable Income

South Plains Museum has the same receipts and expenditures as noted in Appendix B for a private operating foundation; however, contributions of $13,300 received during the year, like previous contributions received, were from the general public rather than from one family. Consequently, the museum would qualify as a public charity under 509(a) (1) and 170(b) (1) (A) (vi). It would file Form 990 for the tax year, as is illustrated. (Form 990 need not be completed if gross receipts are normally not more than $10,000 per year.) Expenditures are broken down as fund-raising expenses, those for program services, and those for management in general. Because total receipts less expenditures are less than $25,000, Part V of Form 990 (which requires a balance sheet for the organization) need only be completed as to total assets and total liabilities. (A nonprofit organization normally uses fund accounting. Fund accounting is a procedure under which an organization segregates its assets, its liabilities, and its net worth into separate funds according to externally imposed restrictions on the use of certain assets, similar designations by the organization's governing board, and other amounts that are unrestricted as to use. Each fund is like a separate entity in that it has a self-balancing set of accounts showing assets, liabilities, equity [fund balance], "income," and expenses. Since these funds are actually part of a single entity, they are all included in that organization's own financial statements. Similar accounts in the various funds may or may not be consolidated in those statements according to the organization's preference and practice. The funds are consolidated on Form 990. Recognition of the separate funds and the net changes within the various funds during the year is accomplished by the fund balances sections of the balance sheet [lines 61 through 65]. The fund balance per books for the current unrestricted funds is listed on line 61(a); the endowment and similar funds balance on line 64, and total fund balances on line 65. The beginning of the year figure in Column A, is carried over to the "total" column in Part I, line 18. The end of the year Part V, line 65, is carried over to the "total" column in Part I, line 18. The end-of-the-year figure in Column B, line 65, should agree with the figure on line 20 of the "total" column in Part I.) Schedule A must be completed by a public charity. It requires information as to activities of charitable organizations in order to ascertain whether activities have been undertaken that might destroy its exempt status and also whether the public charity continues to qualify for nonprivate foundation status.

Part IV, Schedule A. An organization under 501(c) (3) must indicate in Part IV the basis of its claim to public charity status. This part must be completed annually by 501(c) (3) organizations to assure the Internal Revenue Service that the organization continues to meet the requirements for public status. South Plains Museum has been in existence since 1977. Assume that it has obtained funds from the general public in the amounts of $16,000, $15,000, and $20,000 for the years 1979, 1978, and 1977, respectively. Total support, including gross receipts and interest income, totals $62,000. Gross receipts are eliminated from both the numerator and the denominator of the fraction to determine if one-third support is from the general public. Line 20, or $53,500, becomes the denominator of the fraction. Support from disqualified persons is included only to the extent of 2 percent of line 20(e). This would be $1,070. Assume that no contributors donated more than this amount. The numerator would be $51,000 (total gifts from line 11), which is more than one-third. South Plains Museum meets the one-third support test and qualifies as a 509(a) (1) organization.

orm **990**
∍partment of the Treasury
∍ternal Revenue Service

Return of Organization Exempt from Income Tax
Under section 501(c) (except black lung benefit trust or private foundation), 501(e) or (f) of the Internal Revenue Code

or the calendar year 1980, or fiscal year beginning _____ , 1980, and ending _____ , 19 ____

Use IRS label. Other-wise, please print or type.	Name of organization South Plains Museum	A Employer identification number (see instructions) 75 : 1000000
	Address (number and street) 1000 - 10th Street	B If exemption application is pending, check here. . . . . ▶
	City or town, State, and ZIP code Anytown, Texas 79300	C If address changed check here. . . ▶

▶ Check applicable box—Exempt under section ▶ ☒ 501(c) (**3**) (insert number), ☐ 501(e) OR ☐ 501(f).

⸚ Is this a group return (see instruction I) filed for affiliates? . . ☐ Yes ☒ No If "Yes" to either, give four-digit group exemption
⸚ Is this a separate return filed by a group affiliate? . . . . . ☐ Yes ☒ No number (GEN) ▶

☐ Check here if gross receipts are normally not more than $10,000 and do not complete the rest of this return (see instruction B(11)).
☐ Check here if gross receipts are normally more than $10,000 and line 12 is $25,000 or less. Complete Parts I, II, IV, and VI and only the indicated items in Parts III and V (see instruction H). If line 12 is more than $25,000, complete the entire return.

ll section 501(c)(3) organizations must also complete Schedule A (Form 990) and attach it to this return.

These columns are optional— see Instructions

Part I Analysis of Revenue, Expenses, and Fund Balances	(A) Total	(B) Restricted/ Nonexpendable	(C) Unrestricted/ Expendable
1 Contributions, gifts, grants, and similar amounts received:			
(a) Directly from the public	13,300		
(b) Through professional fundraisers			
(c) As allotments from fundraising organizations .			
(d) As government grants			
(e) Other			
(f) Total (add lines 1(a) through 1(e)) (attach schedule—see instructions) .	13,300		
2 Membership dues and assessments	4,000		
3 Interest	1,200		
4 Dividends.			
5 (a) Gross rents			
(b) Minus: Rental expenses			
(c) Net rental income (loss)			
6 Royalties			
7 (a) Gross amount received from sale of assets other than inventory			
(b) Minus: Cost or other basis and sales expenses .			
(c) Net gain (loss) (attach schedule)			
8 Special fundraising events and activities (itemize):			

Type of event	Receipts	Expenses		
(a) Total receipts				
(b) Total expenses.				

	(A) Total	(B) Restricted/ Nonexpendable	(C) Unrestricted/ Expendable
(c) Net income (line 8(a) minus line 8(b))			
9 (a) Gross sales minus returns and allowances . .			
(b) Minus: Cost of goods sold (attach schedule) .			
(c) Gross profit (loss)			
10 Program service revenue (from Part II, line (f))			
11 Other revenue (from Part II, line (g))			
12 Total revenue (add lines 1(f), 2, 3, 4, 5(c), 6, 7(c), 8(c), 9(c), 10, and 11) . . .	18,500		
13 Fundraising (from line 40(B))	4,500		
14 Program services (from line 40(C))	6,400		
15 Management and general (from line 40(D))	500		
16 Total expenses (from line 40(A))	11,400		
17 Excess (deficit) for the year (subtract line 16 from line 12)	7,100		
18 Fund balances or net worth at beginning of year (from line 65(A)) . .	111,000		
19 Other changes in fund balances or net worth (attach explanation) . .	-0-		
20 Fund balances or net worth at end of year (add lines 17, 18, and 19) .	118,100		

Left margin labels: Revenue, Expenses, Fund Balances

Form 990 (1980)   Page

Part II Program Service Revenue and Other Revenue (State Nature)	Program service revenue	Other revenue
(a)		
(b)		
(c)		
(d)		
(e)		
(f) Total program service revenue (Enter here and on line 10)		
(g) Total other revenue (Enter here and on line 11)		

Part III Allocation of Expenses by Function

If line 12, Part I is $25,000 or less, you should complete only the line items for columns (A) and (B), Part III. If line 12 is more than $25,000, complete columns (A), (B), (C), and (D).

Do not include amounts reported on line 5(b), 7(b), 8(b), or 9(b) of Part I.	(A) Total	(B) Fundraising	(C) Program services	(D) Management and general
21 Contributions, gifts, grants, and similar amounts awarded (attach schedule) . . .				
22 Benefits paid to or for members				
23 Compensation of officers, directors, and trustees	3,000	1,500	1,000	500
24 Other salaries and wages	2,000	1,000	1,000	
25 Pension plan contributions				
26 Other employee benefits				
27 Payroll taxes				
28 Fees for fundraising				
29 Other professional services				
30 Interest				
31 Occupancy				
32 Rental and maintenance of equipment . . .	500		500	
33 Printing and postage				
34 Telephone				
35 Supplies	500		500	
36 Travel				
37 Other expenses (itemize):				
Insurance	200		200	
Taxes	200		200	
Purchase of Artifacts	2,000		2,000	
38 Total expenses before depreciation (add lines 21 through 37)	8,400	2,500	5,400	500
39 Depreciation, depletion, etc.	3,000	2,000	1,000	
40 Total (add lines 38 and 39). Enter here and on lines 13 through 16	11,400	4,500	6,400	500

Part IV List of Officers, Directors, and Trustees (See Instructions)

(A) Name and address	(B) Title and time spent on position	(C) Compensation	(D) Contributions to employee benefit plans	(E) Expense account and other allowances
John Doe, Jr.	10%	3,000		

art V Balance Sheet If line 12, Part I is $25,000 or less, you should complete only lines 53 and 60 and, if you do not use fund accounting, line 64. If line 12 is more than $25,000, complete the entire balance sheet.

Assets

	(A) Beginning of tax year	(B) End of tax year
Cash:		
(a) Savings and interest-bearing accounts		
(b) Other		
Accounts receivable:		
(a) Beginning receivables ▶ _____ minus allowance for doubtful accounts ▶ _____		
(b) Ending receivables ▶ _____ minus allowance for doubtful accounts ▶ _____		
Notes receivable:		
(a) Beginning receivables ▶ _____ minus allowance for doubtful accounts ▶ _____		
(b) Ending receivables ▶ _____ minus allowance for doubtful accounts ▶ _____		
(c) Loans to officers, directors, and trustees (attach schedule)		
Inventories		
Government obligations:		
(a) U.S. and instrumentalities		
(b) State and its subdivisions		
Investments in corporate bonds, etc. (attach schedule)		
Investments in corporate stocks (attach schedule)		
Mortgage loans (number of loans ▶ _____)		
Other investments (attach schedule)		
Depreciable (depletable) assets (attach schedule):		
(a) Beginning assets ▶ _____ minus accumulated depreciation ▶ _____		
(b) Ending assets ▶ _____ minus accumulated depreciation ▶ _____		
Land		
Other assets (attach schedule)		
Total assets	111,000	118,100
Liabilities		
Accounts payable		
Contributions, gifts, grants, etc., payable		
Bonds and notes payable (attach schedule)		
Mortgages payable		
Loans from officers, directors, and trustees (attach schedule)		
Other liabilities (attach schedule)		
Total liabilities	-0-	

Fund Balances and Net Worth

mplete this section of the balance sheet based on the accounting method you normally use. se check either "Fund Accounting" or "All Others," and give the information requested under box you checked.

Fund Accounting	All Others		
ck here ▶ ☐	Check here ▶ ☐		
Current funds:			
(a) Unrestricted			
(b) Restricted			
Land, buildings, and equipment	Capital stock or trust principal		
Endowment and similar funds	Paid-in or capital surplus		
Other	Retained earnings or accumulated income		
Total fund balances	Total net worth	111,000	118,100
Total liabilities and fund balances or net worth		111,000	118,100

Form 990 (1980)

Pa

Part VI Statements About Activities

Yes

67 Describe each significant program service activity and indicate the total expenses paid or incurred in connection with each:

Expenses

(a) ....

(b) ....

(c) ....

(d) ....

68 Has the organization engaged in any activities not previously reported to the Internal Revenue Service? . . . .
If "Yes," attach a detailed description of the activities.

69 Have any changes been made in the organizing or governing documents, but not reported to IRS? . . . .
If "Yes," attach a conformed copy of the changes.

70 (a) Did the organization have unrelated business gross income of $1,000 or more during the year covered by this return? .
(b) If "Yes," have you filed a tax return on Form 990–T, Exempt Organization Business Income Tax Return, for this year? .
(c) If the organization has gross sales or receipts from business activities not reported on Form 99ᴄ–ˉ attach a statement explaining your reason for not reporting them on Form 990–T.

71 Was there a liquidation, dissolution, termination, or substantial contraction during the year (see instructions)? . . . . .
If "Yes," attach a statement as described in the instructions.

72 Is the organization related (other than by association with a statewide or nationwide organization) through common membership, governing bodies, trustees, officers, etc., to any other exempt or nonexempt organization (see instructions)? . . . .
If "Yes," enter the name of organization ▶ ....
.... and check whether it is ☐ exempt OR ☐ nonexempt.

73 (a) Enter any political expenditures, direct or indirect, as described in the instructions . . . . . |
(b) Did you file Form 1120–POL, U.S. Income Tax Return of Certain Political Organizations, for this year? . . . . . .

74 Did your organization receive donated services or the use of facilities or equipment at no charge or at substantially less than fair rental value? . . . .
If "Yes," you may, if you choose, indicate the value of these items here. Do not include this amount elsewhere on this return . . . . ▶ |

The following statements should be completed ONLY for the organizations indicated.

75 Section 501(c)(5) or (6) organizations.—Did the organization spend any amounts in an attempt to influence public opinion about legislative matters or referendums (see instructions and Regulations section 1.162–20(c))? . . . .
If "Yes," enter the total amount spent for this purpose . . . . |

76 Section 501(c)(7) organizations.—Enter amount of:
(a) Initiation fees and capital contributions included on line 12 . . . . |
(b) Gross receipts, included in line 12, for public use of club facilities (see instructions) . . . . |
(c) Does the club's governing instrument or any written policy statement provide for discrimination against any person because of race, color, or religion? . . . .

77 Section 501(c)(12) organizations.—Enter amount of:
(a) Gross income received from members or shareholders . . . . |
(b) Gross income received from other sources (do not net amounts due or paid to other sources against amounts due or received from them) . . . . |

78 Public interest law firms.—Attach information described in instructions.

79 The books are in care of ▶ .... Telephone No. ▶ ....
Located at ▶

Please Sign Here
Under penalties of perjury, I declare that I have examined this return, including accompanying schedules and statements, and to the best of my knowledge and it is true, correct, and complete. Declaration of preparer (other than taxpayer) is based on all information of which preparer has any knowledge.

▶ _____ Signature of officer _____ Date ┃▌Title

Paid Preparer's Use Only
Preparer's signature and date ▶
Firm's name (or yours, if self-employed) and address ▶
Check if self-employed ▶ ☐
ZIP code ▶

☆U.S. GOVERNMENT PRINTING OFFICE: 1980-313-050 E.I. 43-0787287

SCHEDULE A
(Form 990)
Department of the Treasury
Internal Revenue Service

Organization Exempt Under 501(c)(3)

(Except Private Foundation) Supplementary Information
► Attach to Form 990.

Name	Employer identification number
South Plains Museum	75 ⋮ 1000000

Part I — Compensation of Five Highest Paid Employees
(Other than Officers, Directors, and Trustees—see specific instructions)

Name and address of employees paid more than $30,000	Title and time devoted to position	Compensation	Contributions to employee benefit plans	Expense account and other allowances
None				

Total number of other employees paid over $30,000 ►

Part II — Compensation of Five Highest Paid Persons for Professional Services
(See specific instructions)

Name and address of persons paid more than $30,000	Type of service	Compensation
None		

Total number of others receiving over $30,000 for professional services . . . . ►

Part III — Statements About Activities

	Yes	No
During the year have you attempted to influence national, State or local legislation, including any attempt to influence public opinion on a legislative matter or referendum?		X

If "Yes," enter the total of the expenses paid or incurred in connection with the legislative activities $..................
Complete Part VI of this form for organizations that made an election under section 501(h) on Form 5768 or other statement. For other organizations checking "Yes," attach a statement giving a detailed description of the legislative activities and a classified schedule of the expenses paid or incurred.

During the year have you, either directly or indirectly, engaged in any of the following acts with a trustee, director, principal officer or creator of your organization, or any organization or corporation with which such person is affiliated as an officer, director, trustee, majority owner or principal beneficiary:

	Yes	No
(a) Sale, exchange, or leasing of property?		X
(b) Lending of money or other extension of credit?		X
(c) Furnishing of goods, services, or facilities?		X
(d) Payment of compensation (or payment or reimbursement of expenses if more than $1,000)?		X
(e) Transfer of any part of your income or assets?		X

If the answer to any question is "Yes," attach a detailed statement explaining the transactions.

Attach a statement explaining how you determine that individuals or organizations receiving disbursements from you in furtherance of your exempt programs qualify to receive payments. (See specific instructions.)

	Yes	No
Do you make grants for scholarships, fellowships, student loans, etc.?		X

313–052–1

Schedule A (Form 990) 1980

Page

Part IV Reason for Non-Private Foundation Status (See instructions for definitions)

The organization is not a private foundation because it is (check applicable box; please check only ONE box):

1 ☐ A church. Section 170(b)(1)(A)(i).

2 ☐ A school. Section 170(b)(1)(A)(ii). (Also complete Part V, page 3.)

3 ☐ A hospital. Section 170(b)(1)(A)(iii).

4 ☐ A governmental unit. Section 170(b)(1)(A)(v).

5 ☐ A medical research organization operated in conjunction with a hospital. Section 170(b)(1)(A)(iii). Enter name and address

hospital ▶ ....

....

6 ☐ An organization operated for the benefit of a college or university owned or operated by a governmental unit. Section 170(b)(1)(A)(i (Also complete Support Schedule.)

7 ☒ An organization that normally receives a substantial part of its support from a governmental unit or from the general public. Sect 170(b)(1)(A)(vi). (Also complete Support Schedule.)

8 ☐ An organization that normally receives: (a) no more than ⅓ of its support from gross investment income and unrelated busin taxable income (less section 511 tax) from businesses acquired by the organization after June 30, 1975, and (b) more than ⅓ of support from contributions, membership fees, and gross receipts from activities related to its exempt functions—subject to cert exceptions. Section 509(a)(2). (Use cash receipts and disbursements method of accounting; also complete Support Schedule.)

9 ☐ An organization that is not controlled by any disqualified persons (other than foundation managers) and supports organizatic described in (1) boxes 1 through 8 above or (2) sections 501(c)(4), (5), or (6) if they meet the test of section 509(a)(2). Sect 509(a)(3).

Provide the following information about the supported organizations. (See instructions for Part IV, box 9.)

(a) Name of supported organizations	(b) Box numbe from above

(c) Relationship of supported organizations to your organization:

    (1) Check here ▶ ☐ if the supported organizations appoint a majority of your governing board.

    (2) Check here ▶ ☐ if a majority of your governing board belong to governing boards of the supported organizations.

    (3) Check here ▶ ☐ if (1) or (2) above does not apply. (See Regulations 1.509(a)-4.)

(d) If applicable, enter the number of supported organizations exempt under:

    (1) Section 501(c)(4) . . . .

    (2) Section 501(c)(5) . . . .

    (3) Section 501(c)(6) . . . .

(e) Check here ▶ ☐ if your organization's main function is to provide funds to the supported organizations.

10 ☐ An organization organized and operated to test for public safety. Section 509(a)(4). (See specific instructions.)

Support Schedule (Complete only if you checked box 6, 7, or 8 above)

Calendar year (or fiscal year beginning in) ▶	(a) 1979	(b) 1978	(c) 1977	(d) 1976	(e) Total
11 Gifts, grants, and contributions received. (Do not include unusual grants. See line 24 below.) . . .	16,000	15,000	20,000		51,000
12 Membership fees received . . .					
13 Gross receipts from admissions, merchandise sold or services performed, or furnishing of facilities in any activity that is not a business unrelated to the organization's exempt purpose	3,500	3,000	2,000		8,500
14 Gross income from interest, dividends, amounts received from payments on securities loans (section 512(a)(5)), rents, royalties, and unrelated business taxable income (less section 511 taxes) from businesses acquired by the organization after June 30, 1975	1,000	1,000	500		2,500
15 Net income from unrelated business activities not included in line 14 . .					

313-052-3

art IV   Support Schedule (continued) (Complete only if you checked box 6, 7, or 8 on page 2)

Calendar year (or fiscal year beginning in) ▶	(a) 1979	(b) 1978	(c) 1977	(d) 1976	(e) Total
Tax revenues levied for your benefit and either paid to you or expended on your behalf					
The value of services or facilities furnished to you by a governmental unit without charge. Do not include the value of services or facilities generally furnished to the public without charge					
Other income. Attach schedule. Do not include gain (or loss) from sale of capital assets					
Total of lines 11 through 18 . . .	20,500	19,000	22,500		62,000
Line 19 minus line 13	17,000	16,000	20,500		53,500
Enter 1% of line 19	205	190	225		

Organizations described in box 6 or 7, page 2:

(a) Enter 2% of amount in column (e), line 20   1,070

(b) Attach a list showing the name of and amount contributed by each person (other than a governmental unit or publicly supported organization) whose total gifts for 1976 through 1979 exceeded the amount shown in 22(a). Enter the sum of all excess amounts here . . . .   -0-

Organizations described in box 8, page 2:

(a) Attach a list, for amounts shown on lines 11, 12, and 13, showing the name of, and total amounts received in each year from each "disqualified person," and enter the sum of such amounts for each year:

(1979)......................................   (1978)....................................   (1977)............. ....   (1976)...............................

(b) Attach a list showing, for 1976 through 1979, the name and amount included in line 13 for each person (other than "disqualified persons") from whom the organization received more, during that year, than the larger of: the amount on line 21 for the year or $5,000. Include organizations described in boxes 1 through 7 as well as individuals. Enter the sum of these excess amounts for each year:

(1979)   (1978)   (1977)   (1976)

For an organization described in boxes 6, 7, or 8, page 2, that received any unusual grants during 1976 through 1979, attach a list for each year showing the name of the contributor, the date and amount of the grant, and a brief description of the nature of the grant. Do not include these grants in line 11 above. (See specific instructions.)

art V   Private School Questionnaire
            To Be Completed ONLY by Schools that Checked Box 2 in Part IV

	Yes	No
Do you have a racially nondiscriminatory policy toward students by statement in your charter, bylaws, other governing instrument, or in a resolution of your governing body?		
Do you include a statement of your racially nondiscriminatory policy toward students in all your brochures, catalogues, and other written communications with the public dealing with student admissions, programs, and scholarships?		
Have you publicized your racially nondiscriminatory policy by newspaper or broadcast media during the period of solicitation for students or during the registration period if you have no solicitation program, in a way that makes the policy known to all parts of the general community you serve?		
If "Yes," please describe; if "No," please explain. (If you need more space, attach a separate statement.)		
Do you maintain the following:		
(a) Records indicating the racial composition of the student body, faculty, and administrative staff?		
(b) Records documenting that scholarships and other financial assistance are awarded on a racially nondiscriminatory basis? (See instructions.)		
(c) Copies of all catalogues, brochures, announcements, and other written communications to the public dealing with student admissions, programs, and scholarships?		
(d) Copies of all material used by you or on your behalf to solicit contributions?		
If you answered "No," to any of the above, please explain. (If you need more space, attach a separate statement.)		

Appendix D

Income Tax Return of a Private Operating Foundation with Unrelated Business Taxable Income

Return of Organization Exempt from Income Tax
(Form 990)
Exempt Organization Business Income Tax Return (Form
990-T), with Schedule of Depreciation

Public Charity with Unrelated Business Taxable Income

Assume the same facts as in Appendix C, but assume that South Plains Museum received rents of $30,000 during 1980 from land it purchased on January 4, 1980, for $100,000; rents of $20,000 from the equipment and from part of the building. The land was not used to further the exempt purposes of the museum. It was purchased by a down payment in cash of $25,000 and by execution of a mortgage in the amount of $75,000. Expenses incurred on the land totaled $11,500. The equipment and part of the building were rented for $20,000, $5,000 of which was for the equipment. Expenses incurred to produce the rent were $4,000, $1,200 of which was on the equipment.

Because the land is debt-financed property (it is not being used in carrying out the exempt purposes of the museum and is subject to acquisition indebtedness), the museum must pay tax on a portion of the net income received from the property. In addition, rent on the equipment (personal property) exceeds 10 percent of total rent on the equipment and building; consequently, rent from the equipment becomes unrelated taxable income. South Plains Museum must file Form 990-T and pay tax on its unrelated business taxable income.

Debt-financed income is computed on Schedule E, part 3, of Form 990-T. Land is not depreciable property; however, if it were a building, only straight-line depreciation could be used. In determining debt-financed income, a percentage is applied to both the income and the expenses from the equipment, computed as follows:

$$\frac{\text{Average acquisition indebtedness for the year}}{\text{Average amount of adjusted basis of property for period held}} = \text{Percentage}$$

The average acquisition indebtedness is $75,000 because nothing was paid on the principal of the debt in 1980. The average adjusted basis of the land is $100,000 because the property is not subject to depreciation. The debt/basis percentage, then, is 75 percent.

Assuming that $1,000 of the foundation manager's salary is used to collect rents and depreciation on the equipment is $2,000, unrelated business taxable income would be $14,675. The museum would deduct $1,000 to arrive at taxable income of $13,675. Because the museum is incorporated, this income is taxed at 17 percent (tax rate for 1980), for total tax of $2,325.

When Form 990 is prepared for South Plains Museum, gross rents of $50,000 [$30,000 for the land and $20,000 for the building and equipment are entered on line 5(a)]. Expenses in connection with the rental property total $20,825 ($11,500 on the land, $4,000 for the building and equipment, $2,000 depreciation, $1,000 salary, and $2,325 in taxes).

A balance sheet must now be prepared, as line 12 of Part I exceeds $25,000. Refer to Appendix A for a determination of ending cash balance before purchase of land and receipt of rental income. Ending cash balance in Appendix A (see Form 990-PF) was $20,100. This amount will be increased $9,500 [$34,500 net increase from net rentals ($50,000 rentals less $15,500 expenses) less a $25,000 down payment on the land.] Land will be increased $100,000. Liabilities will total $77,325, representing the tax liability of $2,325 and the $75,000 mortgage on the land. Net worth will increase $39,275, representing the excess of revenue over expenses from line 17, part 1, of Form 990. (Total expenses on line 16 will have decreased $3,000 over the amount entered on line 16 in Appendix B. This decrease represents $1,000 of the manager's salary and $2,000 depreciation which were deducted on Form 990-T.) Total net worth of $150,275 plus total liabilities of $77,325 equals total assets of $227,600.

Form **990**
Department of the Treasury
Internal Revenue Service

Return of Organization Exempt from Income Tax
Under section 501(c) (except black lung benefit trust or private foundation), 501(e) or (f) of the Internal Revenue Code

For the calendar year 1980, or fiscal year beginning _____ , 1980, and ending _____ , 19____

Use IRS label. Other-wise, please print or type.	**Name of organization** South Plains Museum Association
	Address (number and street) 1000 - 10th Street
	City or town, State, and ZIP code Anytown, Texas 79300

A Employer identification number (see instructions)
75 ⋮ 1000000

B If exemption application is pending, check here . . . . ▶

C If address changed check here . . . ▶

D Check applicable box—Exempt under section ▶ [X] 501(c) (**3**) (insert number), ☐ 501(e) OR ☐ 501(f).

E Is this a group return (see instruction I) filed for affiliates? . . ☐ Yes [X] No   If "Yes" to either, give four-digit group exemptio
Is this a separate return filed by a group affiliate? . . . . . . ☐ Yes [X] No   number (GEN) ▶

☐ Check here if gross receipts are normally not more than $10,000 and do not complete the rest of this return (see instruction B(11)).
☐ Check here if gross receipts are normally more than $10,000 and line 12 is $25,000 or less. Complete Parts I, II, IV, and VI and only the indicated items in Parts II
and V (see instruction H). If line 12 is more than $25,000, complete the entire return.

All section 501(c)(3) organizations must also complete Schedule A (Form 990) and attach it to this return.

These columns are optional—see instructions

			(A) Total	(B) Restricted/ Nonexpendable	(C) Unrestricted/ Expendable
Part I	**Analysis of Revenue, Expenses, and Fund Balances**				
	1 Contributions, gifts, grants, and similar amounts received:				
	(a) Directly from the public	13,300			
	(b) Through professional fundraisers				
	(c) As allotments from fundraising organizations .				
	(d) As government grants				
	(e) Other				
	(f) Total (add lines 1(a) through 1(e)) (attach schedule—see instructions) .		13,300		
	2 Membership dues and assessments		4,000		
	3 Interest		1,200		
	4 Dividends.				
	5 (a) Gross rents	50,000			
	(b) Minus: Rental expenses	20,825			
	(c) Net rental income (loss).		29,175		
	6 Royalties				
	7 (a) Gross amount received from sale of assets other than inventory				
	(b) Minus: Cost or other basis and sales expenses .				
	(c) Net gain (loss) (attach schedule)				
	8 Special fundraising events and activities (itemize):				

Type of event	Receipts	Expenses			
(a) Total receipts					
(b) Total expenses					
(c) Net income (line 8(a) minus line 8(b))				
9 (a) Gross sales minus returns and allowances . .				
(b) Minus: Cost of goods sold (attach schedule) .				
(c) Gross profit (loss)				
10 Program service revenue (from Part II, line (f))				
11 Other revenue (from Part II, line (g))				
12 Total revenue (add lines 1(f), 2, 3, 4, 5(c), 6, 7(c), 8(c), 9(c), 10, and 11) . . .	47,675		

Expenses	13 Fundraising (from line 40(B))	2,000
	14 Program services (from line 40(C))	5,900
	15 Management and general (from line 40(D))	500
	16 Total expenses (from line 40(A))	8,400
Fund Balances	17 Excess (deficit) for the year (subtract line 16 from line 12)	39,275
	18 Fund balances or net worth at beginning of year (from line 65(A)) . .	111,000
	19 Other changes in fund balances or net worth (attach explanation) . .	
	20 Fund balances or net worth at end of year (add lines 17, 18, and 19) .	150,275

art II Program Service Revenue and Other Revenue (State Nature)	Program service revenue	Other revenue
Total program service revenue (Enter here and on line 10)		
Total other revenue (Enter here and on line 11)		

art III Allocation of Expenses by Function

If line 12, Part I is $25,000 or less, you should complete only the line items for columns (A) and (B), Part III. If line 12 is more than $25,000, complete columns (A), (B), (C), and (D).

Do not include amounts reported on line 5(b), 7(b), 8(b), or 9(b) of Part I.	(A) Total	(B) Fundraising	(C) Program services	(D) Management and general
21 Contributions, gifts, grants, and similar amounts awarded (attach schedule) . . .				
22 Benefits paid to or for members				
23 Compensation of officers, directors, and trustees	2,000	1,000	500	500
24 Other salaries and wages	2,000	1,000	1,000	
25 Pension plan contributions				
26 Other employee benefits				
27 Payroll taxes				
28 Fees for fundraising				
29 Other professional services				
30 Interest				
31 Occupancy				
32 Rental and maintenance of equipment . . .	500		500	
33 Printing and postage				
34 Telephone				
35 Supplies				
36 Travel	500		500	
37 Other expenses (itemize):				
Insurance	200		200	
Taxes	200		200	
Purchase of Artifacts	2,000		2,000	
38 Total expenses before depreciation (add lines 21 through 37)	7,400	2,000	4,900	500
39 Depreciation, depletion, etc.	1,000		1,000	
40 Total (add lines 38 and 39). Enter here and on lines 13 through 16.	8,400	2,000	5,900	500

art IV List of Officers, Directors, and Trustees (See Instructions)

(A) Name and address	(B) Title and time spent on position	(C) Compensation	(D) Contributions to employee benefit plans	(E) Expense account and other allowances

Form 990 (1980)   Page

Part V Balance Sheet | If line 12, Part I is $25,000 or less, you should complete only lines 53 and 60 and, if you do not use fu accounting, line 64. If line 12 is more than $25,000, complete the entire balance sheet.

Assets	(A) Beginning of tax year	(B) End of tax year
41 Cash:		
(a) Savings and interest-bearing accounts	20,000	20,000
(b) Other	10,000	29,600
42 Accounts receivable:		
(a) Beginning receivables ▶................... minus allowance for doubtful accounts ▶..............		
(b) Ending receivables ▶................... minus allowance for doubtful accounts ▶..............		
43 Notes receivable:		
(a) Beginning receivables ▶................... minus allowance for doubtful accounts ▶..............		
(b) Ending receivables ▶................... minus allowance for doubtful accounts ▶..............		
(c) Loans to officers, directors, and trustees (attach schedule)................		
44 Inventories		
45 Government obligations:		
(a) U.S. and instrumentalities		
(b) State and its subdivisions		
46 Investments in corporate bonds, etc. (attach schedule)		
47 Investments in corporate stocks (attach schedule)		
48 Mortgage loans (number of loans ▶..................)		
49 Other investments (attach schedule)		
50 Depreciable (depletable) assets (attach schedule):		
(a) Beginning assets ▶......60,000...... minus accumulated depreciation ▶....9,000.....	51,000	
(b) Ending assets ▶......60,000...... minus accumulated depreciation ▶...12,000.....		48,000
51 Land	30,000	130,000
52 Other assets (attach schedule)		
53 Total assets . . . . ▶	111,000	227,600
Liabilities		
54 Accounts payable		2,325
55 Contributions, gifts, grants, etc., payable		
56 Bonds and notes payable (attach schedule)		
57 Mortgages payable		75,000
58 Loans from officers, directors, and trustees (attach schedule)		
59 Other liabilities (attach schedule)		
60 Total liabilities	-0-	77,325

Fund Balances and Net Worth

Complete this section of the balance sheet based on the accounting method you normally use. Please check either "Fund Accounting" or "All Others," and give the information requested under the box you checked.

Fund Accounting		All Others			
Check here . . . . ▶ ☐		Check here . . . . ▶ ☐			
61 Current funds:					
(a) Unrestricted	. . . .			100,000	100,000
(b) Restricted	. . . .				
62 Land, buildings, and equipment	Capital stock or trust principal				
63 Endowment and similar funds	Paid-in or capital surplus				
64 Other	Retained earnings or accumulated income .			11,000	50,275
65 Total fund balances	Total net worth			111,000	150,275
66 Total liabilities and fund balances or net worth				111,000	227,600

Part VI   Statements About Activities | Yes | No

Describe each significant program service activity and indicate the total expenses paid or incurred in connection with each: | **Expenses**

a) .... | ------------

b) .... | ------------

c) .... | ------------

d) ....

Has the organization engaged in any activities not previously reported to the Internal Revenue Service? . . . . . | | X
If "Yes," attach a detailed description of the activities.

Have any changes been made in the organizing or governing documents, but not reported to IRS? . . . . | | X
If "Yes," attach a conformed copy of the changes.

a) Did the organization have unrelated business gross income of $1,000 or more during the year covered by this return? . | X |

b) If "Yes," have you filed a tax return on Form 990–T, Exempt Organization Business Income Tax Return, for this year? . | X |

c) If the organization has gross sales or receipts from business activities not reported on Form 990–T, attach a statement explaining your reason for not reporting them on Form 990–T.

Was there a liquidation, dissolution, termination, or substantial contraction during the year (see instructions)? . . . . . | | X
If "Yes," attach a statement as described in the instructions.

Is the organization related (other than by association with a statewide or nationwide organization) through common membership, governing bodies, trustees, officers, etc., to any other exempt or nonexempt organization (see instructions)? . . . . | | X
If "Yes," enter the name of organization ▶... and check whether it is ☐ exempt OR ☐ nonexempt.

a) Enter any political expenditures, direct or indirect, as described in the instructions . . . . . |

b) Did you file Form 1120–POL, U.S. Income Tax Return of Certain Political Organizations, for this year? . . . . . .

Did your organization receive donated services or the use of facilities or equipment at no charge or at substantially less than fair rental value? . . . . | | X
If "Yes," you may, if you choose, indicate the value of these items here. Do not include this amount elsewhere on this return . . . . ▶ |

Following statements should be completed ONLY for the organizations indicated.

Section 501(c)(5) or (6) organizations.—Did the organization spend any amounts in an attempt to influence public opinion about legislative matters or referendums (see instructions and Regulations section 1.162–20(c))? . . . .
If "Yes," enter the total amount spent for this purpose . . . . |

Section 501(c)(7) organizations.—Enter amount of:

a) Initiation fees and capital contributions included on line 12 . . . . |

b) Gross receipts, included in line 12, for public use of club facilities (see instructions) . . . . . |

c) Does the club's governing instrument or any written policy statement provide for discrimination against any person because of race, color, or religion? . . . . |

Section 501(c)(12) organizations.—Enter amount of:

a) Gross income received from members or shareholders . . . . |

b) Gross income received from other sources (do not net amounts due or paid to other sources against amounts due or received from them) . . . . |

Public interest law firms.—Attach information described in instructions.

The books are in care of ▶... Telephone No. ▶...
Located at ▶

Under penalties of perjury, I declare that I have examined this return, including accompanying schedules and statements, and to the best of my knowledge and belief it is true, correct, and complete. Declaration of preparer (other than taxpayer) is based on all information of which preparer has any knowledge.

▶
Signature of officer | Date | ▶ Title

Preparer's signature and date ▶

Preparer's Only

Firm's name (or yours, if self-employed) and address ▶ | Check if self-employed ▶ ☐
| ZIP code ▶

Form 990-T

Department of the Treasury
Internal Revenue Service

Exempt Organization Business Income Tax Return (Under Section 511 of the Internal Revenue Code)

For calendar year 1980 or fiscal year beginning_____
1980, and ending_____ , 19

Name of organization	A Employer identification number (emplo trust see instruction for Block A)
South Plains Museum Association	75 ¦ 1000000
Address (number and street)	
1000 - 10th Street	B Enter unrelated business act codes from page 8 of instructions
City or town, State, and ZIP code	
Anytown, Texas 79300	

C Check box if address changed . . . . ▶ ☐   D Exempt under section . . . . . . ▶ 501 (c)(3

E Check applicable box . . . . ▶ ☒ Corporation ☐ Trust   F Group exemption number (see instructions for Block F) ▶

Complete page 1, Schedule K on page 2, and sign the return if the unrelated trade or business gross income is $10,000 or less.
Complete all applicable parts of the form (except lines 1 through 5) if unrelated trade or business gross income is over $10,000.

Unrelated Business Taxable Income Computation—When Unrelated Trade or Business Gross Income is $10,000 or ▮

1 Unrelated trade or business gross income. (State sources _____)	1	
2 Minus deductions	2	
3 Unrelated business taxable income before specific deduction	3	
4 Minus specific deduction (see instructions for line 32)	4	
5 Unrelated business taxable income	5	

Tax Computation

Organizations Taxable as Corporations (See Instructions for Tax Computation)

6 (a) Are you a member of a controlled group? . . . . ☐ Yes . . . . ☐ No

   (b) If "Yes," see instructions and enter your share of the $25,000 amount in each taxable income bracket:

     (i) $_____ (ii) $_____ (iii) $_____ (iv) $_____

7 Income tax on amount on line 5 above, or line 33, page 2, whichever applies. Check here ▶ ☐ if alternative tax from Schedule D (Form 1120) is used . . . . | **7** | 2,325

Trusts Taxable at Trust Rates (See Instructions for Tax Computation) Section 401(a) trust, check here ▶ ☐

8 Enter the tax from the tax rate schedule in instructions on amount on line 5 above, or line 33 on page 2, whichever applies . | **8** |

Total Income Tax

9 (a) Foreign tax credit (corporations attach Form 1118, trusts attach Form 1116)	9(a)		
(b) Investment credit (attach Form 3468)	9(b)		
(c) Work incentive (WIN) credit (attach Form 4874)	9(c)		
(d) Other credits (see instructions)	9(d)		
10 Total (add lines 9(a) through (d))		10	
11 Subtract line 10 from line 7 or line 8		11	2,325
12 Increase in tax from refiguring an earlier year investment credit (attach Form 4255)		12	
13 Minimum tax on tax preference items (see instructions for line 13)		13	
14 Alternative minimum tax (see instructions for line 14)		14	
15 Total tax (add lines 11 through 14)		15	2,325
16 Credits and payments: (a) Tax deposited with Form 7004	16(a)		
(b) Tax deposited with Form 7005 (attach copy)	16(b)		
(c) Foreign organizations—Tax paid or withheld at the source (see instructions) .	16(c)		
(d) Credit from regulated investment companies (attach Form 2439)	16(d)		
(e) Federal tax on special fuels and oils (attach Form 4136)	16(e)		
(f) Other payments and credits (see instructions)	16(f)		
(g) Total credits and payments (add lines 16(a) through 16(f))		16(g)	
17 TAX DUE (Subtract line 16(g) from line 15). See instructions for depository method of payment ▶		17	2,325
18 If line 16(g) is more than line 15, enter OVERPAYMENT . . . . ▶		18	

Statements Regarding Certain Activities

	Yes
1 At any time during the tax year, did you have an interest in or a signature or other authority over a bank account, securities account, or other financial account in a foreign country (see instructions)?	
2 Were you the grantor of or transferor to a foreign trust which existed during the current tax year, whether or not you have any beneficial interest in it? . If "Yes," you may have to file Forms 3520, 3520–A or 926.	

Please Sign Here

Under penalties of perjury, I declare that I have examined this return, including accompanying schedules and statements and to the best of knowledge and belief, it is true, correct, and complete. Declaration of preparer (other than taxpayer) is based on all information of which prep has any knowledge.

_____   _____   _____
Signature of officer   Date   Title

Paid Preparer's Use Only

Preparer's signature and date ▶		Check if self-employed ▶ ☐	Preparer's social security
Firm's name (or yours, if self-employed) ▶ and address		E.I. No. ▶	
		ZIP code ▶	

Unrelated Business Taxable Income Computation

Unrelated Trade or Business Income

Gross receipts or gross sales ...., minus returns and allowances........................ Balance ►	1		
Minus: Cost of goods sold (Schedule A) and operations (attach schedule)	2		
Gross profit	3		
(a) Capital gain net income (attach separate Schedule D)	4(a)		
(b) Net gain or (loss) from Part II, Form 4797 (attached)	4(b)		
(c) Capital loss deduction for trusts	4(c)		
Income or (loss) from partnerships (attach statement)	5		
Rent income (Schedule C)	6	3,800	00
Unrelated debt-financed income (Schedule E, line 2)	7	13,875	00
Investment income of a section 501(c)(7) or (9) organization (Schedule F)	8		
Interest, annuities, royalties, and rents from controlled organizations (Schedule G)	9		
Exploited exempt activity income (Schedule H)	10		
Advertising income (Schedule I, Part III, Column A)	11		
Other income (see instructions for line 12—attach schedule)	12		
TOTAL unrelated trade or business income (add lines 3 through 12)	13	17,675	00

Deductions Not Taken Elsewhere

(Except for contributions, deductions must be directly connected with the unrelated business income)

Compensation of officers, directors and trustees (Schedule J)	14	1,000	00
Salaries and wages ...., minus WIN credit .... Balance ►	15		
Repairs (see instructions)	16		
Bad debts (see instructions)	17		
Interest (attach schedule)	18		
Taxes	19		
Contributions (see instructions for line 20)	20		
Depreciation (attach Form 4562)	21	2,000	00
Amortization (attach schedule)	22		
Depletion	23		
(a) Contributions to deferred compensation plans (see instructions for line 24(a))	24(a)		
(b) Employee benefit programs (see instructions for line 24(b))	24(b)		
Other deductions (attach schedule)	25		
TOTAL deductions (add lines 14 through 25)	26	3,000	00
Unrelated business taxable income before allowable advertising loss (subtract line 26 from line 13) . . .	27	14,675	00
Minus: Advertising loss (Schedule I, Part III, Column B)	28		
Unrelated business taxable income before net operating loss deduction (subtract line 28 from line 27) . .	29		
Minus: Net operating loss deduction (see instructions for line 30)	30		
Unrelated business taxable income before specific deduction (subtract line 30 from line 29)	31	14,675	00
Minus: Specific deduction (see instructions for line 32)	32	1,000	00
Unrelated business taxable income (subtract line 32 from line 31)	33	13,675	00

Schedule A—COST OF GOODS SOLD (See Instructions for Line 2 above)		Schedule K—RECORD OF FEDERAL TAX DEPOSIT FORMS 503 (List deposits in order of date made—See Instruction for line 17, page 1)	
Method of inventory valuation (specify) ►		Date of deposit	Amount
Inventory at beginning of year			
Merchandise bought for manufacture or sale . . .			
Salaries and wages			
Other costs (attach schedule)			
TOTAL			
Minus inventory at end of year			
Cost of goods sold (enter here and on line 2, above) .			

Books are in care of ►   John Doe, Jr.   Telephone number ►   806-742-2000

Form **4562**
Department of the Treasury
Internal Revenue Service

Depreciation
▶ See instructions on back.
▶ Attach this form to your return.

Name(s) as shown on return	Identifying number
South Plains Museum Association	75-1000000

For grouping assets, see instructions for line 3.

a. Description of property	b. Date acquired	c. Cost or other basis	d. Depreciation allowed or allowable in earlier years	e. Method of figuring depreciation	f. Life or rate	g. Depreciation for this year
1 Total additional first-year depreciation. See instructions for limitation. ───────▶						
2 Class Life Asset Depreciation Range (CLADR) System depreciation from Form 4832 . .						
3 Other depreciation: Buildings						
Furniture and fixtures . . .						
Transportation equipment . .						
Machinery and other equipment .	1977	20,000	6,000	SL	10%	2,000
Other (Specify)						
4 a Totals (add amounts in columns c and g) .		20,000				2,000
b Total current year acquisitions (included in line 4a, column c)						

Individual and partnership filers enter the totals from line 4a on the corresponding lines of their regular depreciation schedule. Other filers should attach Form 4562 to their return and enter line 4a, column g, on the depreciation expense line in the "Deductions" section of their return.

Schedule C—RENT INCOME FROM REAL PROPERTY AND PERSONAL PROPERTY LEASED WITH REAL PROPERTY
(See Instructions for line 6 of page 2)

1. Description of property	2. Rent received or accrued	3. Percentage of rent for personal property
Building and Equipment	20,000	25 %
		%
		%
		%
		%

4. Complete for any item if the entry in column 3 is more than 50%, or if the rent is based on profit or income		5. Complete for any item if the entry in column 3 is more than 10% but not more than 50%		
(a) Deductions directly connected (Attach schedule)	(b) Income includible (Column 2 minus column 4(a))	(a) Gross income reportable (Column 2 × column 3)	(b) Deductions directly connected with personal property (Attach schedule)	(c) Income includible (Column 5(a) minus column 5(b))
5,000		1,200		3,800

Add columns 4(b) and 5(c) and enter total here and on line 6, page 2 . . . . | **3,800**

Schedule E—UNRELATED DEBT-FINANCED INCOME. (See Instructions for line 7 of page 2)

1. Description of debt-financed property	2. Gross income from or allocable to debt financed property	3. Deductions directly connected with or allocable to debt-financed property	
		(a) Straight line depreciation (Attach schedule)	(b) Other deductions (Attach schedule)
1. Land	30,000	-0-	11,500

4. Amount of average acquisition indebtedness on or allocable to debt financed property (Attach schedule)	5. Average adjusted basis of or allocable to debt financed property (Attach schedule)	6. Percentage which column 4 is of column 5	7. Gross income reportable (Column 2 × column 6)	8. Allocable deductions (Total of columns 3(a) and 3(b) × column 6)	9. Net income or (loss) includible (Column 7 minus column 8)
75,000	100,000	75 %	22,500	8,625	13,875
		%			
		%			
		%			

2 Total (enter here and on line 7, page 2) . . . .
3 Total dividends-received deductions included in column 8 . . . . | **13,875**

Schedule F—INVESTMENT INCOME OF A SECTION 501(c)(7) OR (9) ORGANIZATION (See Instructions for Line 8 of Page 2)

(a) Description	(b) Amount	(c) Deductions directly connected (Attach schedule)	(d) Net investment income (Column (b) minus column (c))	(e) Set-asides (Attach schedule)	(f) Balance of investment income (Column (d) minus column (e))

Total (enter here and on line 8, page 2) . . . .

Schedule G—INCOME (ANNUITIES, INTEREST, RENTS AND ROYALTIES) FROM CONTROLLED ORGANIZATIONS
(See Instructions for Line 9 of Page 2)

1. Name and address of controlled organization(s)	2. Gross income from controlled organization(s)	3. Deductions of controlling organization directly connected with column 2 income (Attach schedule)	4. Exempt controlled organizations		
			(a) Unrelated business taxable income	(b) Taxable income computed as though not exempt under section 501(a) or the amount in column (a), whichever is more	(c) Percentage column (a) is of column (b)
					%
					%
					%

5. Nonexempt controlled organizations			6. Gross income reportable (Column 2 × column 4(c) or column 5(c))	7. Allowable deductions (Column 3 × column 4(c) or column 5(c))	8. Net income includible (Column 6 minus column 7)
(a) Excess taxable income	(b) Taxable income or amount in column (a), whichever is more	(c) Percentage which column (a) is of column (b)			
		%			
		%			
		%			

Total (enter here and on line 9, page 2) . . . .

Schedule H—EXPLOITED EXEMPT ACTIVITY INCOME, OTHER THAN ADVERTISING INCOME
(See Instructions for Line 10 of Page 2)

1. Description of exploited activity	2. Gross unrelated business income from trade or business	3. Expenses directly connected with production of unrelated business income	4. Net Income from unrelated trade or business (Column 2 minus column 3)	5. Gross income from activity that is not unrelated business income	6. Expenses attributable to column 5	7. Excess exempt expenses (Column 6 minus column 5 but not more than column 4)	8. Net income includible (Column 4 minus column 7)

Total (enter here and on line 10, page 2) . . . .

Schedule I—ADVERTISING INCOME AND ADVERTISING LOSS (See Instructions for Line 11 of Page 2)
Part I—Income from periodicals reported on consolidated basis

1. Name of periodical	2. Gross advertising income	3. Direct advertising costs	4. Advertising gain or loss (col. 2 minus col. 3). If loss, enter in col. B, Part III. Do not complete cols. 5, 6 and 7. If gain, complete cols. 5, 6 and 7.	5. Circulation income	6. Readership costs	7. If col. 5 exceeds col. 6, enter in col A, Part III, the gain shown in col. 4. If col 6 exceeds col. 5, subtract col. 6 plus col. 3 from col. 5 plus col. 2. Enter gain in col. A, Part III.

Totals . . . .

Part II—Income from periodicals reported on a separate basis

Part III—Column A—Advertising Income

(a) Enter "consolidated periodical" or names of non-consolidated periodicals	(b) Enter total amount from column 4 or 7, Part I and amounts listed in cols. 4 and 7, Part II

Enter total here and on line 11, page 2 . . . .

Part III—Column B—Advertising Loss

(a) Enter "consolidated periodical" or names of non-consolidated periodicals	(b) Enter total amount from column 4, Part I and amounts listed in column 4, Part II

Enter total here and on line 28, page 2 . . . .

Schedule J—COMPENSATION OF OFFICERS, DIRECTORS AND TRUSTEES

1. Name	2. Title	3. Time devoted to business	4. Total compensation
John Doe, Jr.			1,000

Total compensation of officers (enter total here and on line 14, page 2) . . . .　|　1,000

Appendix E

Application to the Internal Revenue Service for Special Consideration

Application for Recognition of Exemption (Form 1023)
Consent Fixing Period of Limitation upon Assessment of
  Tax under Section 4940 of the Internal Revenue Code
  (Form 872-C)
Election/Revocation of Election by an Eligible Section
  501(c) (3) Organization to Make Expenditures to
  Influence Legislation (Form 5768)
Return of Certain Excise Taxes on Charities and Other
  Persons under Chapters 41 and 42 of the Internal
  Revenue Code (Form 4720)

Form **1023** (Rev. July 1981) Department of the Treasury Internal Revenue Service	**Application for Recognition of Exemption** Under Section 501(c)(3) of the Internal Revenue Code For Paperwork Reduction Act Notice, see page 1 of the instructions.	OMB No. 1545–0056 Expires May 31, 1984 To be filed in the key district for the area in which the organization has its principal office or place of business.

This application, when properly completed, constitutes the notice required under section 508(a) of the Internal Revenue Code so that an applicant may be treated as described in section 501(c)(3) of the Code, and the notice required under section 508(b) for an organization claiming not to be a private foundation within the meaning of section 509(a). **(Read the instructions for each part carefully before making any entries.)** The organization must have an organizing instrument (see Part II) before this application may be filed.

Part I—Identification

1 Full name of organization	2 Employer identification number (If none, attach Form SS–4)

3(a) Address (number and street)	Check here if applying under section: ☐ 501(e) ☐ 501(f)

3(b) City or town, State, and ZIP code	4 Name and phone number of person to be contacted ( )

5 Month the annual accounting period ends	6 Date incorporated or formed	7 Activity codes		

8(a) Has the organization filed Federal income tax returns? . . . . ☐ Yes ☐ No

If "Yes," state the form number(s), year(s) filed, and Internal Revenue office where filed ▶ _____

8(b) Has the organization filed exempt organization information returns? . . . . ☐ Yes ☐ No

If "Yes," state the form number(s), year(s) filed, and Internal Revenue office where filed ▶ _____

Part II.—Type of Entity and Organizational Documents (see instructions)

Check the applicable entity box below and attach a conformed copy of the organization's organizing and operational documents as indicated for each entity.

☐ Corporation—Articles of incorporation, bylaws.   ☐ Trust—Trust indenture.   ☐ Other—Constitution or articles, bylaws.

Part III.—Activities and Operational Information

1 What are or will be the organization's sources of financial support? List in order of magnitude. If a part of the receipts is or will be derived from the earnings of patents, copyrights, or other assets (excluding stock, bonds, etc.), identify the item as a separate source of receipts. Attach representative copies of solicitations for financial support.

2 Describe the organization's fund-raising program, both actual and planned, and explain to what extent it has been put into effect. (Include details of fund-raising activities such as selective mailings, formation of fund-raising committees, use of professional fund raisers, etc.)

I declare under the penalties of perjury that I am authorized to sign this application on behalf of the above organization and I have examined this application, including the accompanying statements, and to the best of my knowledge it is true, correct, and complete.

_____   _____   _____
(Signature)   (Title or authority of signer)   (Date)

Part III.—Activities and Operational Information (Continued)

3 Give a narrative description of the activities presently carried on by the organization, and those that will be carried on. If the organization is not fully operational, explain what stage of development its activities have reached, what further steps remain for the organization to become fully operational, and when such further steps will take place. The narrative should specifically identify the services performed or to be performed by the organization. (Do not state the purposes of the organization in general terms or repeat the language of the organizational documents.) If the organization is a school, hospital, or medical research organization, include enough information in your description to clearly show that the organization meets the definition of that particular activity that is contained in the instructions for Part VII–A.

4 The membership of the organization's governing body is:

(a) Names, addresses, and duties of officers, directors, trustees, etc.	(b) Specialized knowledge, training, expertise, or particular qualifications

Part III.—Activities and Operational Information (Continued)

4 (c) Do any of the above persons serve as members of the governing body by reason of being public officials or being appointed by public officials? . . . . □ Yes □ No

If "Yes," name those persons and explain the basis of their selection or appointment.

(d) Are any members of the organization's governing body "disqualified persons" with respect to the organization (other than by reason of being a member of the governing body) or do any of the members have either a business or family relationship with "disqualified persons?" (See specific instruction 4(d).) . . □ Yes □ No

If "Yes," explain.

(e) Have any members of the organization's governing body assigned income or assets to the organization? . □ Yes □ No

If "Yes," attach a copy of assignment(s) and a list of items assigned.

(f) Is it anticipated that any current or future member of the organization's governing body will assign income or assets to the organization? . . . . □ Yes □ No

If "Yes," explain fully on an attached sheet.

5 Does the organization control or is it controlled by any other organization? . . . . □ Yes □ No

Is the organization the outgrowth of another organization, or does it have a special relationship to another organization by reason of interlocking directorates or other factors? . . . . □ Yes □ No

If either of these questions is answered "Yes," explain.

6 Is the organization financially accountable to any other organization? . . . . □ Yes □ No

If "Yes," explain and identify the other organization. Include details concerning accountability or attach copies of reports if any have been submitted.

7 (a) What assets does the organization have that are used in the performance of its exempt function? (Do not include property producing investment income.) If any assets are not fully operational, explain their status, what additional steps remain to be completed, and when such final steps will be taken.

(b) To what extent have you used, or do you plan to use contributions as an endowment fund, i.e., hold contributions to produce income for the support of your exempt activities?

8 (a) What benefits, services, or products will the organization provide that are related to its exempt function?

Part III.—Activities and Operational Information (Continued)

8 (b) Have the recipients been required or will they be required to pay for the organization's benefits, services, or products? . . . . □ Yes □ No

If "Yes," explain and show how the charges are determined.

9 Does or will the organization limit its benefits, services, or products to specific classes of individuals? . . . □ Yes □ No

If "Yes," explain how the recipients or beneficiaries are or will be selected.

10 Is the organization a membership organization? . . . . □ Yes □ No

If "Yes," complete the following:

(a) Describe the organization's membership requirements and attach a schedule of membership fees and dues.

(b) Describe your present and proposed efforts to attract members, and attach a copy of any descriptive literature or promotional material used for this purpose.

(c) Are benefits, services, or products limited to members? . . . . □ Yes □ No

If "No," explain.

11 Does or will the organization engage in activities tending to influence legislation or intervene in any way in political campaigns? . . . . □ Yes □ No

If "Yes," explain. (**Note:** *You may wish to file Form 5768, Election/Revocation of Election by an Eligible Section 501(c) (3) Organization to Make Expenditures to Influence Legislation.*)

12 Does the organization have a pension plan for employees? . . . . □ Yes □ No

13 (a) Are you filing Form 1023 within 15 months from the end of the month in which you were created or formed as required by section 508(a) and the related Regulations? (See general instructions.) . . □ Yes □ No

(b) If you answer "No," to 13(a) and you claim that you fit an exception to the notice requirements under section 508(a), attach an explanation of your basis for the claimed exception.

(c) If you answer "No," to 13(a) and section 508(a) does apply to you, you may be eligible for relief under section 1.9100 of the Income Tax Regulations from the application of section 508(a). Do you wish to request relief? . . . . □ Yes □ No

(d) If you answer "Yes," to 13(c) attach a detailed statement that satisfies the requirements of Rev. Proc. 79–63.

(e) If you answer "No," to both 13(a) and 13(c) and section 508(a) does apply to you, your exemption can be recognized only from the date this application is filed with your key District Director. Therefore, do you want us to consider your application as a request for recognition of exemption from the date the application is received and not retroactively to the date you were formed? . . . . □ Yes □ No

Part IV.—Statement as to Private Foundation Status

1 Is the organization a private foundation? . . . . □ Yes □ No

2 If you answer "Yes," to question 1 and the organization claims to be a private operating foundation, check here □ and complete Part VIII.

3 If you answer "No," to question 1 indicate the type of ruling you are requesting regarding the organization's status under section 509 by checking the box(es) that apply below:

(a) Definitive ruling under section 509(a)(1), (2), (3), or (4) ▶ □. Complete Part VII.

(b) Advance ruling under section ▶ □ 170(b)(1)(A)(vi) or ▶ □ 509(a)(2)—see instructions.

(c) Extended advance ruling under section ▶ □ 170(b)(1)(A)(vi) or ▶ □ 509(a)(2)—see instructions.

(**Note:** If you want an extended advance ruling **you must check** the appropriate boxes for **both** 3(b) and 3(c).)

Form 1023 (Rev. 7-81)   **Part V.—Financial Data**   Page **5**

Statement of Support, Revenue, and Expenses for period ending ...., 19........

1 Gross contributions, gifts, grants, and similar amounts received	1	
2 Gross dues and assessments of members	2	
3 (a) Gross amounts derived from activities related to organization's exempt purpose		
(b) Minus cost of sales	3	
4 (a) Gross amounts from unrelated business activities		
(b) Minus cost of sales	4	
5 (a) Gross amount received from sale of assets, excluding inventory items (attach schedule)		
(b) Minus cost or other basis and sales expenses of assets sold	5	
6 Investment income (see instructions)	6	
7 Total support and revenue	7	

(Support and Revenue)

8 Fund raising expenses	8	
9 Contributions, gifts, grants, and similar amounts paid (attach schedule)	9	
10 Disbursements to or for benefit of members (attach schedule)	10	
11 Compensation of officers, directors, and trustees (attach schedule)	11	
12 Other salaries and wages	12	
13 Interest	13	
14 Rent	14	
15 Depreciation and depletion	15	
16 Other (attach schedule)	16	
17 Total expenses	17	
18 Excess of support and revenue over expenses (line 7 minus line 17)	18	

(Expenses)

Balance Sheets	Enter dates ▶	Beginning date	Ending date

Assets

19 Cash (a) Interest bearing accounts			
(b) Other	19		
20 Accounts receivable, net	20		
21 Inventories	21		
22 Bonds and notes (attach schedule)	22		
23 Corporate stocks (attach schedule)	23		
24 Mortgage loans (attach schedule)	24		
25 Other investments (attach schedule)	25		
26 Depreciable and depletable assets (attach schedule)	26		
27 Land	27		
28 Other assets (attach schedule)	28		
29 Total assets	29		

Liabilities

30 Accounts payable	30		
31 Contributions, gifts, grants, etc., payable	31		
32 Mortgages and notes payable (attach schedule)	32		
33 Other liabilities (attach schedules)	33		
34 Total liabilities	34		

Fund Balances or Net Worth

35 Total fund balances or net worth	35		
36 Total liabilities and fund balances or net worth (line 34 plus line 35)	36		

Has there been any substantial change in any aspect of your financial activities since the period ending date shown above? . . . . ☐ Yes ☐ No
If "Yes," attach a detailed explanation.

Part VI.—Required Schedules for Special Activities

	If "Yes," check here;	And, complete schedule—
1 Is the organization, or any part of it, a school?		A
2 Does the organization provide or administer any scholarship benefits, student aid, etc.?		B
3 Has the organization taken over, or will it take over, the facilities of a "for profit" institution?		C
4 Is the organization, or any part of it, a hospital or a medical research organization?		D
5 Is the organization, or any part of it, a home for the aged?		E
6 Is the organization, or any part of it, a litigating organization (public interest law firm or similar organization)?		F
7 Is the organization, or any part of it, formed to promote amateur sports competition?		G

Part VII.—Non-Private Foundation Status (Definitive ruling only)

A.—Basis for Non-Private Foundation Status

The organization is not a private foundation because it qualifies as:

✓	Kind of organization	Within the meaning of	Complete
1	a church	Sections 509(a)(1) and 170(b)(1)(A)(i)	/////
2	a school	Sections 509(a)(1) and 170(b)(1)(A)(ii)	/////
3	a hospital	Sections 509(a)(1) and 170(b)(1)(A)(iii)	/////
4	a medical research organization operated in conjunction with a hospital	Sections 509(a)(1) and 170(b)(1)(A)(iii)	/////
5	being organized and operated exclusively for testing for public safety	Section 509(a)(4)	/////
6	being operated for the benefit of a college or university which is owned or operated by a governmental unit	Sections 509(a)(1) and 170(b)(1)(A)(iv)	Part VII.–B
7	normally receiving a substantial part of its support from a governmental unit or from the general public	Sections 509(a)(1) and 170(b)(1)(A)(vi)	Part VII.–B
8	normally receiving not more than one-third of its support from gross investment income and more than one-third of its support from contributions, membership fees, and gross receipts from activities related to its exempt functions (subject to certain exceptions)	Section 509(a)(2)	Part VII.–B
9	being operated solely for the benefit of or in connection with one or more of the organizations described in 1 through 4, or 6, 7, and 8 above	Section 509(a)(3)	Part VII.–C

B.—Analysis of Financial Support

	(a) Most recent tax year 19......	(b) 19......	(c) 19......	(d) 19......	(e) Total
1 Gifts, grants, and contributions received					
2 Membership fees received .					
3 Gross receipts from admissions, sales of merchandise or services, or furnishing of facilities in any activity which is not an unrelated business within the meaning of section 513					
4 Gross investment income (see instructions for definition)					
5 Net income from organization's unrelated business activities not included on line 4					
6 Tax revenues levied for and either paid to or spent on behalf of the organization . .					
7 Value of services or facilities furnished by a governmental unit to the organization without charge (not including the value of services or facilities generally furnished the public without charge)					
8 Other income (not including gain or loss from sale of capital assets)—attach schedule.					
9 Total of lines 1 through 8 .					
10 Line 9 minus line 3 . . .					

11 Enter 2% of line 10, column (e) only . . . .

12 If the organization has received any unusual grants during any of the above tax years, attach a list for each year showing the name of the contributor, the date and amount of grant, and a brief description of the nature of such grant. Do not include such grants on line 1 above—(See instructions).

Part VII.—Non-Private Foundation Status (Definitive ruling only) (Continued)

B.—Analysis of Financial Support (Continued)

13 If the organization's non-private foundation status is based on:
   (a) Sections 509(a)(1) and 170(b)(1)(A)(iv) or (vi).—Attach a list showing the name and amount contributed by each person (other than a governmental unit or "publicly supported" organization) whose total gifts for the entire period were more than the amount shown on line 11.
   (b) Section 509(a)(2).—For each of the years included on lines 1, 2, and 3, attach a list showing the name of and amount received from each person who is a "disqualified person."
       For each of the years on line 3, attach a list showing the name of and amount received from each payor (other than a "disqualified person") whose payments to the organization were more than $5,000. For this purpose, "payor" includes but is not limited to, any organization described in sections 170(b)(1)(A)(i) through (vi) and any government agency or bureau.

C.—Supplemental Information Concerning Organizations Claiming Non-Private Foundation Status Under Section 509(a)(3)

1 Organizations supported by applicant organization: Name and address of supported organization	Has the supported organization received a ruling or determination letter that it is not a private foundation by reason of section 509(a)(1) or (2)?
	☐ Yes ☐ No
	☐ Yes ☐ No
	☐ Yes ☐ No
	☐ Yes ☐ No
	☐ Yes ☐ No

2 To what extent are the members of your governing board elected or appointed by the supported organization(s)?

3 What is the extent of common supervision or control that you and the supported organization(s) share?

4 To what extent do(es) the supported organization(s) have a significant voice in your investment policies, the making and timing of grants, and in otherwise directing the use of your income or assets?

5 Does the mentioning of the supported organization(s) in your governing instrument make you a trust that the supported organization(s) can enforce under State law and compel to make an accounting? . . . . . ☐ Yes ☐ No
   If "Yes," explain.

6 What portion of your income do you pay to each supported organization and how significant is the support to each?

7 To what extent do you conduct activities which would otherwise be carried out by the supported organization(s)? Explain why these activities would otherwise be carried on by the supported organization(s).

8 Is the applicant organization controlled directly or indirectly by one or more "disqualified persons" (other than one who is a disqualified person solely because he or she is a manager) or by an organization which is not described in section 509(a)(1) or (2)?   . . . . ☐ Yes ☐ No
   If "Yes," explain.

Part VIII.—Basis for Status as a Private Operating Foundation

If the organization—
  (a) bases its claim to private operating foundation status on normal and regular operations over a period of years; or
  (b) is newly created, set up as a private operating foundation, and has at least one year's experience;
provide the information under the income test and under one of the three supplemental tests (assets, endowment, or support). If the organization does not have at least one year's experience, complete line 21. If the organization's private operating foundation status depends on its normal and regular operations as described in (a) above, attach a schedule similar to the one below showing the data in tabular form for the three years next preceding the most recent tax year.

	Income Test	Most recent tax year
1	Adjusted net income, as defined in section 4942(f)	
2	Qualifying distributions:	
	(a) Amounts (including administrative expenses) paid directly for the active conduct of the activities for which organized and operated under section 501(c)(3) (attach schedule)	
	(b) Amounts paid to acquire assets to be used (or held for use) directly in carrying out purposes described in sections 170(c)(1) or 170(c)(2)(B) (attach schedule)	
	(c) Amounts set aside for specific projects which are for purposes described in section 170(c)(1) or 170(c)(2)(B) (attach schedule)	
	(d) Total qualifying distributions (add lines 2(a), (b), and (c))	
3	Percentage of qualifying distributions to adjusted net income (divide line 2(d) by line 1—percentage must be at least 85%)	%
	Assets Test	
4	Value of organization's assets used in activities that directly carry out the exempt purposes. Do not include assets held merely for investment or production of income (attach schedule)	
5	Value of any stock of a corporation that is controlled by applicant organization and carries out its exempt purposes (attach statement describing corporation)	
6	Value of all qualifying assets (add lines 4 and 5)	
7	Value of applicant organization's total assets	
8	Percentage of qualifying assets to total assets (divide line 6 by line 7—percentage must exceed 65%) .	%
	Endowment Test	
9	Value of assets not used (or held for use) directly in carrying out exempt purposes:	
	(a) Monthly average of investment securities at fair market value	
	(b) Monthly average of cash balances	
	(c) Fair market value of all other investment property (attach schedule)	
	(d) Total (add lines 9(a), (b), and (c))	
10	Subtract acquisition indebtedness related to line 9 items (attach schedule)	
11	Balance (subtract line 10 from line 9(d))	
12	For years beginning on or after January 1, 1976, multiply line 11 by a factor of 3⅓% (⅔ of the applicable percentage for the minimum investment return computation under section 4942(e)). Line 2(d) above must equal or exceed the result of this computation	
	Support Test	
13	Applicant organization's support as defined in section 509(d)	
14	Subtract amount of gross investment income as defined in section 509(e)	
15	Support for purposes of section 4942(j)(3)(B)(iii) (subtract line 14 from line 13)	
16	Support received from the general public, five or more exempt organizations, or a combination of these sources (attach schedule)	
17	For persons (other than exempt organizations) contributing more than 1% of line 15, enter the total amounts that are more than 1% of line 15	
18	Subtract line 17 from line 16	
19	Percentage of total support (divide line 18 by line 15—must be at least 85%)	%
20	Does line 16 include support from an exempt organization that is more than 25% of the amount on line 15?	☐ Yes ☐ No

21 Newly created organizations with less than one year's experience: Attach a statement explaining how the organization is planning to satisfy the requirements of section 4942(j)(3) for the income test and one of the supplemental tests during its first year's operation. Include a description of plans and arrangements, press clippings, public announcements, solicitations for funds, etc.

Department of the Treasury—Internal Revenue Service

Form **872–C**

(Rev. July 1981)

Consent Fixing Period of Limitation Upon Assessment of Tax Under Section 4940 of the Internal Revenue Code
(See instruction 2 of Part IV—Form 1023 instructions.)

OMB No. 1545–0056

Expires May 31, 1984

To be used with Form 1023. Submit in duplicate.

Under section 6501(c)(4) of the Internal Revenue Code, and as part of a request filed with Form 1023 that the organization named below be treated as a publicly supported organization under section 170(b)(1)(A)(vi) or section 509(a)(2) during an extended advance ruling period,

----
(Name of organization)

District Director

and the

(Number, street, city or town, State, and ZIP code)

consent and agree that: (check one)

☐ If the first tax year in the extended advance ruling period is at least 8 months long, then the period for assessing tax (imposed under section 4940 of the Code) for any of the 5 tax years in the extended advance ruling period will extend 8 years, 4 months, and 15 days beyond the end of the first tax year.

☐ If the first tax year in the extended advance ruling period is less than 8 months long, then the period for assessing tax (imposed under section 4940 of the Code) for any of the 6 tax years in the extended advance ruling period will extend 9 years, 4 months, and 15 days beyond the end of the first tax year.

However, if a notice of deficiency in tax for any of these years is sent to the organization before the period expires, then the time for making an assessment will be further extended by the number of days the assessment is prohibited, plus 60 days.

Ending date of first tax year...

Name of organization	Date
Officer or trustee having authority to sign	

Signature ▶

District Director	Date

By ▶

For Paperwork Reduction Act Notice, see page 1 of the Form 1023 instructions.

Form **5768**

(March 1977)

Department of the Treasury
Internal Revenue Service

Election/Revocation of Election by an Eligible Section 501(c)(3) Organization to Make Expenditures to Influence Legislation
(Under Section 501 of the Internal Revenue Code)

For IRS
Use Only ▶

Name of organization	Employer identification number

Address (number and street)

City or town, State and ZIP code

1 Election.—As an eligible organization we hereby elect to have the provisions of the applicable subsection of 501 of the Code, relating to expenditures by public charities to influence legislation, apply to our taxable year ending
...., and all subsequent taxable years until revoked.
(Month, day, and year)

Note: This election must be signed and postmarked within the first taxable year to which it applies.

2 Revocation.—As an eligible organization we hereby revoke our election to have the provisions of the applicable subsection of 501 of the Code, relating to expenditures to influence legislation, apply to our taxable year ending ....

....
(Month, day, and year)

Note: This revocation must be signed and postmarked before the first day of the taxable year to which it applies.

Under penalties of perjury, I declare that I am authorized to make this (check applicable box) ▶ ☐ election/☐ revocation on behalf of the above named organization.

....
(Signature of officer or trustee)   (Title)   (Date)

Instructions

(References are to the Internal Revenue Code)

Section 501(c)(3) of the Code provides that an organization exempt under that section will lose its tax-exempt status and its qualification to receive deductible charitable contributions if a substantial part of its activities are carried on to influence legislation. The applicable subsection under section 501, however, permits certain eligible 501(c)(3) organizations to elect to make limited expenditures to influence legislation. The election is only applicable to taxable years beginning after December 31, 1976. An organization making the election will, however, be subject to an excise tax under section 4911 if it spends more than the amounts permitted by that section. Furthermore, the organization may lose its exempt status if its lobbying expenditures exceed the permitted amounts by more than 50 percent over a four-year period. For any taxable year in which an election under section 501 is in effect, an electing organization must report the actual and permitted amounts of its lobbying expenditures and grass roots expenditures (as defined in section 4911(c)) on its annual return required under section 6033. Each electing member of an affiliated group must report the above amounts as to both itself and the affiliated group as a whole.

The election or revocation of election is made by entering the ending date of the taxable year for the Election or Revocation applies in item 1 or 2 as is applicable and by entering the date signed and the signature and title of the officer or trustee authorized to make the election or revocation in the appropriate spaces on this form.

Eligible Organizations.—A 501(c)(3) organization is permitted to make the election if it is not a disqualified organization (see below) and is described in:

(a) section 170(b)(1)(A)(ii) (relating to educational institutions),

(b) section 170(b)(1)(A)(iii) (relating to hospitals and medical research organizations),

(c) section 170(b)(1)(A)(iv) (relating to organizations supporting government schools),

(d) section 170(b)(1)(A)(vi) (relating to organizations publicly supported by charitable contributions),

(e) section 509(a)(2) (relating to organizations publicly supported by admissions, sales, etc.), or

(f) section 509(a)(3) (relating to organizations supporting certain types of public charities other than those section 509(a)(3) organizations that support section 501(c)(4), (5) or (6) organizations).

Disqualified Organizations.—The following types of organizations are not permitted to make the election:

(a) section 170(b)(1)(A)(i) organizations (relating to churches),

(b) an integrated auxiliary of a church or a convention or association of churches, or

(c) a member of an affiliated group of organizations if one or more members of such group is described in (a) or (b) above.

Affiliated Organizations.—Organizations are members of an affiliated group of organizations only if—(1) the governing instrument of one such organization requires it to be bound by the decisions of the other organization on legislative issues, or (2) the governing board of one such organization includes persons who (i) are specifically designated representatives of another such organization or are members of the governing board, officers, or paid executive staff members of such other organization and (ii) by aggregating their votes have sufficient voting power to cause or prevent action on legislative issues by the first such organization.

For further details, see section 4911 and the applicable subsection of section 501.

Note: A private foundation (including a private operating foundation) is not an eligible organization.

Where to File.—

If principal office of the organization is located in:	Send election/revocation form to:
Connecticut, New Hampshire, Maine, Massachusetts, Rhode Island, and Vermont	Internal Revenue Service Center 310 Lowell Street Andover, Mass. 01812
Indiana, Kentucky, Michigan, Ohio, and West Virginia	Internal Revenue Service Center Cincinnati, Ohio 45298
Arizona, California, Hawaii, Nevada, and Utah	Internal Revenue Service Center 5045 East Butler Avenue Fresno, Calif. 93888
All other States, U.S. possessions and foreign countries	Internal Revenue Service Center 11601 Roosevelt Boulevard Philadelphia, Pa. 19155

Form **4720**	**Return of Certain Excise Taxes on Charities and Other Persons Under Chapters 41 and 42 of the Internal Revenue Code**
Department of the Treasury Internal Revenue Service	(Sections 4911, 4941, 4942, 4943, 4944, and 4945)

For the calendar year 1980 or other tax year beginning ...., 1980 and ending ...., 19.......

Name of foundation or charity	Employer identification number
Number and street	Check box for type of annual return ☐ Form 990
City or town, State and ZIP code	☐ Form 990–PF ☐ Form 5227

Public charities complete only the heading; Part III, line 4; signature section; and Schedule F. Enter N/A in all other parts.

		Yes	No
A.	Is the foundation a foreign private foundation within the meaning of section 4948(b)?		
B.	Has corrective action been taken with respect to any transaction which resulted in Chapter 42 taxes being reported on this form?		

If "Yes," attach a detailed documentation and description of the corrective action taken and, if applicable, enter the Fair Market Value of any property recovered as a result of the correction ▶ $.................................... (for any uncorrected acts, attach explanation) (see instructions).

Part I.—Initial Taxes on Private Foundation

1. Tax on undistributed income—Schedule B, line 4 . . . . _____
2. Tax on excess business holdings—Schedule C, line 7 . . . . _____
3. Tax on investments that jeopardize charitable purpose—Schedule D, Part I, col. 5 . . . . _____
4. Tax on taxable expenditures—Schedule E, Part I, col. 7 . . . . _____
5. Total . . . .

Part II.—Initial Taxes on Self-dealers and Foundation Managers

	1. Name and address of person subject to tax	2. Taxpayer identifying number
(a)		
(b)		
(c)		
(d)		

	3. Tax on self-dealing—Schedule A, Part II, col. 4 and Part III, col. 4	4. Tax on investments that jeopardize charitable purpose—Schedule D, Part II, col. 4	5. Tax on taxable expenditures—Schedule E, Part II, col. 4	6. Total tax—Total of cols. 3, 4, and 5
(a)				
(b)				
(c)				
(d)				
Total				

Part III.—Summary of Taxes (See General Instruction H)

1. Enter total from Part I, line 5 . . . . _____
2. Enter here the total of those taxes listed in Part II, column 6, which apply to foundation managers and disqualified persons who sign this form. If all sign, enter the total from Part II, column 6 . . . . . _____
3. Chapter 42 tax—total of lines 1 and 2. Pay in full with return. (Make check or money order payable to Internal Revenue Service.) (See General Instruction H.) . . . .
4. Lobbying expenditures tax—enter amount from Schedule F, line 4. (Make check or money order payable to Internal Revenue Service.) . . . .

Under penalties of perjury I declare that I have examined this return, including accompanying schedules and statements, and to the best of my knowledge and belief it is true, correct, and complete. Declaration of preparer (other than taxpayer) is based on all information of which preparer has any knowledge.

Signature of officer or trustee	Title	Date

Signature (and organization name if applicable) of disqualified person or foundation manager	Date

Signature (and organization name if applicable) of disqualified person or foundation manager	Date

Signature (and organization name if applicable) of disqualified person or foundation manager	Date

Signature of individual or firm preparing the return	Address of preparer	Date

SCHEDULE A.—Initial Taxes on Self-dealing (Section 4941)

Part I.—Acts of Self-dealing and Tax Computation

1. Act no.	2. Date of act	3. Description of act
1		
2		
3		
4		
5		

4. Question no. from Form 990–PF, Part V, or Form 5227, Part V, applicable to the act	5. Amount involved in act	6. Initial tax on self-dealing (5% of col. 5)	7. Tax on foundation managers (if applicable) (Lesser of $10,000 or 2½% of col. 5)

Part II.—Summary of Tax Liability of Disqualified Persons and Proration of Payments

1. Names of disqualified persons liable for tax	2. Act no. from Part I, col. 1	3. Amount of tax from Part I, col. 6 or prorated amount	4. Disqualified person's total tax liability (Total of amounts in col. 3)

Part III.—Summary of Tax Liability of Foundation Managers and Proration of Payments

1. Names of foundation managers liable for tax	2. Act no. from Part I, col 1	3. Amount of tax from Part I, col. 7 or prorated amount	4. Manager's total tax liability (Total of amounts in col. 3)

SCHEDULE B.—Tax on Undistributed Income (Section 4942)

1. Undistributed income for years prior to 1979, from Part XI, Form 990–PF (or Part X, Form 5227) for 1980.
   (a) Enter year ....
   (b) Enter year ....
   (c) Enter year ....
2. Undistributed income for 1979, from Part XI, Form 990–PF (or Part X, Form 5227) for 1980 . .
3. Total undistributed income as of end of current tax year beginning in 1980 and subject to tax under section 4942 (add lines 1(a), (b), (c), and 2) . . . .
4. Tax under section 4942—Enter 15% of amount on line 3 here and in Part I, line 1, page 1 . . .

Page

SCHEDULE C.—Initial Tax on Excess Business Holdings (Section 4943)

Business Holdings and Computation of Tax

If you have taxable excess holdings in more than one business enterprise, attach a separate schedule for each enterprise. Refer to the instructions for each line item before making any entries.

Name and address of business enterprise

Employer Identification Number

Form of enterprise (corporation, partnership, trust, joint venture, sole proprietorship, etc.)

	Voting stock (profits interest, or beneficial interest) A	Value B	Nonvoting stock (capital interest) C
1. Foundation holdings in business enterprise	%	%	
2. Permitted holdings in business enterprise	%	%	
3. Value of excess holdings in business enterprise			
4. Value of excess holdings disposed of within 90 days; or, other value of excess holdings not subject to section 4943 tax (attach explanation) . .			
5. Taxable excess holdings in business enterprise, line 3 minus line 4 . .			
6. Tax—5% of line 5			
7. Total tax—Enter total of columns A, B, and C, line 6 here and in Part I, line 2, page 1			

SCHEDULE D.—Taxes on Investments Which Jeopardize Charitable Purpose (Section 4944)

Part I.—Investments and Tax Computation

1. Investment number	2. Date of investment	3. Description of investment	4. Amount of investment	5. Initial tax on foundation (5% of col. 4)	6. Initial tax on foundation managers (if applicable)—(lesser of $5,000 or 5% of col. 4)
1					
2					
3					
4					
5					
Total .					

Part II.—Summary of Tax Liability of Foundation Managers and Proration of Payments

1. Names of foundation managers liable for tax	2. Investment no. from Part I, col. 1	3. Amount of tax from Part I, col. 6 or prorated amount	4. Manager's total tax liability (Total of amounts in col. 3)

SCHEDULE E.—Taxes on Taxable Expenditures (Section 4945)

Part I.—Expenditures and Computation of Tax

1. Item number	2. Amount	3. Date paid or incurred	4. Name and address of recipient	5. Description of expenditure and purposes for which made
1				
2				
3				
4				
5				

6. Question number from Form 990–PF, Part V, or Form 5227, Part V, applicable to the expenditure	7. Tax imposed on foundation (10% of col. 2)	8. Tax imposed on foundation managers (if applicable)—(lesser of $5,000 or 2½% of col. 2)
Total		

Part II.—Summary of Tax Liability of Foundation Managers and Proration of Payments

1. Names of foundation managers liable for tax	2. Item no. from Part I, col. 1	3. Amount of tax from Part I, col. 8 or prorated amount	4. Manager's total tax liability (Total of amounts in col. 3)

SCHEDULE F.—Tax on Excess Lobbying Expenditures (Section 4911)

1. Excess of grass roots expenditures over grass roots nontaxable amount, from Schedule A (Form 990), Part VI, column (b), line 8 (see instructions before making entry) . . . .

2. Excess of lobbying expenditures over lobbying nontaxable amount, from Schedule A (Form 990), Part VI, column (b), line 9 (see instructions before making entry) . . . .

3. Taxable lobbying expenditures—enter the larger of line 1 or line 2 . . . .

4. Tax—Enter 25% of line 3 here and in Part III, line 4, Page 1 . . . .

☆ U.S. GOVERNMENT PRINTING OFFICE : 1980—O-313-180   23 0916750

Appendix F
Documents Affording Protection against Liability

Release (Agreement to Hold Harmless)
Sample Licensing Agreement
Application for Copyright Registration (Form VA)

AGREEMENT TO HOLD HARMLESS

I, _____ , agree to assume full responsibility for my own safety while participating in a travel tour of _____ arranged by _____ _____ . I hereby release South Plains Museum, its officials, employees, and agents from any and all claims or actions resulting from any injury that may occur while participating in this travel tour. I agree to reimburse South Plains Museum for any damages it is compelled to pay, arising from any such claim, demand, action or cause of action.

_____
Date

_____
Participant

_____
Parent or Guardian if Participant is
under Eighteen Years of Age

LICENSING AGREEMENT

This Licensing Agreement is made and entered into this _____ day of _____ , by and between South Plains Museum, a nonprofit corporation of the State of _____ , having an address at _____ _____ , hereinafter referred to as "Licensor," and _____ , a corporation of the

State of _____ , having an address at _____
_____ , hereinafter referred to as "Licensee."

Whereas, Licensor asserts and warrants that it is the owner of all right, title, and interest in and to _____ , hereinafter called Product.

Whereas, Licensee desires to acquire an exclusive license to make, use, and sell reproductions of Product in the following territory: _____ .

Now therefore, in consideration of the mutual covenants, conditions and limitations hereinafter set forth, the Parties hereto agree as follows:

1. Licensor grants to Licensee permission to manufacture, distribute, advertise, and market the product, which shall consist of the following _____ _____ . The license herein granted to the Licensee by the Licensor shall be exercised only in the following territory: ___ _____ .

2. Licensee agrees to pay Licensor as royalties or license fees, _____ percent (_____) of Licensee's gross selling price of Product. Royalties paid on sales which are not accepted by the customer shall be credited against further royalty payments to be made. All costs incurred in the manufacturing and promoting of Product shall be the obligation of Licensee. Royalties shall not be reduced by costs incurred by Licensee for manufacturing and promoting of Product.

3. On or before the first days of March and September of each year, Licensee shall render a report to Licensor indicating the quantity of Products sold by Licensee during the preceding six months' period ending on the last days of December and June of each year, and with each of said reports, Licensee shall make payment to Licensor of the royalty which shall be due and payable in accordance with paragraph 2. At all times, Licensor or its duly authorized agent or attorney shall have access to the books of Licensee insofar as the books shall be pertinent to the subject matter of this agreement, and Licensor shall have the right to have a representative present when any examination of the books of Licensee shall be made.

4. Licensee agrees to have all licensed Products which it shall manufacture and sell stamped with the word "copyrighted" or an abbreviation thereof.

5. Licensor will furnish Licensee in writing standards of quality for Product, and Licensee agrees to meet the standards of quality established by Licensor. Licensee recognizes the substantial value of the goodwill associated with Product and acknowledges that all rights therein and goodwill pertaining thereto belong exclusively to Licensor. Licensee acknowledges that if the Product manufactured and sold were of inferior quality in design, material or workmanship, the reputation and goodwill of Licensor would be impaired. Accordingly, Licensee warrants that the licensed Product shall be of high quality. Licensor shall be the sole judge of whether or not Licensee has met or is meeting the standards of quality so established. Licensee agrees to deliver a specimen of the product to Licensor for inspection, and the written approval of the Licensor's

designated employee as to the design standards of workmanship, quality of presentation, and intrinsic merit of the product shall be necessary before Licensee begins sales of the product. Licensor shall have the right to withhold approval, but Licensor is deemed to have approved the product unless Licensee is notified to the contrary within two weeks of receipt of the specimen of the product. At periodic intervals beginning with the date of this Agreement, Licensee agrees to send Licensor evidence of the continued quality of the product, for the approval of Licensor.

6. Licensee agrees to supply Licensor free of charge with _____ specimens of the product not later than the first day of issue to the public.

7. Licensee shall not make use of the name of the Licensor in any respect without prior written consent of Licensor. Licensee acknowledges it is not an agent of Licensor and agrees it will not in any manner represent itself as such in the course of this License.

8. All art work and designs involving the product, or any reproduction thereof, shall be and remain the property of Licensor, and Licensor shall be entitled to use the same and to license their use by others.

9. Licensor grants this license on the express condition that the prices, terms, and conditions of sale for use or sale of licensed products shall be no more favorable to the customer than those which from time to time Licensor establishes and maintains for its own sales of similar or competing products. Licensee shall be notified of all such prices, terms, and conditions of sale fixed by Licensor.

10. Licensor assumes no liability to the Licensee or third parties with respect to the licensed product manufactured or sold by Licensee. Licensee agrees to indemnify Licensor against all actions, claims, costs, damages and expenses which Licensor may sustain as a result of the use or reproduction by Licensee of any trademark, copyright, patent, method, or device in connection with the product. Licensee will secure at its own cost an adequate policy of product liability insurance covering the Licensor as well as the Licensee and will furnish a copy of the certificate to Licensor.

11. The license herein granted shall not be assignable or transferable in any manner whatsoever by Licensee.

12. This agreement shall terminate in the event of the bankruptcy or insolvency of Licensee. In any event, this agreement shall terminate on _____ _____ ; however, Licensor has the option to renew this agreement for another _____ year period.

13. If either party fails to observe or perform any term of this Agreement, the nondefaulting party shall have the right to elect to terminate this agreement if such default is not cured within thirty (30) days after the nondefaulting party shall have given the defaulting party written notice specifying such default. In this regard, if Licensee fails to produce Product for sale by _____ _____ , Licensor has the option to terminate this agreement. In the event of

termination for failure to produce Product for sale by _____
___ , all development costs shall be the obligation of Licensee.

14. This agreement shall be governed by and construed and enforced in accordance with and subject to the laws of the State of _____ .

In witness whereof the parties above named have hereunto set their hands the day and year first above written.

Licensee: Licensor:
X Manufacturing   South Plains Museum

By_____   By_____

APPLICATION FOR COPYRIGHT REGISTRATION

for a Work of the Visual Arts

HOW TO APPLY FOR COPYRIGHT REGISTRATION:

- **First:** Read the information on this page to make sure Form VA is the correct application for your work.

- **Second:** Open out the form by pulling this page to the left. Read through the detailed instructions before starting to complete the form.

- **Third:** Complete spaces 1-4 of the application, then turn the entire form over and, after reading the instructions for spaces 5-9, complete the rest of your application. Use typewriter or print in dark ink. Be sure to sign the form at space 8.

- **Fourth:** Detach your completed application from these instructions and send it with the necessary deposit of the work (see below) to: Register of Copyrights, Library of Congress, Washington, D.C. 20559. Unless you have a Deposit Account in the Copyright Office, your application and deposit must be accompanied by a check or money order for $10, payable to: *Register of Copyrights.*

WHEN TO USE FORM VA: Form VA is the appropriate form to use for copyright registration covering works of the visual arts. Both published and unpublished works can be registered on Form VA.

WHAT IS A "WORK OF THE VISUAL ARTS"? This category consists of "pictorial, graphic, or sculptural works," including two-dimensional and three-dimensional works of fine, graphic, and applied art, photographs, prints and art reproductions, maps, globes, charts, technical drawings, diagrams, and models.

WHAT DOES COPYRIGHT PROTECT? Copyright in a work of the visual arts protects those pictorial, graphic, or sculptural elements that, either alone or in combination, represent an "original work of authorship." The statute declares: "In no case does copyright protection for an original work of authorship extend to any idea, procedure, process, system, method of operation, concept, principle, or discovery, regardless of the form in which it is described, explained, illustrated, or embodied in such work."

WORKS OF ARTISTIC CRAFTSMANSHIP AND DESIGNS: "Works of artistic craftsmanship" are registrable on Form VA, but the statute makes clear that protection extends to "their form" and not to "their mechanical or utilitarian aspects." The "design of a useful article" is considered copyrightable "only if, and only to the extent that, such design incorporates pictorial, graphic, or sculptural features that can be identified separately from, and are capable of existing independently of, the utilitarian aspects of the article."

LABELS AND ADVERTISEMENTS: Works prepared for use in connection with the sale or advertisement of goods and services are registrable if they contain "original work of authorship." Use Form VA if the copyrightable material in the work you are registering is mainly pictorial or graphic; use Form TX if it consists mainly of text. *NOTE:* Words and short phrases such as names, titles, and slogans cannot be protected by copyright, and the same is true of standard symbols, emblems, and other commonly-used graphic designs that are in the public domain. When used commercially, material of that sort can sometimes be protected un-

der State laws of unfair competition or under the Federal trademark laws. For information about trademark registration, write to the Commissioner of Patents and Trademarks, Washington, D.C. 20231.

DEPOSIT TO ACCOMPANY APPLICATION: An application for copyright registration must be accompanied by a deposit representing the entire work for which registration is to be made. The following are the general deposit requirements for works of the visual arts, as set forth in the statute:

Unpublished work: Deposit one complete copy.

Published work: Deposit two complete copies of the best edition.

Work first published outside the United States: Deposit one complete copy of the first foreign edition.

Contribution to a collective work: Deposit one complete copy of the best edition of the collective work.

These general deposit requirements will vary in particular situations. In most cases, where the copies in which the work has been reproduced are three-dimensional, the Copyright Office Regulations provide for the deposit of identifying material (such as photographs or drawings) meeting certain requirements. For further information about the deposit requirements for works of the visual arts, see the reverse side of this sheet. For general information about copyright deposit, write to the Copyright Office.

DURATION OF COPYRIGHT: For works that were created after the effective date of the new statute (January 1, 1978), the basic copyright term will be the life of the author and fifty years after the author's death. For works made for hire, and for certain anonymous and pseudonymous works, the duration of copyright will be 75 years from publication or 100 years from creation, whichever is shorter. These same terms of copyright will generally apply to works that had been created before 1978 but had not been published or copyrighted before that date. For further information about the duration of copyright, including the terms of copyrights already in existence before 1978, write for Circular R15a.

FORM VA
UNITED STATES COPYRIGHT OFFICE

REGISTRATION NUMBER
VA   VAU
EFFECTIVE DATE OF REGISTRATION
....
(Month)   (Day)   (Year)

DO NOT WRITE ABOVE THIS LINE. IF YOU NEED MORE SPACE, USE CONTINUATION SHEET (FORM VA/CON)

(1) Title

TITLE OF THIS WORK: | **NATURE OF THIS WORK:** (See instructions)

Previous or Alternative Titles:

PUBLICATION AS A CONTRIBUTION: (If this work was published as a contribution to a periodical, serial, or collection, give information about the collective work in which the contribution appeared.)

Title of Collective Work: .... Vol. ...... No. ...... Date .... Pages ....

(2) Author(s)

IMPORTANT: Under the law, the "author" of a "work made for hire" is generally the employer, not the employee (see instructions). If any part of this work was "made for hire" check "Yes" in the space provided, give the employer (or other person for whom the work was prepared) as "Author" of that part, and leave the space for dates blank.

NAME OF AUTHOR: | **DATES OF BIRTH AND DEATH:**

Was this author's contribution to the work a "work made for hire"? Yes ...... No ......
Born .... Died ....
(Year)   (Year)

1

AUTHOR'S NATIONALITY OR DOMICILE:
Citizen of .... } or { Domiciled in ....
(Name of Country)   (Name of Country)

WAS THIS AUTHOR'S CONTRIBUTION TO THE WORK:
Anonymous? Yes ...... No ......
Pseudonymous? Yes ...... No ......

AUTHOR OF: (Briefly describe nature of this author's contribution)

If the answer to either of these questions is "Yes," see detailed instructions attached.

NAME OF AUTHOR: | **DATES OF BIRTH AND DEATH:**

Was this author's contribution to the work a "work made for hire"? Yes ...... No ......
Born .... Died ....
(Year)   (Year)

2

AUTHOR'S NATIONALITY OR DOMICILE:
Citizen of .... } or { Domiciled in ....
(Name of Country)   (Name of Country)

WAS THIS AUTHOR'S CONTRIBUTION TO THE WORK:
Anonymous? Yes ...... No ......
Pseudonymous? Yes ...... No ......

AUTHOR OF: (Briefly describe nature of this author's contribution)

If the answer to either of these questions is "Yes," see detailed instructions attached.

NAME OF AUTHOR: | **DATES OF BIRTH AND DEATH:**

Was this author's contribution to the work a "work made for hire"? Yes ...... No ......
Born .... Died ....
(Year)   (Year)

3

AUTHOR'S NATIONALITY OR DOMICILE:
Citizen of .... } or { Domiciled in ....
(Name of Country)   (Name of Country)

WAS THIS AUTHOR'S CONTRIBUTION TO THE WORK:
Anonymous? Yes ...... No ......
Pseudonymous? Yes ...... No ......

AUTHOR OF: (Briefly describe nature of this author's contribution)

If the answer to either of these questions is "Yes," see detailed instructions attached.

(3) Creation and Publication

YEAR IN WHICH CREATION OF THIS WORK WAS COMPLETED: | **DATE AND NATION OF FIRST PUBLICATION:**

Year ....
(This information must be given in all cases.)

Date ....
(Month)   (Day)   (Year)
Nation ....
(Name of Country)
(Complete this block ONLY if this work has been published.)

(4) Claimant(s)

NAME(S) AND ADDRESS(ES) OF COPYRIGHT CLAIMANT(S):

TRANSFER: (If the copyright claimant(s) named here in space 4 are different from the author(s) named in space 2, give a brief statement of how the claimant(s) obtained ownership of the copyright.)

- Complete all applicable spaces (numbers 5-9) on the reverse side of this page
- Follow detailed instructions attached • Sign the form at line 8

DO NOT WRITE HERE
Page 1 of .... pages

	EXAMINED BY:	APPLICATION RECEIVED:	
	CHECKED BY:		
	CORRESPONDENCE: ☐ Yes	DEPOSIT RECEIVED:	FOR COPYRIGHT OFFICE USE ONLY
	DEPOSIT ACCOUNT FUNDS USED: ☐	REMITTANCE NUMBER AND DATE:	

DO NOT WRITE ABOVE THIS LINE. IF YOU NEED ADDITIONAL SPACE, USE CONTINUATION SHEET (FORM VA/CON)

PREVIOUS REGISTRATION:

⑤ Previous Registration

- Has registration for this work, or for an earlier version of this work, already been made in the Copyright Office? Yes....... No ....

- If your answer is "Yes," why is another registration being sought? (Check appropriate box)
  ☐ This is the first published edition of a work previously registered in unpublished form.
  ☐ This is the first application submitted by this author as copyright claimant.
  ☐ This is a changed version of the work, as shown by line 6 of the application.

- If your answer is "Yes," give: Previous Registration Number............................ Year of Registration........................

COMPILATION OR DERIVATIVE WORK: (See instructions)

⑥ Compilation or Derivative Work

⌈ PREEXISTING MATERIAL: (Identify any preexisting work or works that this work is based on or incorporates.)
  ....
  ....
  ....
  ....

⌈ MATERIAL ADDED TO THIS WORK: (Give a brief, general statement of the material that has been added to this work and in which copyright is claimed.)
  ....
  ....
  ....
  ....

DEPOSIT ACCOUNT: (If the registration fee is to be charged to a Deposit Account established in the Copyright Office, give name and number of Account.)

Name: ....

Account Number: ....

CORRESPONDENCE: (Give name and address to which correspondence about this application should be sent.)

Name: ....

Address: ....
                                          (Apt.)
(City)   (State)   (ZIP)

⑦ Fee and Correspondence

CERTIFICATION: ✱ I, the undersigned, hereby certify that I am the: (Check one)
☐ author ☐ other copyright claimant ☐ owner of exclusive right(s) ☐ authorized agent of: ....
                                       (Name of author or other copyright claimant, or owner of exclusive right(s))
of the work identified in this application and that the statements made by me in this application are correct to the best of my knowledge.

      ☞ Handwritten signature: (X) ....

      Typed or printed name: .... Date: ....

⑧ Certification (Application must be signed)

⌈ ....
               (Name)
....
       (Number, Street and Apartment Number)
....
   (City)   (State)   (ZIP code)

MAIL CERTIFICATE TO

(Certificate will be mailed in window envelope)

⑨ Address For Return of Certificate

Appendix G
Documents Pertaining to Acquisitions

Contract of Bailment
Gift of Personalty
New York State Association of Museums, Guidelines
Declaration for Importation or Exportation of Fish or
    Wildlife (U.S. Fish and Wildlife Service, Form 3-177)
Federal Fish and Wildlife License/Permit Application
    (U.S. Fish and Wildlife Service, Form 3-200)
Application for Permit under the Antiquities Act (U.S.
    Department of the Interior, Form 10-70)

CONTRACT OF BAILMENT

State of _____

County of _____
    By this agreement, made and entered into by and between _____
_____ , hereinafter called Bailor, and South Plains Museum, Inc.,
hereinafter called Bailee, the Bailor, for and in consideration of the sum of____
Dollars, paid by Bailee to Bailor, the receipt of which is hereby acknowledged,
lets to Bailee the following described property:

Article	Valuation by Owner	Condition

subject to the terms and conditions hereinafter set forth.
    1. Delivery of the property shall be made to Bailee at _____
_____ . Acceptance or retention by Bailee of said property shall
constitute acknowledgment that such property was received in good order and
repair.
    2. The term of this bailment shall commence on _____
and shall terminate on _____ .

    The sample contract shown here was adapted from *Texas Forms*, vol. 17:1–28:8 (San
Francisco: Bancroft-Whitney, 1969), pp. 15–18.

237

3. The bailed property shall at all times remain and be the sole and exclusive property of Bailor, and Bailee shall have no right of property therein. The bailed property shall not be transferred or delivered to any other person or corporation without prior written consent or instruction of Bailor, and neither this agreement nor the bailment hereby granted may be assigned by Bailee, either by its own act or by operation of law.

4. The property shall remain in the possession of Bailee for the time specified in this agreement, but it may be withdrawn from exhibition at any time by Bailee.

5. Bailee binds itself to keep and maintain said property with proper care so that the same shall not be injured, ordinary wear and tear excepted. Bailee shall not be liable for damage or loss caused by war, confiscation, order of any government or public authority, or discoloration from natural or inherent causes or by any and all causes beyond the control of Bailee.

6. The property accepted by Bailee will be protected by Bailee by insurance against loss by fire and theft, payable to Bailor to the full amount of the valuation declared by Bailor and so noted opposite each item listed herein. Bailee shall not be liable for any loss or damage to the property in excess of the value declared by the owner at the time of signing this contract, and if a valuation is not declared, the liability of Bailee as to all items hereby hired shall be limited to _____ Dollars.

7. The amount of space allotted to display of the bailed property is _____ _____ . The method of exhibition and any publicity given the exhibition is to be determined and controlled by Bailee.

8. All shipping and packaging costs for the bailed property are to be paid by _____ .

9. On the expiration of the term of this bailment, Bailee shall redeliver the property hereby bailed to Bailor, in accordance with the terms and conditions set forth in this agreement. The delivery of the bailed property to a common carrier, or to any address directed by Bailor or Bailor's representative, shall be considered delivery to Bailor. If, after reasonable efforts, Bailee is unable to return the work within ninety days after termination of this agreement, Bailee shall have the right to place the work in storage and to charge regular storage fees and insurance and to have a lien for such fees and costs. If the property is not reclaimed after two years, the work shall become a gift to Bailee.

10. On termination of this bailment in any manner, Bailor or its agents are hereby authorized to enter upon premises of Bailee and to remove and take possession of the property. Bailor may inspect the property before taking possession or accepting delivery, and if the inspection establishes that any part of the property is not in the condition above required, Bailee will do all things necessary to place it in such condition.

11. Bailor and Bailee agree that no modification of this agreement shall be

binding unless such modification shall be in writing duly accepted and executed by both parties.

Dated _____ .

Bailor _____

Bailee _____

GIFT OF PERSONALTY

State of _____
County of _____
Know all men by these presents, that I, _____ of _____ , State of _____ , own the items described below. I desire to give the described property to South Plains Museum, Inc., of Anytown, Texas.

To carry out my purpose, I do hereby give and deliver to South Plains Museum, Inc., the property described as follows:

It is distinctly understood by me that it is my purpose and intention to vest all the incidents of absolute ownership of the property in South Plains Museum, Inc., from this time forward.

Dated _____ .

Donor _____

Acceptance

The gift above described is accepted by South Plains Museum, Inc.

Dated _____ .

South Plains Museum, Inc. _____

By _____

NEW YORK STATE ASSOCIATION OF MUSEUMS,

GUIDELINES

The Ethics and Responsibilities of Museums
with Respect to the Acquisition and Disposition
of Collection Materials

April 1974

The following Guidelines were formulated to assist member institutions of NYSAM in reviewing their policies and practices relative to the acquisition and disposition of collection materials. These Guidelines may also serve to assist institutions in formulating and adopting written standards to govern their own practices, if such written standards do not already exist.

It is recognized that these Guidelines may not be binding on individual institutions without specific approval and adoption by their governing authorities. However, they do represent the official position of NYSAM on the ethics and responsibilities that ought to be followed by museums on such matters. It is expected that the adoption of these Guidelines by NYSAM will place some responsibility on the operating personnel of member institutions to observe them in their practices, to the extent that they are not in conflict with the requirements and policy of the museum's governing authority.

The New York State Association of Museums strongly urges each of its member institutions to adopt these Guidelines, or to formulate and adopt, with the approval of their governing authority, written standards with respect to the matters they cover. The written standards adopted by member institutions should reflect the principles set forth in the Guidelines, modified or amplified as necessary to meet local conditions.

I. *Acquisition of Objects for Museum Collections*
    (1) Objects should not be accepted or otherwise acquired for museum collections unless the following conditions are met:
        a. The objects are relevant to and consistent with the purposes and activities of the museum.
        b. The museum can provide for the storage, protection, and preservation of the objects under conditions that insure their availability for museum purposes and are in keeping with professionally accepted standards.
        c. It is intended that the objects shall have permanency in the collections as long as they retain their physical integrity, their identity, and their authenticity, and as long as they remain useful for the purposes of the museum.
    (2) Title to all objects acquired for the collections should be obtained free and clear, without restrictions as to use or future disposition. If objects

are accepted with restrictions or limitations, however, the conditions should be stated clearly in an instrument of conveyance, should be made part of the accession records for the objects, and should be strictly observed by the museum.

(3) A legal instrument of conveyance, setting forth an adequate description of the objects involved and the precise conditions of transfer, should accompany all gifts and purchases and should be kept on file at the museum. In the case of sales and conditional gifts, this document should be signed by the seller or donor and by an authorized museum representative; in the case of unconditional gifts, it need be signed only by the donor.

(4) Records of accession should be made and retained for all objects acquired for the collections.

II. *Deaccessioning and Disposing of Objects from the Collections*

(1) Objects in the collections should be retained permanently if they continue to be relevant and useful to the purposes and activities of the museum and if they can be properly stored, preserved, and used. Deaccessioning of objects may be considered when these conditions no longer prevail or in the interest of improving the collections for the museum's purposes and activities.

(2) Objects in the collections should be deaccessioned only upon the recommendation of the appropriate curator or a responsible authority approved by the curator, upon the approval of the museum's chief operating officer, and in accordance with policies approved by the museum's governing authority. Boards of trustees are urged to adopt specific policies with respect to such matters, including the conditions under which transactions must be reported to and approved by the board.

(3) In considering various alternatives for the disposition of deaccessioned objects, museums should be concerned that:

a. the manner of disposition is in the best interests of the museum, the public it serves, the public trust it represents in owning the collections, and the scholarly or cultural communities that it represents.

b. preference should be given to retaining in the state or nation material that is part of the historical, cultural, or scientific heritage of New York State or of the United States, respectively.

c. consideration should be given to placing the objects, through gift, exchange, or sale, in another tax-exempt public institution wherein they may serve the purpose for which they were acquired initially by the museum. If objects are offered for sale elsewhere, preference should be given to sale at advertised public auction or at the public marketplace in a manner that will best protect the interests, objectives, and legal status of the museum.

   d. objects should not be given or sold privately to museum employees,
      officers, members of the governing authority, or to their representa-
      tives.
   (4) Before disposing of any objects from the collections, the museum
       should make reasonable efforts to ascertain that it is free to so do.
       Where restrictions as to use or disposition of the objects under question
       are found to apply, the museum should act as follows:
       a. Mandatory restrictions should be observed strictly unless deviation
          from their terms is authorized by a court of competent jurisdiction.
       b. Objects to which precatory restrictions apply should not be dis-
          posed of until reasonable efforts have been made to comply with the
          restricting conditions. If it is practical and reasonable to do so, con-
          sidering the value of the objects under question, the museum should
          notify the donor if it intends to dispose of such objects within ten
          years of receiving the gift or within the donor's lifetime, whichever
          is less.
       c. If there is any question as to the intent or force of restrictions, the
          museum should seek the advice of its legal counsel.
   (5) An adequate record of the conditions and circumstances under which
       objects are deaccessioned and disposed of should be made and retained
       as part of the museum's collection records.

III. *Public Disclosure*
   (1) A written statement of the policy and procedures adopted and followed
       by museums with respect to the acquisition and disposition of collec-
       tion materials should be prepared and should be made available to
       donors or other responsible persons on request.
   (2) In reply to responsible inquiry, museums should make available the
       identity and description of collection materials acquired or deacces-
       sioned. All other facts pertaining to the circumstances of acquisition,
       deaccession, and disposal should be adequately documented in the
       museum's records.

Form 3-177

USFWS Form 3-177
(revised Sept. 1978)

Form Approved O.M.B. No. 42-R1476

U.S. FISH AND WILDLIFE SERVICE

DECLARATION FOR IMPORTATION

OR EXPORTATION OF

FISH OR WILDLIFE

Indicate One:
☐ import   ☐ export

Port of:

Date:

For Imports Only

Customs Identification No.:

Name of Carrier:

Airway Bill or Bill of Lading No.:

Imported or Exported via:
☐ air cargo   ☐ ocean cargo   ☐ truck
☐ rail   ☐ mail   ☐ personal baggage
☐ automobile: license no. _____
state _____

Location where wildlife is available for inspection:

Package or Bale Marks and Nos.:

(indicate one)

Please Type or Print Legibly

☐ U.S. Importer of Record

☐ U.S. Exporter _____
(name)

_____
(address - street, city, state, zip code)

Foreign Consignor
or Consignee _____
(name)

_____
(address - street, city, country)

Customs Broker
or Agent _____

Shipping Agent or
Freight Forwarder _____

Furnish All Information Below (invoices or lists providing required information may be attached)

QUANTITY	SCIENTIFIC NAME Genus	Species	COMMON NAME	DESCRIPTION If live, so state. If product, describe.	DECLARED VALUE	COUNTRY OF ORIGIN

U.S. License and/or Permit Nos.:

Foreign License and/or Permits:
Country   No.

I certify the information contained herein is true and complete to the best of my knowledge and belief.

_____   _____
signature   date

FOR OFFICIAL USE ONLY

Action Taken: **Date:**
☐ cleared
☐ clearance refused
☐ seized

_____ % of Wildlife Inspected:

Officer Signature and Badge No.:

SEE REVERSE OF THIS FORM FOR INSTRUCTIONS AND PRIVACY ACT NOTICE

FILING INSTRUCTIONS

File original declaration only. Copies may be retained by importer or broker if desired. Print or type legibly. Provide all relevant information. Declared value need not be shown for scientific specimens, game, or game trophies not imported or exported for a commercial purpose.

"Country of Origin" means the country where the animal was taken from the wild or the country of natal origin of the animal.

When And Where To File.

At Designated Ports: File with the U.S. Fish and Wildlife Service Office serving the designated port. For imports, file declarations when requesting wildlife clearance. For exports, file declaration in sufficient time in advance of actual departure of wildlife from U.S. to allow reasonable time for inspection.

At Nondesignated Ports: File with U.S. Customs. For imports, file declaration prior to removal of wildlife from Customs custody. For exports, file prior to departure of wildlife from U.S.

Note To Customs Officers. Mail all Forms 3-177 collected to Special Agent in Charge, U.S. Fish and Wildlife Service for your district at end of each month.

Regulations concerning the importation and exportation of wildlife may be found in 50 CFR Part 14. Specific regulations concerning the filing of declarations for the importation or exportation of wildlife may be found in 50 CFR 14.61-14.64.

Failure to file a declaration for importation or exportation of fish or wildlife when required by the regulations in 50 CFR 14.61-14.64 is a violation of the Endangered Species Act of 1973 (16 USC 1531-1543).

Knowingly making a false statement in a Declaration for Importation or Exportation of Fish or Wildlife may subject the declarant to the penalty provided by 18 USC 1001.

NOTICE

In accordance with the Privacy Act of 1974 (P.L. 93-579), please be advised that:

1. The gathering of information on the importation or exportation of wildlife, including any wild mammal, bird, fish, amphibian, reptile, mollusk, or crustacean, is authorized by the Endangered Species Act of 1973 (16 USC 1531-1543) and Title 50, Parts 14 and 17, of the Code of Federal Regulations.

2. The disclosure of the requested information is required to provide information about wildlife imports or exports, including products and parts, to facilitate enforcement of the act and to carry out the provisions of the Convention on International Trade in Endangered Species of Wild Fauna and Flora.

3. Failure to provide all of the requested information is sufficient cause for the U.S. Fish and Wildlife Service to deny you permission to import or export wildlife.

4. In the event there is indicated a violation of a statute, regulation, rule, order, or license, whether civil, criminal, or regulatory in nature, the requested information may be transferred to the appropriate Federal, State, local, or foreign agency charged with investigating or prosecuting such violations.

5. In the event of litigation involving the records or the subject matter of the records, the requested information may be transferred to the U.S. Department of Justice.

6. The requested information may be subject to disclosure under provisions of the Freedom of Information Act, 5 USC 552.

Form 3-200

OMB NO. 42-R1670

DEPARTMENT OF THE INTERIOR **U.S. FISH AND WILDLIFE SERVICE** **FEDERAL FISH AND WILDLIFE** **LICENSE/PERMIT APPLICATION**	1. APPLICATION FOR *(Indicate only one)* ☐ IMPORT OR EXPORT LICENSE ☐ PERMIT 2. BRIEF DESCRIPTION OF ACTIVITY FOR WHICH REQUESTED LICENSE OR PERMIT IS NEEDED.

3. APPLICANT. *(Name, complete address and phone number of individual, business, agency, or institution for which permit is requested)*

4. IF "APPLICANT" IS AN <u>INDIVIDUAL</u>, COMPLETE THE FOLLOWING:	5. IF "APPLICANT" IS A <u>BUSINESS</u>, <u>CORPORATION</u>, <u>PUBLIC AGENCY</u>, OR <u>INSTITUTION</u>, COMPLETE THE FOLLOWING:
☐ MR. ☐ MRS. ☐ MISS ☐ MS.	EXPLAIN TYPE OR KIND OF BUSINESS, AGENCY, OR INSTITUTION
HEIGHT / WEIGHT	
DATE OF BIRTH / COLOR HAIR / COLOR EYES	
PHONE NUMBER WHERE EMPLOYED / SOCIAL SECURITY NUMBER	
OCCUPATION	
ANY BUSINESS, AGENCY, OR INSTITUTIONAL AFFILIATION HAVING TO DO WITH THE WILDLIFE TO BE COVERED BY THIS LICENSE/PERMIT	NAME, TITLE, AND PHONE NUMBER OF PRESIDENT, PRINCIPAL OFFICER, DIRECTOR, ETC. IF "APPLICANT" IS A CORPORATION, INDICATE STATE IN WHICH INCORPORATED

6. LOCATION WHERE PROPOSED ACTIVITY IS TO BE CONDUCTED	7. DO YOU HOLD ANY CURRENTLY VALID FEDERAL FISH AND WILDLIFE LICENSE OR PERMIT? ☐ YES ☐ NO *(If yes, list license or permit numbers)* 8. IF REQUIRED BY ANY STATE OR FOREIGN GOVERNMENT, DO YOU HAVE THEIR APPROVAL TO CONDUCT THE ACTIVITY YOU PROPOSE? ☐ YES ☐ NO *(If yes, list jurisdictions and type of documents)*

9. CERTIFIED CHECK OR MONEY ORDER *(if applicable)* PAYABLE TO THE U.S. FISH AND WILDLIFE SERVICE ENCLOSED IN AMOUNT OF $ 25.00	10. DESIRED EFFECTIVE DATE	11. DURATION NEEDED

12. ATTACHMENTS. THE SPECIFIC INFORMATION REQUIRED FOR THE TYPE OF LICENSE/PERMIT REQUESTED *(See 50 CFR 13.12(b))* MUST BE ATTACHED. IT CONSTITUTES AN INTEGRAL PART OF THIS APPLICATION. LIST SECTIONS OF 50 CFR UNDER WHICH ATTACHMENTS ARE PROVIDED.

SEE REVERSE SIDE

CERTIFICATION

I HEREBY CERTIFY THAT I HAVE READ AND AM FAMILIAR WITH THE REGULATIONS CONTAINED IN TITLE 50, PART 13, OF THE CODE OF FEDERAL REGULATIONS AND THE OTHER APPLICABLE PARTS IN SUBCHAPTER B OF CHAPTER I OF TITLE 50, AND I FURTHER CERTIFY THAT THE INFORMATION SUBMITTED IN THIS APPLICATION FOR A LICENSE/PERMIT IS COMPLETE AND ACCURATE TO THE BEST OF MY KNOWLEDGE AND BELIEF. I UNDERSTAND THAT ANY FALSE STATEMENT HEREIN MAY SUBJECT ME TO THE CRIMINAL PENALTIES OF 18 U.S.C. 1001.

SIGNATURE *(In ink)*	DATE

3-200
(6/74)

ENDANGERED OR THREATENED SPECIES

I. COMPLETE THE FOLLOWING:

 a. Species: _____ _____ Number____ Age____ Sex____
              (Scientific name)   (Common name)

 b. At the time of application, the wildlife sought to be covered:

 ____ is still in the wild

 ____ has been removed from the wild _____
                                        (country and place of removal)

 ____ was raised in captivity _____
                                (country and place where wildlife was born)

 c. Attempts to obtain wildlife in a manner which would not cause the death or removal from the wild.

 d. A complete description and address of the institution or facility where the wildlife will be used, displayed, or maintained.

II. ATTACH THE FOLLOWING INFORMATION ON PLAIN WHITE PAPER:

 f. Copies of contracts and agreements relating to the permit, including the identity of all persons who will engage in the activities and the dates of such activities.

 g. A statement justifying the permit, including:
    (1) Details of the activities (attach research proposals, if appropriate)
    (2) How the activities will be carried out.
    (3) The relationship to scientific objectives or to enhancing the propagation or survival of the wildlife involved.
    (4) Planned disposition of the wildlife upon termination of the activities.

III. IF LIVE WILDLIFE IS TO BE COVERED BY THE PERMIT:

 1) Attach photographs or diagrams of the area and facilities where wildlife will be housed and cared for.

 2) Give a brief resume of the technical expertise of the persons who will care for such wildlife including any experience the applicant or his personnel have had in raising, caring for, and propagating similar wildlife or any closely related wildlife.

 3) Indicate your willingness to participate in a cooperative breeding program or to contribute data to a studbook.

 4) Describe the type, size and construction of all containers wildlife will be placed in during transportation or temporary storage, if any, and the arrangements for feeding, watering, and otherwise caring for it during that period.

 5) Provide a detailed description of all mortalities during the preceding 5 years involving the species covered in the application and held by the applicant (or any other wildlife of the same genus or family held by the applicant), including the causes of such mortalities and the steps taken to avoid or decrease such mortalities.

Form 10-70
(March 1970)

UNITED STATES
DEPARTMENT OF THE INTERIOR

APPLICATION FOR PERMIT
UNDER THE ANTIQUITIES ACT

(P.L. 59-209 (34 Stat. 225; 16 U.S.C. 431-433))

FOR OFFICIAL USE ONLY
DATE RECEIVED _____
DISPOSITION _____
DATE _____

INSTRUCTIONS: Application must be signed by director or other responsible official (Item 14) of the applicant institution (Item 1) other than the person named in direct charge of field work (Item 8B). All information requested must be completed before application will be considered. Use separate sheet of paper if more space is needed to complete a section.

1. NAME OF INSTITUTION	2. DATE OF APPLICATION

3. ADDRESS *(Include Zip Code)*

4. NATURE, STATUS, AND SCIENTIFIC AFFILIATIONS OF APPLICANT ORGANIZATION:

5. TYPE OF PERMIT REQUESTED:

A. ☐ To conduct preliminary explorations in areas described in 6A and 6B below.

B. ☐ To excavate, collect, and make intensive studies of specific sites described as:

6. LANDS OF THE UNITED STATES FOR WHICH PERMIT IS REQUESTED:

A. Description: *(If on surveyed lands, descriptions must be by subdivisions of the Public Land Surveys. If on unsurveyed lands, description must be by metes and bounds with ties to some topographic feature.)*

B. Map, sketch, or plan, showing specific sites or areas for which permit is desired. *(Use separate sheet, if necessary, and attach to each copy of application submitted.)*

7. AIMS, PURPOSES, AND EXACT CHARACTER OF WORK PROPOSED:

8. NAME, ADDRESS, AND OFFICIAL STATUS OF PERSONS IN "A" AND "B" BELOW: *(Name a DIFFERENT person for each.)*

A. In general charge of project:

B. In direct charge of field work: *(Include qualifications.)*

9. DATE FIELD WORK WILL BEGIN:	10. LENGTH OF TIME WORK WILL BE IN PROGRESS:

11. PUBLIC MUSEUM IN WHICH MATERIALS COLLECTED WILL BE PERMANENTLY PRESERVED AND AVAILABLE FOR SCIENTIFIC STUDY AND PUBLIC OBSERVATION: *(Name and Location)*

12. RESULTS OF WORK DONE TO BE PUBLISHED AS FOLLOWS: *(Name of publication and date of issuance.)*

13. FUNDS AVAILABLE FOR FIELD WORK, EXCLUSIVE OF REGULAR STAFF SALARIES:

14. INSTITUTION OFFICIAL REQUESTING PERMIT: *(MUST BE SIGNED)*

_____   _____
        (Signature)   *(Title)*

15. COMPLETE FOUR (4) COPIES OF THIS APPLICATION AND RETURN TO:

GENERAL INFORMATION FOR COMPLETING APPLICATION FORM FOR

DEPARTMENT OF THE INTERIOR ANTIQUITIES ACT PERMITS

Numbers in the brackets (10) refer to the specific sections on the
application form.

A. Antiquities Act permits are granted only to qualified scientific or
   educational institutions (1). They cannot be issued to or in the
   name of an individual. If the field investigations are to be
   carried out by an organization or group affiliated with a qualified
   institution, other than one of its departments, the nature of the
   affiliation must be clearly indicated (4). The address of the
   affiliated organization or group must also be included if it is
   not the same as the applying institution (3).

B. All applications are to be submitted in quadruplicate and mailed to:

   > Departmental Consulting Archeologist
   > Department of the Interior
   > Office of Archeology and Historic Preservation
   > Interagency Archeological Services Division
   > Washington, D.C. 20240

   unless otherwise stated on the application form (15).

C. All copies of the application must be signed (14) by the Director or
   other responsible official of the applicant institution. Unsigned or
   improperly signed applications will be returned.

D. The application should indicate if the requestered permit is for
   archeological or paleontological investigations (5). Separate permit
   applications are required for preliminary explorations or surveys (5A)
   and for permits to excavate or make intensive studies and collections
   from specific sites (5B). The specific sites to be excavated must
   be adequately identified.

E. Lands of the United States for which a permit is requested (6) must
   be clearly identified. This should be by Township, Range, Section,
   and Quarter Section whenever possible (6A). Descriptions from an
   appropriate U.S.G.S. topographic map, or its equivalent, is advised.
   If a portion of an U.S.G.S. or other topographic map is attached to
   the application (6B), it should be identified by name. County maps,
   State highway department maps (other than the tourist variety), and
   etc., can be used if topographic maps are not available, as long as
   they clearly define or identify the area or sites proposed for study.
   Oil company road maps should be avoided, if at all possible, unless
   no other suitable map is available. State the specific Federal land
   manageing agency that administers the lands in the proposed permit area.

F. The application should define as accurately as possible the nature and scope of the project (7). If the project is for research purposes, a brief discussion of the problem and anticipated results should be provided. This should also include the reasons the particular site(s) were selected over alternate sites on applications for excavation permits. If the purpose of the work is salvage, there should be a brief explanation of the threat to the resource.

G. Avoid submitting applications with the same individual listed in general charge of the project (8A) and in direct charge of the field work (8B). If it is necessary that the same individual be listed for both, explain on a separate sheet and attach a copy to each copy of the application. Applications will not be accepted if the institution official requesting the permit (14) is the same as the person in direct charge of the field work (8B).

H. Permits are issued to cover only the time field investigations are being conducted on Federal lands (9) and (10), but no permit can be issued for a period longer than three calendar years. Applications for permits to exceed 1 year must contain adequate justification. The time granted may be extended upon written request showing proper cause and diligence in pursuing the work. Extensions can be granted for up to one year at a time. Failure to begin work within six months after a permit is granted, or failure to diligently keep on with the work after it has been started, shall make the permit void without any further action.

I. All applications must be reviewed by Interagency Archeological Services and the Federal agency administering the lands involved. It generally takes 60 days to review an application and issue the permit from the date it is received, if it is approved. Applications, therefore, should be submitted well in advance of the date on which the field investigations are proposed to begin. Applications for permits in Alaska generally take up to 10 weeks for review. Applications for permits for Indian lands can take much longer.

J. Within approximately 6 weeks of the conclusion of field work carried out under an Antiquities Act permit, a preliminary report on work performed under the permit is to be furnished to the Secretary, Smithsonian Institution, and the Departmental Consulting Archeologist. The number of copies of the report required will be specified in Sec. 9 of the permit.

K. The application must contain vita, in quadruplicate, for each individual cited on the application as being in direct charge of field work.

Appendix H
Codes of Ethics

Association of Art Museum Directors, Code of Ethics
American Association of Museums, Code of Ethics for
  Museum Workers

CODE OF ETHICS
of the Association of Art Museum Directors
as adopted in 1966 and revised in 1972

The position of a Museum Director is one of trust, involving great responsibilities. It is the moral obligation of a Museum Director, in implementing the policies of his governing board, to accept and discharge these to the best of his ability for the benefit of his institution and the public. It is assumed that, in all his activities, he will act with integrity and in accordance with the highest moral principles; that he will assiduously avoid any and all activities which could in any way compromise him or the institution which he directs. It is further assumed that, in all undertakings within his jurisdiction, he will be personally responsible for the highest standards and excellence of performance. Through his own professional integrity he will set an example to his staff, to whom he should communicate the contents of this Code of Ethics, in substance and detail, upon assuming the position of Director, and to each member of his professional staff hired subsequent to that occasion before the latter's acceptance of employment by the museum.

The members of the Association of Art Museum Directors, maintaining that the position of a Museum Director is dependent upon his professional competence and integrity, and that it requires impartiality and a sense of public responsibility, especially in the area of museum acquisitions, declare that it should be unprofessional for a Museum Director

(a) to use his influence or position in the art market for personal gain. He should not traffic in works of art for monetary reasons nor be party to the recommendation of works of art for purchase by museums or collectors

Reprinted from pages 27–28 of *Professional Practices in Art Museums*, by the Association of Art Museum Directors, by permission of the Association of Art Museum Directors.

in which he has any undisclosed financial interest, nor should he accept any commission or gift from any seller or buyer of works of art. If he himself is a collector he should exercise extraordinary discretion to assure that no conflict of interest arises between himself and the concerns of his museum. If such an occasion should arise, it must be resolved by granting the museum's governing board the first option to acquire the work or works of art in question.

(b) to give, for a fee or on a retainer, any certificate or statement as to the authenticity or authorship of a work of art, or any statement of the monetary value of a work of art, except where authorized by and in accordance with the lawful purposes of his own or other nonprofit institutions concerned or government agencies.

Infractions of these canons of professional conduct, when duly established, will render a member of the Association of Art Museum Directors subject to discipline by reprimand, suspension, or expulsion from the Association.

CODE OF ETHICS FOR MUSEUM WORKERS
adopted by the American Association of Museums

Museums, in the broadest sense, are institutions which hold their possessions in trust for mankind and for the future welfare of the race. Their value is in direct proportion to the service they render the emotional and intellectual life of the people.

The life of the museum worker, whether he be an humble laborer or a responsible trustee, is essentially one of service. His conduct rests on a threefold ethical basis:

1. devotion to the cause he serves
2. faith in the unselfish motives of his coworkers
3. honor based on a high sense of justice as the controlling motive of his thoughts and actions.

RELATIONS OF MUSEUMS TO THE PUBLIC

Courtesy

A museum worker will always be courteous to the visitor, thoughtful even to the extent of great personal inconvenience upon occasion. It may be helpful to remember that one is in a sense the host to a visiting guest.

Service

A museum worker will always give his best service to the public. Every member, in so doing, approximates most fully the ideals and purposes for which the museum stands. This service may be performed indirectly or by direct contact with the people. He will at no time allow jealousy to prevent him from transferring a call to a colleague, if by so doing he can render better and more proper service.

Business Dealings

The maintenance of a museum involves business relationships with many different persons including such individuals as lecturers, architects, lawyers, and physicians.

No museum official or worker may honorably accept any commission, gift, or tip which may be offered by a business concern as an inducement to do business with it. Only the museum itself is entitled to the discounts customarily allowed on a large volume of business or for prompt payment of bills.

Business Independence

A museum should avoid any business relationship which shall put it under any obligation, financial or otherwise, to deal exclusively with any particular person or concern, but should rather base its business dealings on quality of goods, promptness of service, and fairness of price. In the long run a museum will prosper if it keeps its business dealings clearly separated from its public support regardless of the source from which it may be derived.

A museum should carefully scrutinize the titles to objects offered for sale and refuse to acquire those obtained through vandalism.

A museum may feel free to ask or accept service of a nonprofessional lecturer, but it should pay a suitable fee to him whose livelihood in part or whole is derived from his lecture service.

The Public

The public should be slow to demand a service which will be freely given, and should be mindful of the fact that unnecessary expenditure of time in serving one reduces the amount and quality of service the museum can render all.

Relations between Museums

The relations between museums are essentially those between presidents, trustees, or directors.

Employees

A museum may not properly offer a position to an employee of another museum with which it has regular and intimate relations without having first notified the director of its intentions so to do. If, however, an employee of a museum shall apply for a position at another museum, that museum shall not be under any obligation to confer with the museum by which the applicant is then employed, the obligation in such cases resting with the employee.

A museum shall regard the advancement of an employee qualified to assume larger responsibilities as a matter of first importance, both from the point of view of the welfare of the employee and the cause of museums, and if it is unable for financial or other reasons to offer the enlarged opportunity, it not only should put nothing in the way of that employee going elsewhere, but if the occasion should arise, it may encourage such an employee to make application for a better position which it knows to be open.

Collection and Acquisition

If a museum has under negotiation the acceptance of a gift or the purchase of an object or collection of objects, another museum knowing of such negotiations may not with honor make an offer, either for whole or part of the collection, until the first museum has reached a decision in the matter. On occasion where two or more museums may be interested in the purchase of a collection in whole or in part, the highest ethical standards shall require that they cooperate through correspondence, conference, or otherwise toward the consummation of the purchase.

Explorations

Where two or more museums conduct explorations in the same region for the same kind of material, they not only duplicate effort but needlessly expend funds. It is highly desirable that museums establish an intimate cooperative practice in the matter of fieldwork so that an exploration party may have financial support from a number of institutions with freedom to carry on exhaustive exploration in its chosen field, making collections in such quantities that all museums contributing to the work may have representative collections, while that museum which has the work in charge may retain the rarer finds. It shall be considered unethical for a museum not to report every specimen collected to the museums concerned. The material should be placed where it will be of greatest value to science or to art or to history and to mankind.

Collections and Exchanges

Museums should cooperate by exchange, sale, or otherwise so that a very rare object or specimen may be placed where it can best be studied and kept in association with closely related objects. A museum should not "corner the market" by refusing to dispose of duplicate specimens to other museums. It, however, should not release valuable specimens until after they have been studied, and it should make those studies as promptly as possible so that an early distribution of material may be made.

Duplication of Effort

Two or more museums should not attempt to do the same service for the same community. They should so arrange the work that the effort of one should not duplicate that of the other, and it should be considered dishonorable for a museum, knowing the tentative plans of another museum, to take any action whatsoever to forestall or prevent the carrying out of such plans unless it shall be clearly in the interest of the public so to do, and then not until the matter has been discussed between the two museums and, if possible, an agreement reached as to division of labor. The most honorable action which one museum may take toward the work of another is that of sympathetic understanding and hearty cooperation.

Information

A museum will always give willingly and courteously, insofar as its rules and regulations will permit, any information regarding its finances, methods, and researches which may be asked of it by another museum. That museum to which such information has been given shall make use of it only for its own individual needs, it being dishonorable for it to make use of such information either for publication or for money except by permission. A free exchange of ideas and facts between museums is highly desirable if museums are to render their best service to mankind.

Relations of the Director to the Trustees

Responsibility

A museum director is responsible to his trustees for the treasures within the museum, the character of the service it renders, and the expenditure of the funds it receives. He should, therefore, expect, and the trustee should grant, a wide range of freedom in carrying on the work of the museum. He, in return, should make a strict accounting to the trustees at frequent intervals of the condition and activities of the museum, should make no large expenditure of funds without their approval, and should obtain their sanction of all changes in policy. He should neither expect nor ask an action from his trustees until he is sure that they thoroughly understand the matter which they are asked to consider, and if the action is contrary to his wishes, he should patiently wait until conditions have changed before presenting the matter again. The trustees should be sharers with the director of his responsibilities and should earnestly endeavor so to acquaint themselves with museum matters that they may fully bear their part of the burden.

Authority

With large responsibility goes large authority. The museum director has always before him the danger that he will abuse the authority vested in him unless he tempers it with wisdom, justice, and sympathy. While on the one hand the trustees should trust to the judgment of the director and give sympathetic consideration to his recommendations, the director must so act as to inspire the confidence of his trustees.

An indiscreet trustee may unconsciously wreck the whole morale of the museum organization through casual conversation with curators or other workers of the museum. It is incumbent on the trustee, therefore, to be discreet in his relationships with staff members, avoiding topics which may be concerned with administrative and executive matters.

Loyalty

A director should be loyal to the trustees and the trustees loyal to the director. When this condition cannot exist, it is time relations were severed. Other than the formality of his election for a term of years to the directorship, there should be no necessity for any written agreement between the director and his trustees. If either are dissatisfied, it should be recognized that his directorship should be terminated upon reasonable notice.

Sincerity

A director should be absolutely sincere with his trustees. To paint a picture in too glowing terms or to minimize the importance of the matter in an attempt to mislead in order to carry one's point is never justifiable.

Tact

To say the right thing at the right time and in the right way often means the success or failure of an undertaking. This is not incompatible with frankness. The better a director knows the individual members of his board of trustees, the more successfully he should be able to bring museum matters to their attention.

Impartiality

It is inevitable that a director shall more frequently consult the president and other officers of his board of trustees in an official capacity, but to show favoritism toward certain trustees and to ignore others will ultimately result in friction.

Relations of the Director to the Staff

Duty

It is the duty of the director to see that members of his staff work under as pleasant and healthful conditions as it is possible for the museum to maintain; that they be paid a suitable salary based upon their training, length of service, and faithful performance of their duty; they they be accorded proper credit for the work they do either in whole or in part; and that they be given every opportunity for advancement within the organization or for service in some other museum.

Fairness

In any organization certain rules are absolutely necessary. In the establishment of such rules the director should consider the welfare not only of the institution but also of its employees. At no time should he feel justified to make a rule to cover an individual case which would work a hardship on others. Ideally it should not be necessary to enforce fair rules, but if it is, they should be enforced impartially and without exception.

Sympathy

A director should show sympathetic interest in the work of his staff. In dealing, as he does, with different individuals, he should endeavor to have a sympathetic understanding of their personalities which is free from sentimentality.

RELATIONS OF THE STAFF TO THE DIRECTOR

Loyalty

A museum employee should be loyal to the director, to the museum, and to the cause it serves. Personal criticism may readily become disloyalty, and it is better that an employee sever his connection with the museum than that he feel disloyal toward it or the director.

Responsibility

A museum employee is responsible for the work he is engaged to do; he should ever keep in mind that his first duty is to care for the collections in his custody, and he should not allow his private interests to interfere with his duties to the museum and the public. Habitual lateness, loafing, or the use of museum time for personal gain are forms of irresponsibility which no director should countenance and no employee should practice.

Respect for Authority

In the last analysis, the director is the final authority. He may ask for suggestions and advice from members of the museum staff to help him toward a final decision, and staff members should respond to such requests with a full realization of the use to which their contribution is to be put. They should carry out to the best of their ability the plans of the director, even though those plans may not appear expedient to them. An employee's attitude toward the museum director and the museum official by whom he is employed should be one of respect for authority.

RELATIONS BETWEEN MEMBERS OF THE STAFF

Comity

Among all the workers in the museum there should exist a goodwill and a friendliness in regard to the rights of each other.

Charity

Where many persons are working together in more or less close contact, each should have for the other a respect for his personality, his intelligence, his feelings, and his work. Jealous acts, gossip, inquisitiveness, sarcasm, and practical jokes, often thoughtless, are always uncharitable, selfish, and often cruel.

Glossary of Legal Terms

A glossary of selected legal and tax terms, most of which are used and defined within the text, is provided here as a quick reference for terms used most often in a study of those laws particularly relevant to a museum organization. For more complete access to the meanings of legal terms and phrases found in statutes or judicial opinions, see *Black's Law Dictionary*, 5th ed. (St. Paul, Minn.: West Publishing, 1979).

ACCORD AND SATISFACTION. An agreement between parties to a contract which serves as a discharge of the contract. If a party to a contract enters into a different, later agreement with the other party to the contract, the later agreement is called an accord. When the party performs the duty under the subsequent agreement, he performs the accord, this being deemed satisfaction. The satisfaction operates as a discharge of the original contract.

ACQUISITION INDEBTEDNESS. Tax term referring to indebtedness on property incurred before the acquisition or improvement of the property, in instances where income from the property constitutes unrelated taxable income for an otherwise exempt organization. The amount of income from such property which is subject to income taxation is determined by multiplying the gross income from the property by a fraction, the numerator of which is the "average acquisition indebtedness" on the property and the denominator of which is the "average adjusted basis" of the property.

ADJUSTED BASIS. Cost or other basis of property reduced by depreciation and increased for capital improvements.

AGENCY. Those relationships in which one person represents another by the latter's authority.

AGENT. A person who is authorized to act for another (called a principal). A representative who transacts business with third persons on behalf of his principal.

ANSWER. Pleading filed by the defendant in a suit at law to deny allegations made by the plaintiff in plaintiff's pleading, which is called a petition or a complaint.

APPELLATE COURT. Courts of appeal and the Supreme Court. A losing party at the trial court level may appeal the trial court's decision to a court of appeals. The role of appellate courts is limited to a review of the record of trial compiled by the trial court. Thus, the appellate process involves a determination of whether or not the trial court applied the proper law in arriving at its decision. For the federal system, there are eleven circuit courts of appeals. Each state is within one of the eleven circuits, and appeals from each state must be to the appropriate court of appeals. New York, for example, is within the Second Circuit; California, the Ninth Circuit; Texas, the Fifth Circuit; and Virginia, the Fourth Circuit. An appeal from the court of appeals may be made to the United States Supreme Court by writ of certiorari.

ASSETS. The aggregate of available property to the museum organization. The value of all assets of an organization, less all indebtedness of the organization, reflects the worth of the organization.

ASSOCIATION. An unincorporated organization composed of a number of persons who have united together for some business purpose.

ASSUMPTION OF RISK. A defense to a plaintiff's allegation that the defendant's negligence caused injury to the plaintiff. It is a form of consent on the part of the plaintiff. If the plaintiff assumes the risk of defendant's negligence, the defendant is relieved from liability. (Assumption of risk is no longer a defense in some states.)

BAILEE. The person to whom goods are delivered pursuant to a contract of bailment.

BAILMENT. A contract, express or implied, whereby goods are to be delivered for a specific purpose to another person with the agreement that the goods will be returned or accounted for by the party to whom the goods are delivered.

BAILOR. Person who delivers property pursuant to a contract of bailment.

BEQUEST. A gift by will of personal property upon death.

CAPITAL GAIN. Tax term meaning a gain from the sale or exchange of a capital asset. All assets are capital assets for tax purposes except for the following: property held for resale in the normal course of business (inventory), trade accounts and notes receivable, and depreciable property and real estate used in a trade or business (though such real estate may still provide a capital gain).

CAUSE OF ACTION. A right to recover a debt or damages or a right to possession of property.

CHARITABLE TRUST. A fiduciary relationship causing the holder of property to administer it for the benefit of the public or for a charitable purpose.

CIRCUMSTANTIAL EVIDENCE. Evidence of an indirect nature; evidence from which the existence of facts in issue may be inferred.

COMMON LAW. That body of law which was adopted from the laws of England in force in the United States at the time of the Revolution and recognized as the foundation of jurisprudence in the United States. It is that law in the United States which is of general and universal application.

COMPLAINANT. One who files a lawsuit in the courts. The term "plaintiff" is used more frequently.

COMPLAINT. First or initial pleading on the part of the plaintiff in a civil action. It states the facts regarding the plaintiff's demand.

CONDITION PRECEDENT. Something that must be performed before an agreement becomes effective. Some act must be performed, or some event must occur, before the terms of an agreement are binding.

CONDITION SUBSEQUENT. A requirement attached to an agreement that must continually be met in order for the agreement to remain in effect. The happening of such a condition causes the agreement or obligation to be binding no longer.

CONTRACT. An agreement which creates obligations. Its essentials are competent parties, subject matter, a legal consideration, mutuality of agreement, and mutuality of obligations.

CONTRIBUTORY NEGLIGENCE. A defense in a negligence suit. If the plaintiff was also negligent and the plaintiff's negligence was a proximate cause of plaintiff's injury, the defendant is excused from liability.

CONVERSION. An unauthorized exercise of right of ownership over personal property belonging to another.

CORPORATION. A separate legal entity created by and under the laws of a particular state. Corporations can be public or private. A public corporation is one created by the state to act as an agency in the administration of civil government. A private corporation is one founded by and composed of private individuals for private purposes, as distinguished from governmental purposes.

CORPUS. The principal amount or capital of a trust, as distinguished from income of the trust.

CY PRES DOCTRINE. Rule for construction of a trust instrument which requires that the intention of the donor be carried out "as nearly as possible." The basic premise for application of cy pres is to defeat the failure of a charitable bequest. The cy pres power is the power of the court alone to direct the application of trust property to some other charitable purpose which can be attributed to the donor should the initial intent of the donor fail.

DEBT-FINANCED PROPERTY. Tax term referring to property which is held to produce income unrelated to an exempt organization's exempt purpose and on which there is an acquisition indebtedness at any time during the year.

DEFAULT. Failure of any party to take steps required in a cause of action. If a defendant fails to answer a complaint or petition within the time allowed him; the court will render judgment by default against him.

DEFENDANT. Person against whom relief is sought in a lawsuit.

DEPOSITION. Testimony of a witness taken outside the court upon notice to the adverse party. Testimony is reduced to writing and may be used in court at the trial.

DEPRECIATION. Tax or accounting term referring to the write-off for tax or accounting purposes of the cost or other basis of a business asset, over the estimated useful life of the asset. Annual amount of the cost of an asset which is charged as expense for the period.

DEVISE. A gift by will of real property upon death.

DISCOVERY. Disclosure by a party in a lawsuit of facts or documents which are necessary to the party seeking such documents but which are in the exclusive possession of the other party. Proceedings prior to trial to obtain facts or documents in the possession of another party.

DISTRICT COURT. Court of original jurisdiction. A trial court. A jury or the judge in the district court is the trier of the facts in a case.

EVIDENCE. All matters of fact by which any alleged fact, the truth of which is submitted to investigation, is established or disproved. Documents and other exhibits which may properly be submitted are evidence. Facts admitted upon trial become evidence. Reasonable inferences drawn from affirmative facts proven are evidence.

FELONY CRIME. A crime generally punishable by imprisonment in the penitentiary. It is a crime of a more severe nature and requires more severe punishment than a misdemeanor.

FIDUCIARY. Person holding the position of a trustee. A relationship founded upon a trust or confidence. Person who is required to act in good faith and with due regard to the interests of another.

INTERROGATORIES. Series of written questions propounded to a party in a lawsuit, or to a witness, for the purpose of judicial examination of the party or witness.

INTER VIVOS. Between the living. An inter vivos transfer of property is made during the life of the owner. It is distinguished from a gift which passes upon death.

INVASION OF PRIVACY. Intrusion upon one's right of physical solitude or seclusion. A tort in most states for which a person has a right of redress. To be an invasion of privacy, a matter which is offensive and objectionable to a reasonable man of ordinary sensibilities must be made public. Publicity which places a person in a false light in the public eye is an invasion of privacy.

INVITEE. One who is on another's premises by invitation.

JUDGMENT. The official decision of a court of law which determines the respective rights of the parties to a cause of action.

LEASE. An agreement for exclusive possession of property for a certain period of time.

LIBEL. An action in torts. A defamation of a person's reputation expressed in writing.

LICENSEE. A person permitted on another's property for his own interest but with the toleration of the owner.

LICENSING AGREEMENT. An agreement giving another permission to do something. A contract authorizing a firm or person to manufacture and market a product.

MISDEMEANOR CRIME. A crime punishable by a lesser degree than a felony. Punishment is usually by fine or imprisonment in jail rather than in a penitentiary.

NEGLIGENCE. Failure to do that which an ordinary prudent person under the same circumstances would have done or the doing of something which a prudent person would not have done.

PAROL EVIDENCE. Oral evidence. When an agreement is reduced to writing, the parol evidence rule provides that the written contract cannot be modified by parol evidence in the absence of mistake or fraud in the preparation of the agreement.

PASSIVE INCOME. Tax term referring to income from investments, such as royalties, rents, dividends, interest, annuities, and gains from the sale of stock and securities. It is distinguished from a person's earned income, or his income from personal services.

PERSONAL PROPERTY. Everything subject to ownership except land and that which is attached to the land—land being denoted as real property.

PETITION. An application to a court asking the court to provide redress for, or to grant a favor to, the person filing the petition (called the plaintiff, complainant, or petitioner).

PLAINTIFF. One who files a lawsuit. One who seeks redress in a civil action against another, called the defendant.

PLEADINGS. The documents filed by parties to a lawsuit disclosing to the court the allegations of the parties.

PRIMA FACIE. A fact presumed to be true unless and until it is contradicted. Prima facie evidence is that evidence which is sufficient to establish a fact.

PRINCIPAL. Under the law of agency, the employer of an agent or the one who gives authority to the agent.

PRIVATE FOUNDATION. Tax term referring to a charitable organization controlled by private groups or by a few persons, as distinguished from public charities which are more responsive to the general public. Private foundations are subject to close scrutiny by the Internal Revenue Service and often to substantial penalties. In addition, contribution deductions are more limited for gifts to private foundations than for those to public charities.

PROPERTY. That which is subject to ownership by a person. Property is either real or personal. Personal property is all property other than land or buildings. Real property refers to land and whatever is erected on it or to a part of the land, such as a building.

PROXIMATE CAUSE. That which is nearest as the responsible causation of an injury. The dominant or moving cause of an injury.

REAL PROPERTY. Land and that which is a part of the land, such as a building.

RES IPSA LOQUITUR. Presumption that defendant was negligent because the thing causing injury was in the exclusive control of the defendant and the accident was one which would not normally occur in the absence of negligence.

RESPONDEAT SUPERIOR. Doctrine meaning literally that the master will respond in damages; the master is liable for the wrongful acts of his agent which occurred within the scope of employment.

RESPONDENT. Person who must answer in a lawsuit, normally called a defendant. In appellate practice, the person answering an appeal.

SLANDER. The speaking of words which tend to damage another's reputation in the presence of a third party.

STATUTE OF FRAUDS. Rule requiring that most contracts must be in writing to be valid.

SUBPOENA. A command that a person appear before a court to give testimony.

SUBROGATION. The substitution of one party for another regarding a debt or claim. One who pays the debt of another succeeds to the rights of the former creditor against the debtor. The right does not apply to a volunteer in the absence of an agreement for subrogation.

THIRD-PARTY BENEFICIARY. One who is a party to a contract merely because the contract was made and intended for his benefit. Third-party beneficiaries who are donee or creditor beneficiaries normally have enforceable rights under contracts executed by other parties. A donee beneficiary is a third party upon whom a gift is conferred by the contract. A creditor beneficiary is a third party who will have a debt discharged by a contract between two other parties.

TORT. A private wrong, independent of contract, for which a civil action may be maintained.

TRESPASSER. One who enters another's land unlawfully.

TRUST. A confidence imposed upon one person for the benefit of another. An agreement whereby property is transferred to one person, a trustee, who administers for another.

UNFAIR COMPETITION. Wrongful or malicious interference with the formation of a contract or the right to pursue a lawful trade.

VICARIOUS LIABILITY. That liability of an employer for the torts of his employees. Vicarious liability only extends to conduct "within the course of employment."

Table of Selected Cases

Table of Statutes

FEDERAL

STATE

Notes

Chapter 1

1. *Corpus Juris Secundum*, vol. 90, pp. 217–32.
2. *Black's Law Dictionary*, p. 156.
3. *Black's Law Dictionary*, p. 409.
4. Chief Justice Marshall in *Dartmouth College* v. *Woodward*, 4 Wheat 481, 4 L. Ed. 629 (1819).
5. Ibid.
6. Article 6081E, Section 1, V.C.T.S.
7. Article 4413 (32C), V.C.T.S.
8. Article 1269J-4.1, Section 1, V.C.T.S.
9. Article 6081G-1, V.C.T.S.
10. Section 37541, Government Code, West's Ann. Calif. Code.
11. Ibid., Section 37542.
12. Ibid., Section 37563.
13. Ibid., Section 25351.
14. Educ. Code 255, McKinney's Consol. Laws of N.Y., Ann.
15. Educ. Code 254, McKinney's Consol. Laws of N.Y., Ann.

Chapter 2

1. If a museum is a governmental agency, and not separately incorporated, it is automatically an exempt organization as a political subdivision of the state. Its receipts are exempt from income taxation under Section 115 of the Internal Revenue Code. It need not file annual returns unless it receives unrelated business taxable income.
2. The sample articles of incorporation, appendix A, would satisfy the organizational test.
3. Reg. 1.501(c) (3)-1(d) (2).
4. Reg. 1.501(c) (3)-1(d) (5).
5. Reg. 1.501(c) (3)-1(d) (3).
6. Reg. 1.170A-9(e) (6).
7. Section 508(e), Internal Revenue Code of 1954.
8. Reg. 53.4941 (d)-1.
9. Reg. 53.4942 (d).
10. Reg. 53.4943-2(a) (1).
11. Section 4943 (c) (b), Internal Revenue Code of 1954.

12. Reg. 53.4944-1(a) (2) (i).
13. Reg. 53.4945.4.
14. Reg. 53.4945-4(a) (3) (ii).
15. Reg. 53.4942(b)-1.
16. Section 512, Internal Revenue Code of 1954.
17. Section 512(a) (1), Internal Revenue Code of 1954.
18. Reg. 1.513-1(d).
19. Rev. Rul. 69-267, 69-268, and 69-269, 1969-1 C.B. 160.
20. Rev. Rul. 73-104, 1973-1 C.B. 263.
21. Rev. Rul. 73-105, 1973-1 C.B. 264.
22. Rev. Rul. 74-399, 1974-2 C.B. 1972.
23. Rev. Rul. 76-93, 1976-1 C.B. 1970.
24. Section 513(a), Internal Revenue Code of 1954.
25. See Reg. 1.512(b)-1(c) (2) (iv).
26. See Reg. 1.512(b)-1(k) (2) (b) (ii).
27. See Reg. 1.512(b)-1(k) (3) (iii).
28. Reg. 1.514(b)-1(a).
29. Reg. 1.514(a)-1(a) (3).
30. Reg. 1.514(c)-1(a).
31. Reg. 1.514(c)-(b) (3).

Chapter 3

1. *Jones* v. *Hunt*, 74 Texas 657 (1889).
2. *Smith* v. *International Printing*, 190 S.W.2d 769 (Civ. App., Tex., 1945).
3. *Pertzman* v. *City of Ill.*, 141 F.2d 956 (8th Cir., 1944), *cert. den.*, 323 U.S. 718 (1944).
4. *Galveston, H. & S.A. Ry. Co.* v. *Hennigan*, 76 S.W.452 (Civ. App., Tex., 1903).
5. William L. Prosser, *Law of Torts* (St. Paul, Minn.: West Publishing, 1971), p. 27.
6. Prosser, *Law of Torts*, p. 143.
7. Prosser, *Law of Torts*, p. 161.
8. Prosser, *Law of Torts*, p. 211.
9. Prosser, *Law of Torts*, p. 214.
10. Prosser, *Law of Torts*, p. 459.
11. Prosser, *Law of Torts*, p. 445.
12. 28 U.S.C. 1346, 1402, 1504, 2110, 2402, 2671–2680.
13. 28 U.S.C. 2680(h).
14. 28 U.S.C. 2680(a).
15. Prosser, *Law of Torts*, pp. 977–78.
16. *Feofees of Heriot's Hospital* v. *Ross*, 12 C & F 507, 8 Eng. Rep. 1508 (1846).
17. *Davidson* v. *Methodist Hospital of Dallas*, 348 S.W.2d 400 (Ct. of App., Dallas, 1961). See, however, *Howle* v. *Camp Amon Carter*, 470 S.W.2d 629 (1971), in which the Supreme Court of Texas held that with respect to suits arising from events occurring after March 9, 1966, a charitable enterprise is subject to vicarious liability under the rule of respondeat superior applicable to business organizations operated for a profit.
18. Prosser, *Law of Torts*, p. 517.
19. W. Page Keeton, "Products Liability—Design Hazards and the Meaning of Defect," *Cumberland Law Review*, vol. 10, (fall 1979), pp. 297–98.

20. Keeton, "Products Liability," pp. 297–98.

21. 5 U.S.C. 8101–8173. The Federal Employees Compensation Act provides a comprehensive compensation system for federal employees. Each state has enacted its separate compensation act.

22. Prosser, *Law of Torts*, p. 531.

23. Prosser, *Law of Torts*, p. 357.

24. Prosser, *Law of Torts*, p. 364.

25. Restatement of Torts, Section 339.

26. Ibid.

27. Ibid., § 341A, 343.

28. Prosser, *Law of Torts*, p. 399.

29. Prosser, *Law of Torts*, pp. 403–5.

30. Prosser, *Law of Torts*, pp. 403–5.

31. Prosser, *Law of Torts*, pp. 403–5.

32. "Liability of Charitable Organization under Respondeat Superior Doctrine for Tort of Unpaid Volunteer," Allan Manley, 82 American Law Reports, 2d series, 1213, at p. 1216.

33. Ibid.

34. Prosser, *Law of Torts*, p. 737.

35. Prosser, *Law of Torts*, p. 737.

36. Prosser, *Law of Torts*, p. 739.

37. Prosser, *Law of Torts*, p. 776.

38. Prosser, *Law of Torts*, pp. 807–8.

39. Prosser, *Law of Torts*, pp. 807–8.

40. Prosser, *Law of Torts*, p. 812.

41. Prosser, *Law of Torts*, p. 804.

42. *Factors Etc. v. Pro Arts, Inc.*, 579 F.2d 215 (2nd Cir., 1978).

43. *Corpus Juris Secundum*, vol. 86, pp. 954–63.

44. *Corpus Juris Secundum*, vol. 17, p. 545.

45. Ibid., pp. 545–50.

46. Ibid., pp. 554–76.

47. Ibid., pp. 577–81.

48. *Corpus Juris Secundum*, vol. 8, p. 391.

49. Ibid., p. 418.

50. Ibid., pp. 401–3.

51. Ibid., pp. 421–2.

52. *American Jurisprudence*, 2d, vol. 8, pp. 1024–26.

53. 173 Misc. 791, 19 N.Y.S.2d 96 (City Ct., N.Y., 1940).

54. 80 Wash. 662, 141 P. 1153 (S.C., Wash., 1914).

55. *Corpus Juris Secundum*, vol. 8, pp. 425–30.

56. In *Mazer v. Stein*, 347 U.S. 201 (1954), the Supreme Court stated that their term "authors" includes the creator of a picture or a statue. The court in that case held that the fact that statues were intended for use as bases for lamps did not invalidate their copyright registration.

57. 17 U.S.C. 101-702, effective January 1, 1978.

58. 17 U.S.C. 106.

59. "Fair use" is not defined by the code. Section 107 of the act states that in determining whether a use made of a work is a fair use, factors to be considered include: the

purpose and character of the use, including whether such use is of a commercial nature or is for nonprofit educational purposes; the nature of the copyrighted work; the amount and substantiality of the portion used in relation to the copyrighted work as a whole; and the effect of the use upon the potential market for, or value of, the copyrighted work.

60. 17 U.S.C. 201.
61. Ibid.
62. U.S.C. 302.
63. U.S.C. 401.
64. 17 U.S.C. 401.
65. 42 Fed. Reg. 64, 377 (1977).
66. 17 U.S.C. 401.
67. 17 U.S.C. 303.
68. 17 U.S.C. 411.
69. 17 U.S.C. 205.
70. 17 U.S.C. 203.

Chapter 4

1. 320 F. Supp. 1303 (N.D., Ill., 1970).
2. See also *Grossman Designs, Inc.* v. *Bartin*, 347 F. Supp. 1150 (N.D., Ill., 1972). and *Classic Film Museum, Inc.* v. *Warner Bros., Inc.*, 453 F. Supp. 852 (D.C., Mass., 1978).
3. Stephen S. Ashley, "A Critical Comment on California's Droit de Suite, Civil Code Section 986," *Hastings Law Journal*, vol. 29 (1977–78), pp. 249–60.
4. 433 U.S. 562 (1976).
5. William Strauss, "The Moral Right of the Author," *American Journal of Comparative Law*, vol. 4 (1955), p. 506.
6. Strauss, "Moral Right," p. 507.
7. Strauss, "Moral Right," p. 511.
8. Strauss, "Moral Right," p. 508.
9. Strauss, "Moral Right," p. 508.
10. James M. Treece, "American Law Analogues of the Author's 'Moral Right,'" *American Journal of Comparative Law*, vol. 16 (1968), p. 494.
11. Treece, "American Law Analogues," p. 494.
12. 67 Misc. 183, 122 N.Y. Supp. 206 (1910).
13. 164 F.2d 522 (7th Cir., 1947).
14. William Strauss, "Moral Right," p. 525.
15. 194 Misc. 570, 89 N.Y.S.2d 813 (1949).
16. 198 F.2d 585 (2nd Cir., 1952).
17. 538 F.2d 14 (2nd Cir., 1976).
18. 15 U.S.C. § 1125(a).
19. Civil Code, West's Ann. Calif. Code, p. 134.
20. William Strauss, "American Law Analogues," p. 529.
21. 89 N.E.2d 863 (Ct. App., N.Y., 1949).
22. See *Estate of Hemingway* v. *Random House, Inc.*, 244 N.E.2d 250 (Ct. App., N.Y., 1968).
23. Ibid.
24. 25 N.Y.S.2d 32 (S. Ct., 1914).

25. 294 F. Supp. 331 (S.D., N.Y., 1968). The New York Law, Article 12-E, Sections 219-f and 219-g, General Business Law, now provides that right of production of a work of fine art does not pass when the work is sold or otherwise transferred. This right is specifically reserved to the artist unless it is transferred in a written instrument signed by the artist or his agent.

26. 216 F.2d 945 (9th Cir., 1954), *cert. den.*, 348 U.S. 971 (1955).

27. 17 U.S.C. 106.

28. 17 U.S.C. 201(2) (d).

29. 17 U.S.C. 201.

30. 424 F.2d 988 (1st Cir., 1970).

31. 354 U.S. 476 (1957).

32. *A Book Named "John Cleland's Memoirs of a Woman of Pleasure* v. *Attorney General of Massachusetts,"* 383 U.S. 413 (1966).

33. 311 F. Supp. 884, aff'd, 432 F.2d 420 (4th Cir., 1970).

34. 413 U.S. 15 (1973).

35. See *Jenkins* v. *Georgia*, 418 U.S. 153 (1974), wherein the Supreme Court held that the showing of the film *Carnal Knowledge* is not the "public portrayal of hardcore sexual conduct for its own sake and for ensuing commercial gain" which is punishable under *Miller*. The Court held that the film did not depict sexual conduct in a patently offensive way.

36. *Kaplan* v. *California*, 413 U.S. 115 (1973).

37. 436 U.S. 293 (1978).

38. *Stanley* v. *Georgia*, 394 U.S. 557 (1969).

39. *U.S.* v. *Orito*, 413 U.S. 139 (1973).

40. *U.S.* v. *Various Articles of Obscene Merchandise*, 600 F.2d 394 (2nd Cir., 1949).

41. *United States* v. *Reidel, 402 U.S. 351 (1971); U.S.* v. *Twelve 200 Ft. Reels of Super 8 MM Film*, 413 U.S. 123 (1973).

42. Ibid.

Chapter 5

1. All states except Louisiana have adopted the Uniform Commercial Code, but because of omissions and modifications in various parts of it in the various states, the law of the particular state should be examined to determine the applicability of different provisions.

2. Uniform Commercial Code, section 2-204(2).

3. Ibid., Section 2-201(3) (b).

4. Ibid., Section 2-103(1) (b).

5. Ibid., Section 2-612.

6. Section 219-d, General Business Law, McKinney's Consol. Laws of N. Y., Ann.

7. Ibid., Section 291-c.

8. Article 12-F, Section 219-i, General Business Law, McKinney's Consol. Laws of N. Y., Ann.

9. 67 Misc.2d 1077, 325 N.Y.S.2d 576 (Civ. Ct., N.Y. City, 1971).

10. Lawrence Scott Bauman, "Fake Paintings," *Stanford Law Review*, vol. 24 (1972), pp. 932–33.

11. Bauman, "Fake Paintings," pp. 932–33.

12. Bauman, "Fake Paintings," pp. 932–33.
13. Bauman, "Fake Paintings," pp. 932–33.
14. 24 N.Y.2d 91, 298 N.Y.S.2d 979 (1969).
15. *Corpus Juris Secundum*, vol. 38, p. 788.
16. Ibid., p. 811.
17. Ibid., pp. 789–90.
18. Ibid., pp. 790–92.
19. Ibid., pp. 816–17.
20. Ibid., pp. 846–48.
21. *In Re Koons' Will*, 206 Misc. 856, 135 N.Y.S.2d 733 (1954).
22. 440 S.W.2d 719 (Civ. App., El Paso, 1969).
23. 396 U.S. 435 (1969).
24. *In Re Stuart's Estate*, 183 Misc. 20, 46 N.Y.S.2d 911 (1944).
25. See *Lutheran Hospital of Manhattan v. Goldstein*, 182 Misc. 913, 46 N.Y.S.2d 705 (1944). See also *Women's Christian Temperance Union of El Paso v. Cooley*, 25 S.W.2d 171 (Civ. App., El Paso, 1930), wherein a state court ruled that whenever a charitable purpose is limited to a particular object or a particular institution and there is no general charitable intent in connection with the gift, the doctrine of cy pres does not apply and the legacy will lapse. In the *Cooley* case, the decedent left a portion of her property to the Women's Christian Temperance Union to be used for the purpose of securing, to the people of Texas and New Mexico, state and national prohibition. Because state and national prohibition had already been obtained at the date of decedent's death, the court held the legacy lapsed. In *Coffee v. William Marsh Rice University*, 403 S.W.2d 340 (S.C., Tex., 1966), the Supreme Court of Texas discussed the role of the attorney general in the construction of a trust instrument, as well as the general application of the cy pres doctrine to eliminate restriction in a charitable trust. In that case the university instituted an action for application of the cy pres doctrine to eliminate restrictions in a charitable trust providing for the establishment of a university for white citizens.
26. Reg. 1.170A-4(b) (3) (ii) (b).
27. Section 170(f), Internal Revenue Code.
28. Section 170(f) (3), Internal Revenue Code.
29. Reg. 1.170-1(c).
30. Rev. Proc. 66-49, 1966-2 C.B. 1257.
31. Ibid., p. 1258.
32. Ibid., p. 1259.
33. 20 U.S.C. 971–977.
34. 16 U.S.C. 431–433.
35. 499 F.2d 113 (9th Cir., 1974).
36. 596 F.2d 939 (10th Cir., 1979).
37. 569 F.2d 330 (5th Cir., 1978).
38. 16 U.S.C. 461–467.
39. 101 F.2d 295 (8th Cir., 1939).
40. 40 U.S.C. 257.
41. 16 U.S.C. 468.
42. 16 U.S.C. 469, amended in 1974 by the Moss Bennett Bill (Pub. L. 93-291).
43. 16 U.S.C. 470a–470n.
44. 42 U.S.C. 4321–4347.
45. 16 U.S.C. 470aa–470ll.

46. 16 U.S.C. 470ee.

47. National Preservation Act, Amendments of 1980, Public Law 96-515, December 12, 1980.

48. 42 U.S.C. 1996, Pub. L.95-341, Aug. 11, 1978.

49. See note 35.

50. The state of California has passed a statute recognizing the religious freedom of native Americans. Section 5097.9 of the Public Resources Code (West) provides that no public agency nor any private party using or occupying public property may cause damage to any native American sanctified cemetery, place of worship, religious or ceremonial site, or sacred shrine unless a public interest or necessity exists. The public property of all cities and counties is exempt from the act, however.

51. Bowen Blair, "American Indians vs. American Museum—A Matter of Religious Freedom," *American Indian Journal*, part 1, vol. 5 (May 1979), p. 14.

52. Blair, "American Indians," part 2, vol. 5 (June 1979), p. 5.

53. Blair, "American Indians," part 2, p. 5.

54. These expenditures must have been incurred on a certified historic structure that was at least twenty years old and for which any previous costs for rehabilitation had been incurred at least twenty years previous.

55. These credits are available only if the taxpayer elects to use the straight-line method of cost recovery for the expenditures. In addition, the building must be "substantially rehabilitated," i.e., rehabilitation expenditures during the twenty-four-month period ending on the last day of the taxable year must exceed the greater of the basis (cost less depreciation) of the building, or $5,000. The 25 percent credit is available for both residential (except a personal residence) and nonresidential buildings; the 15 and 20 percent credits are limited to nonresidential buildings. For rehabilitation of buildings more than thirty years old but not certified as historic structures, the cost eligible for depreciation must be reduced by the rehabilitation credit. As to a certified historic structure, no credit is available unless approval of the rehabilitation is obtained from the Secretary of the Interior.

56. Section 48(8) (3), Internal Revenue Code.

57. 438 U.S. 104 (1978).

58. See James P. Beckwith, Jr., "Preservation Law 1976–1980: Faction, Property Rights, and Ideology," *North Carolina Central Law Journal*, vol. 11 (spring 1980), pp. 276–40, at page 294. The author has included an appendix which lists the historic preservation statutes of all the states. Following Beckwith's article is an annotated list of major historic preservation court decisions compiled by Stephen N. Dennis (pp. 341ff.).

59. 20 U.S.C. 41–80.

60. *State of California, County of San Bernardino—Museum v. Smithsonian Institution et al.*, 618 F.2d, 618 (9th Cir., 1980).

61. 19 U.S.C. 2091–2095.

62. 545 F.2d 988 (5th Cir., 1977).

63. 18 U.S.C. 2315.

64. *U.S. v. McClain*, 593 F.2d 658 (5th Cir., 1979).

65. See Title 19, Code of Federal Regulations, 10.43–10.49.

66. 19 C.F.R. 10.49(c) and (d).

67. There are criminal sanctions, as well as civil penalties, for obtaining or possessing certain specimens without proper permits. See 18 U.S.C. 42–44, 16 U.S.C. 705–706, 16 U.S.C. 1375, and 16 U.S.C. 1540.

68. See M. Houston McGaugh and Hugh H. Genoways, "State Laws as They Pertain to Scientific Collecting Permits," *Museology*, vol. 2 (1976), for a summary of state laws pertaining to permits.

69. 16 U.S.C. 703–711.

70. 16 U.S.C. 1361–1407.

71. 16 U.S.C. 1531–1543. For a detailed presentation of the permits required for all types of specimens, consult Thomas J. Berger and John D. Phillips, eds., *Index to U.S. Federal Wildlife Regulations* (Lawrence, Kans.: Association of Systematics Collections, 1977). See also Hugh H. Genoways and Jerry R. Choate, "Federal Regulations Pertaining to Collection, Import, Export, and Transport of Scientific Specimens of Mammals," *Journal of Mammalogy*, vol. 57, no. 2, supplement (May 1976), pp. 1–8.

72. 16 U.S.C. 1331–1340.

73. 16 U.S.C. 668.

74. 18 U.S.C. 41–44.

75. 16 U.S.C. 851–856.

76. If the duty-free specimens are transferred within a five-year period, the museum should write U.S. Customs in Washington, D.C., for forms to use in applying for a transfer.

77. To obtain Form 3-177, write U.S. Fish and Wildlife Service, Division of Law Enforcement, P.O. Box 28006, Washington, D.C. 20005. For Forms 3-200, write U.S. Fish and Wildlife Service, Wildlife Permit Office, P.O. Box 3654, Arlington, Va. 22203.

78. 18 U.S.C. 44.

79. Contact U.S. Fish and Wildlife Service, Division of Law Enforcement, Washington, D.C. 20240.

80. 7 U.S.C. 2131. Write Veterinary Services, Department of Agriculture, Hyattsville, Md. 20782. For live animals and endangered species, Form 65 must be filed with the U.S. Department of Agriculture. State permits must also be obtained for those animals listed on the federal list of rare and endangered species.

81. Apply to Biohazards Control Officer, Office of Biosafety, Public Health Service, Center for Disease Control, Department of Health and Human Services, Atlanta, Ga. 30333.

82. Plant Protection and Quarantine, Hyattsville, Md. 20782.

83. See notes 67 and 74.

84. 582 F.2d 159 (2nd Cir., 1978).

Chapter 6

1. 29 U.S.C. 152–169. Federal museums are subject to provisions regulating collective bargaining among federal employees. See 5 U.S.C. 7101–7901.

2. 29 C.F.R. 101.1

3. See *Hughes Tool Co.*, 147 N.L.R.B. 1573 (1964), and *Jubilee Manufacturing Co.*, 202 N.L.R.B. 272 (1973).

4. 42 U.S.C. 1981, 1982, and 1983.

5. 42 U.S.C. 2000.

6. 29 U.S.C. 206(d).

7. 29 U.S.C. 621.

8. 29 U.S.C. 793.

9. *Corpus Juris Secundum*, vol. 51, p. 610.

10. There may be state labor laws covering state employees, however. Further employees of a federal museum would be subject to provisions regulating collective bargaining among federal employees. See 5 U.S.C. 7101–7901.

11. 194 N.L.R.B. 371 (1971). See also *N.L.R.B. v. Natchez Trace Electric Power Association*, 476 F.2d 1042 (5th Cir., 1973).

12. *The Trustees of Columbia University in the City of New York*, 97 N.L.R.B. 424 (1951).

13. *Cornell University*, 183 N.L.R.B. 329 (1970).

14. *Shattuck School*, 189 N.L.R.B. 886 (1971), and *Trustees of Corcoran Gallery of Art*, 186 N.L.R.B. 565 (1970). In the *Corcoran Gallery* case, the board stated that the primary goal of the gallery was education; thus it ruled that the gallery was an educational institution for the public promotion of works of art and was subject to the act.

15. The board's assertion of jurisdiction over religious educational institutions has been clouded by the recent decision of the Supreme Court in *N.L.R.B. v. Catholic Bishop of Chicago*, 440 U.S. 490 (1979), discussed below.

16. In a closed shop an employer and a union agree that only union members will be hired and that any employee not in good standing with the union will be discharged.

17. 61 Stat. 136, 29 U.S.C. 152(2) (1970 ed.).

18. H.R. Rep. No. 245, 80th Cong., 1st Sess. 12 (1947).

19. Pub. L. No. 93-360, 88 Stat. 395 (1974).

20. 440 U.S. 490 (1979).

21. *C. W. Post Center*, 189 N.L.R.B. 904 (1971).

22. 100 S. Ct. 856 (1980).

23. 29 U.S.C. 159.

24. 419 U.S. 301 (1974).

25. 29 C.F.R. 101.17.

26. 324 U.S. 793 (1945).

27. *N.L.R.B. v. Babcock & Wilcox Co.*, 351 U.S. 105 (1956).

28. 29 C.F.R. 101.19.

29. 29 U.S.C. 158(d).

30. See *Minneapolis Society of Fine Arts*, 194 N.L.R.B. 371 (1971).

31. *Corpus Juris Secundum*, vol. 51, pp. 892–98.

32. See 29 C.F.R. 101.1–101.15 for rules and regulations of the National Labor Relations Board.

33. *Corpus Juris Secundum*, vol. 51A, pp. 52–53.

34. 29 U.S.C. 164(b).

35. 42 U.S.C. 1981–1985.

36. 42 U.S.C. 2000e.

37. 29 U.S.C. 206(d).

38. 29 U.S.C. 621.

39. 29 U.S.C. 793.

40. 38 U.S.C. 2012–2014.

41. 42 U.S.C. 2000e-4.

42. 411 U.S. 792 (1973).

43. 438 U.S. 567 (1978).

44. *Davis v. Weidner*, 596 F.2d 726 (7th Cir., 1979).

45. 401 U.S. 424 (1971).
46. See *Washington* v. *Davis,* 426 U.S. 229, at p. 248 (1976).
47. 29 C.F.R. 1604.
48. 29 U.S.C. 206(d).
49. Executive Order 12144, June 22, 1979.
50. See *Schwager* v. *Sun Oil Company of Pennsylvania,* 591 F.2d 58 (10th Cir., 1979).
51. Ibid.
52. 499 F.2d 859 (7th Cir., 1974).
53. 29 U.S.C. 793.
54. 41 C.F.R. 60.741.6(d).
55. 29 U.S.C. 794.
56. 99 S. Ct. 2361 (1979).
57. See *Trageser* v. *Libbie Rehab. Center,* 590 F.2d 87 (4th Cir., 1978).
58. 45 C.F.R. 84.12.
59. U.S.C. 2012–2014.
60. 580 F.2d 1150 (2nd Cir., 1978).
61. 408 U.S. 564 (1972).
62. 408 U.S. 725 (1972).
63. *Palmer* v. *Board of Education of City of Chicago,* 603 F.2d 1271 (7th Cir., 1979).
64. 511 F.2d 697 (5th Cir., 1975).
65. 426 U.S. 341 (1976).
66. See *Haimowitz* v. *University of Nevada,* 579 F.2d 526 (9th Cir., 1978).
67. 591 F.2d 493 (9th Cir., 1978).
68. 535 F.2d 605 (9th Cir., 1976).
69. 430 F.2d 852 (5th Cir., 1970).
70. 29 U.S.C. 651–678.
71. 29 U.S.C. 651.
72. 29 C.F.R. 1975.4.
73. 29 U.S.C. 669(a).
74. See 29 C.F.R. 1910–1919.
75. 540 F.2d 1283 (6th Cir., 1976).
76. 100 S. Ct. 2844 (1980).
77. 29 U.S.C. 657(a).
78. 98 S. Ct. 1916 (1978).

Chapter 7

1. The term "director" as used in this chapter refers to a member of a museum's board of directors as distinguished from the museum director, an employee of the museum serving under a board of directors.
2. Austin Wakeman Scott, *The Law of Trusts,* vol. 2 (Boston: Little, Brown, 1967), pp. 1299–1324.
3. Section 5.
4. Scott, *Law of Trusts,* 2:1408–15.
5. Scott, *Law of Trusts,* 2:1388–99.
6. Scott, *Law of Trusts,* 2:1398.
7. 25 N.Y.S.2d 667 (S.C., N.Y., 1940).
8. See *American Jurisprudence,* vol. 19, pp. 684–90.

9. 248 N.2d 910 (Ct. of App., N.Y., 1969).

10. 584 F.2d 186 (7th Cir., 1978).

11. 313 So.2d 739 (Fla., 1975), 519 F.2d 453 (2nd Cir., 1975).

12. 381 F. Supp. 1003 (S.D., N.Y., 1974).

13. See also *Midlantic National Bank v. Frank Thompson Foundation*, 405 A.2d 866 (N.J., 1979).

Appendix A

1. Publication 557, 1979 ed., Department of the Treasury, Internal Revenue Service.

2. See chapter 2 for an explanation of the Internal Revenue Code provisions.

3. These provisions are a required part of the trust indenture if the trust is a private foundation [Section 508(e), Internal Revenue Code of 1954]. They need not be part of the instrument, however, if state law treats them as being contained in a private foundation's governing instrument. (See the discussion of these provisions in chapter 2.)

4. Provisions (2) through (6) are a required part of the articles of incorporation if the corporation is a private foundation [Section 508(e), Internal Revenue Code]. They need not be part of the instrument if state law treats these required provisions as being contained in a private foundation's governing instrument. (See the discussion of these provisions in chapter 2.)

Selected Bibliography

ARTICLES

Adams, Ben. "Inheritability of the Right of Publicity upon the Death of the Famous." *Vanderbilt Law Review*, vol. 33 (1980), pp. 1251–64.

Ashley, Stephen S. "A Critical Comment on California's Droit de Suite, Civil Code Section 986." *Hastings Law Journal*, vol. 29 (1977–78), pp. 249–60.

Bauman, Lawrence Scott. "Fake Paintings." *Stanford Law Review*, vol. 24 (1972), pp. 930–46.

Beckwith, James P., Jr. "Preservation Law, 1976–1980: Faction Property Rights, and Ideology." *North Carolina Central Law Journal*, vol. 11 (spring 1980), pp. 276–340. (The spring 1980 issue of *North Carolina Central Law Journal* is a symposium issue on historic preservation law.)

Blair, Bowen. "American Indians vs. American Museums—A Matter of Religious Freedom." *American Indian Journal*, vol. 5 (May 1979), pp. 13–21; vol. 5 (June 1979), pp. 2–6.

Cukell, Carole F. "The Author's Moral Right: Can Louisiana Adopt the Doctrine?" *Tulane Law Review*, vol. 51 (1976–77), pp. 308–33.

Genoways, Hugh H., and Choate, Jerry R. "Federal Regulations Pertaining to Collection, Import, Export, and Transport of Scientific Specimens of Mammals." *Journal of Mammalogy*, vol. 57, no. 2, supplement (May 1976), pp. 1–9.

Harris, Kathryn. "The American Indian Religious Freedom Act and Its Promise." *American Indian Journal*, vol. 5 (June 1979), pp. 7–10.

Katz, Arthur S. "The Doctrine of Moral Right and American Copyright Law—A Proposal." *Southern California Law Review*, vol. 24 (1951), pp. 375–427.

Keeton, W. Page. "Products Liability—Design Hazards and the Meaning of Defect." *Cumberland Law Review*, vol. 10, (fall 1979), pp. 293–316.

Manley, Allan. "Liability of Charitable Organization under Respondeat Superior Doctrine for Tort of Unpaid Volunteer." *American Law Reports*, 3rd series, vol. 82, pp. 1213–33.

McGaugh, M. Houston, and Genoways, Hugh H. "State Laws as They Pertain to Scientific Collecting Permits." *Museology*, vol. 2 (1976), pp. 1–81.

Monta, Rudolf. "The Concept of 'Copyright' versus the 'Droit D'Auteur.' " *Southern California Law Review*, vol. 32 (1959), pp. 177–86.

Sarraute, Raymond. "Current Theory on the Moral Right of Authors and Artists under French Law." *American Journal of Comparative Law*, vol. 16 (1968), pp. 465–86.

Strauss, William. "The Moral Right of the Author." *American Journal of Comparative Law*, vol. 4 (1955), pp. 506–38.

"Symposium—Legal Protection of America's Archaeological Heritage." *Arizona Law Review*, vol. 22 (1980), pp. 675–751.

Treece, James M. "American Law Analogues of the Author's 'Moral Right.' " *American Journal of Comparative Law*, vol. 16 (1968), pp. 487–506.

Zegas, Alan. "Personal Letters: A Dilemma for Copyright and Privacy Law." *Rutgers Law Review*, vol. 33 (1980), pp. 134–64.

BOOKS

Berger, Thomas J., and Phillips, John D. *Index to U.S. Federal Wildlife Regulations*. Lawrence, Kan.: Association of Systematics Collections, 1977.

DuBoff, Leonard D. *Deskbook of Art Law*. Washington, D. C.: Federal Publications, 1977.

Duffy, Robert E. *Art Law: Representing Artists, Dealers, and Collectors*. New York: Practicing Law Institute, 1977.

Feldman, Franklin, and Weil, Stephen E. *Art Works: Law, Policy, Practice*. New York: Practicing Law Institute, 1974.

Phelan, Marilyn. *A Practical Guide to Meeting Reporting Requirements of Tax-Exempt Organizations*. Tucson, Ariz.: Lawyers and Judges Publishing, 1978.

Prosser, William L. *Law of Torts*. 4th ed. St. Paul, Minn.: West Publishing, 1971.

Scott, Austin Wakeman. *The Law of Trusts*. 3rd ed. 6 vols. Boston: Little, Brown, 1967.

Index

283